MARKETING to CONSUMERS with DISABILITIES

HOW TO IDENTIFY AND MEET THE GROWING MARKET NEEDS OF 43 MILLION AMERICANS

Joel Reedy

PROBUS PUBLISHING COMPANY
Chicago, Illinois
Cambridge, England

To my wife, Shirley, and children, Chanel and Chandler.
Without their push, I'd be nowhere.

CONTENTS

FOREWORD

Marketing to Consumers with Disabilities outlines how businesses and government agencies can effectively design and market products and services to a large and growing segment of our population—persons with disabilities. Even though the market segment of 43 million disabled Americans is larger than the African-American or Spanish-speaking segments, little attention has been directed toward understanding the needs of this segment and developing marketing programs to satisfy these needs. Joel Reedy has rectified this situation by providing a stimulating "how-to" guide for marketing practitioners interested in exploring this opportunity.

The enactment of the Americans with Disabilities Act (ADA) has heightened interest in the disabled consumer. However, most of this attention has focused on interpreting and complying with the law. The economic potential of this segment of the population has been largely ignored. This book takes a more proactive perspective. It outlines the impact of environmental and demographic forces on the disabled segments—forces that resulted in the ADA—and provides a framework for developing marketing programs directed toward the disabled that benefit both the marketer and the disabled consumer.

As a marketing professor in a wheelchair, I appreciate the insights provided by this book on both a personal and professional level. On the personal level, I have experienced the frustration of being unable to purchase and consume certain goods and services because I could not reach the products on the top shelves or get up the steps to a restaurant. On the other hand, I am a loyal customer of hotel chains that have wheelchair accessible rooms and facilities. By sensitizing marketers to the needs of disabled patrons, this book shows how businesses can tap this important market.

On a professional level, the principles in this book go far beyond simply marketing products and services to disabled consumers. With the advent of flexible manufacturing and targeted marketing communications vehicles, businesses can effectively provide unique offerings to smaller market niches. Micromarketing is the theme for the 1990s.

While this book focuses on the disabled niche, it also provides a general framework that can be used to develop marketing programs for other niches. The book emphasizes the importance of understanding consumer needs from the perspective of the consumer, not the marketer. Many of the problems encountered by disabled consumers also frustrate the able-bodied. Most of us find it difficult to read some labels and open some containers—problems that arise because marketers have not fully appreciated the information consumers want and how they use products.

Another important marketing principle emphasized in this book is that diversity in needs often arises in seemingly homogeneous segments. Effective marketing programs must recognize there are important differences within the disabled consumer market segment, just as there are differences in racial and elderly market segments.

Marketing to Consumers with Disabilities offers valuable insights for marketing professionals who offer or are considering offering products or services to disabled consumers. In addition, the insights in this book are useful for all marketers who are pursuing niche strategies.

Dr. Barton A. Weitz

J.C. Penney Eminent Scholar Chair in Retailing Management
College of Business Administration/University of Florida

and

Editor, *Journal of Marketing Research*
American Marketing Association

ACKNOWLEDGMENTS

In researching and writing on this marketing topic during the last three years, I was fortunate to work with many sensitive and responsive associates. Consumer preferences and attitudes can be difficult to uncover, yet six colleagues helped to keep me on track. My thanks to Tom White, M.B.A., and Tom Scanio, Ph.D., for insights into auditory and speech impairments; also to Sandra Sroka, M.S., and Mike Shahnasarian, Ph.D., for input on sensitivity and mental health issues. At the University of South Florida, Paul Solomon, Ph.D., started me off in the right direction, and Keith Schilit, Ph.D., introduced me to John Willig, the literary agent who became excited enough to bring this book to Probus Publishing. It has been a privilege to work with Marlene Chamberlain and Kevin Thornton at Probus Publishing, as well as with editor Pamela Sourelis. They approached the work seriously and enthusiastically; this combination of values has been a refreshing reaffirmation of today's entrepreneurial spirit.

I also wish to thank the progressive and innovative companies which shared their experiences and materials aimed at improving communications with various consumer segments with disabilities. These proactive organizations have recognized that disabilities marketing is the right thing to do today; this effort also establishes a marketing mechanism for serving tomorrow's market growth.

Practical support can be traced to my parents, Edward and Melissa Reedy, who provided hours of detailed work that makes writing somewhat intimidating. Finally, I appreciate my own family's patience and support as I waded through notepads full of research and experiences.

INTRODUCTION

OBSTACLES AND EVERYDAY EVENTS

The Thoughts of a Mobility-Impaired Antiques Collector

"Mail, mail, and more mail. Bills, magazines. About time for this month's price guide. Here it is, but what's this? What happened to the old brown paper sleeve? This issue is covered in a plastic wrap. Pulling, tearing, I don't have the hand strength to break the plastic open. This is a perfect way to preserve an issue, absolutely adult-proof but how do I read it? Some idiots."

What appears trivial to the nondisabled person can easily be an insurmountable barrier to customers with mobility impairments. But who in the circulation department could have anticipated this problem with the "new, improved" plastic sleeve?

Sight Impairments Stand in the Way

"Is this what I ordered? As I remember, a size three came only in soft gray. This red is atrocious. Where's the invoice? I hate these carbonless invoices; the light blue ink is impossible to read. Here's the customer service number. Wait a minute, is that a 3 or an 8? The type is too small to see. I wonder if this is the first time these people designed a mail-order catalog. Satisfaction guaranteed? Fine, I'll send the whole order back to them and tell them to take my name off their list. Then I'll be satisfied."

Persons with disabilities are prime prospects for mail or telephone ordering, but limitations in communications response have to be recognized, such as making the visuals easily legible or providing ready compatibility for accessing Telecommunications Devices for the Deaf (TDD) or similar hearing enhancements.

Opinions that Fall through the Cracks

"What's this? A postcard from customer service? 'We're interested in what our valued customers think of our new automotive department. A customer service representative will be calling you next week.' Well, unless they have a TDD, they won't be getting through to me. And my rental fleet spends big bucks on auto repair parts."

Surveys and other direct communications are designed to keep the marketer in touch with customers, to learn what the customer likes or dislikes about the organization. Telephone contact is a good method for generating response, but using only the telephone may exclude some important account holders, such as those customers with hearing or speech impairments. Alternate means of soliciting opinions or experiences from the retailer's consumer base should also be used.

People with disabilities present a puzzling array of conflicting demographic and psychographic factors to marketers and manufacturers throughout the nation. There is a huge number of Americans with disabilities, but as a group, they are difficult to contact. They collectively have at least one limitation in a major life function, but individually possess hundreds of different disabilities and injuries. Long ignored by society, they are now protected from intended or unintended discrimination by the equilibrating federal law called the Americans with Disabilities Act (ADA).

Never before have so many consumers become so important so quickly. The previously indiscernible consumer group has become known in aggregate as "Americans with disabilities," and their population is estimated at 43 million persons, a number larger than the population of African-Americans or Spanish-speaking Americans or the entire population of Canada. This is an enormous total that in the mind of a marketer presents an opportunity and a challenge to organize and reduce this diverse populace into smaller, more manageable buyer segments with common interests or needs.

Stereotypes years in the making are being overthrown by the harsh glare of news and entertainment media. While for decades, persons with disabilities have experienced the lowest levels of pervasive unemployment, they are now materializing as an economic strength. Marketers can serve and shape the transformation of the disabilities marketplace.

Helping you gain a better understanding of the motivations and abilities of customers with disabilities is the intention of this book; equally important is learning to develop an evaluation and action process that guides a marketing manager through a new and specialized marketing strategy. The procedure is called "Disabilities Marketing." It provides a step-by-step insight into marketing methods from the view of disabled customers, who recognize many communications and distribution obstacles, and red flags of all sorts, many of which are easily avoidable.

Consumer markets are in confusion today with the waxing of product-line competition and the waning of customer loyalty. Price seems to be the proven weapon to gain attention even though profit margins are spiraling downward. While not a "magic bullet" or "a quick fix," disabilities marketing is an appropriate market development strategy for locating and catering to new customers, or for introducing new products or services, or possibly as a retention strategy for current customers. Companies of all sizes are constantly surveying the marketplace for fresh ideas that offer at least short-term competitive advantage. Disabilities marketing can do better than provide a short-lived advantage; it can produce a lasting relationship, an allegiance that extends past the disabled user to his or her relatives, friends, and associates.

Disabling conditions are frustrating, not only to the individual, but to the spouse, family, friends, classmates, students, or associates of the disabled person. When obstacles are eliminated or at least reduced, disabled and nondisabled persons alike notice and appreciate the effort— not to mention the wealth of community goodwill and acknowledgment generated by excellent service to customers with disabilities.

MORE THAN MEDICAL APPARATUS

Disabilities marketing is more than organizing and distributing health care services and medical equipment. People with disabilities need clothing, jewelry repair, furnishings, and consumer goods of all kinds; they join book clubs, travel clubs, and garden clubs. To help narrow their choices, disabilities marketing—a consumer oriented evaluation and planning strategy—that improves message content and delivery, and encourages feedback from a mix of communications tools, such as advertising, sales promotion, public relations, and personal selling efforts.

These marketing tools are sharpened to eliminate communications barriers; a marketer can employ disabilities communications to embrace old and new customers. Disability communications can address internal and external audiences; it can educate or familiarize. It can be applied to broad product or service categories such as retailing or financial services companies, which have daily encounters with large publics nationwide, and have, therefore, a reasonable propensity to serve disabled customers. The encounter might not be face to face. You might, however, encourage customer service contact by telephone or by written response.

With proper anticipation, none of your prospect groups would be excluded from receiving your messages because of "user-unfriendly" marketing vehicles such as media access, response access, in-store barriers, and sales staff attitudes. Disabilities marketing is devoted to offering more to consumers with disabilities . . . more choice, more exposure, and more opportunity. What's standing in the way now?

OVERCOMING COMMUNICATIONS INTERFERENCE

Most marketing managers have no idea how limiting conventional marketing communications can be to persons with disabilities. Physical impairments such as arthritis or paralysis can prevent readers from holding, opening, or manipulating magazines, newspapers, or direct mail pieces; lower body impairments such as orthopedic conditions or missing limbs can restrict the distance or the amount of time a disabled person can spend on her or his feet. Sensory impairments such as sight or hearing loss can exclude whole categories of auditory (radio, telemarketing, or television) or visual (broadcast or print) vehicles.

Are these exclusions intentional? No, it's most likely that marketers are unaware of the obstacles and partitions they unwittingly add (or overlook) as broad-based marketing efforts are launched. A complement of disabilities marketing tools can probably be blended into your existing product- or service-marketing mix, adapting and strengthening components such as product design, prospect selection, message development, media dissemination, distribution methods, and performance measurements. To take full advantage of the process, an understanding of contemporary disabilities issues is beneficial for the marketer to master; a classification procedure makes the various health conditions easier to empathize with and comprehend, especially for the marketing manager who has never had the opportunity of knowing or working with or serving customers with disabilities. The benefit to the unfamiliar marketer is that this book can shorten the "learning curve" for recognizing communications obstacles. Once identified, "canceling" the barrier is easier and efficient for the customer and marketer alike.

SEGMENTATION BY "PHYSIOGRAPHIC" CHARACTERISTICS

Central to any segmentation process is the classification strategy; most marketers are probably familiar with and currently use various combinations of demographic, psychographic, geographic, or behavioral segmentation as they organize, quantify and prioritize their customer communications. Each of these clustering strategies can produce valuable information about the customer targets.

Take demographic segmentation. Marketers can reach deeper into prospect pools, casting for characteristics such as age, sex, income, education, working versus nonworking persons, home owners or renters. Adding physical or sensory input such as the type of health condition, the frequency of the condition by age, by sex, by total adults, or by the ability to work, for example, helps the marketer in critical decisions concerning attractiveness or convenience of product or service design, distribution channels, or media strategies when evaluating target groups.

Equally valuable is knowing which submarkets aren't interested in your marketing offerings. Disabilities marketing builds on past segmentation methods such as age or income characteristics, yet opens a new "window" through which to better visualize and appreciate the needs of buyers with disabilities. It evokes a new taxonomy of **physiographic segmentation**, which classifies prospects, customers, or account holders by four physical or sensory-limiting attributes:

- *Mobility impairments* These are limitations to movement, ranging from restricted upper body motions such as reaching, typing, or grasping to restricted lower body motions such as walking or climbing. Mobility impairments may result from many conditions such as injury or disease. These impairments may be caused by amputation of limbs, neuromuscular disease or arthritis, for example, and these limitations might reduce the ability of customers in accessing, handling, or responding to your advertisements or getting to your location or around in your store.

Sensory impairments form the next three categories:

- *Hearing impairments* These include diminished hearing abilities ranging from deafness to being hard of hearing. The degree of limitation can range from mild to severe; many cases respond well to amplification by a hearing aid. Sensitivity to the audio element of television or radio messages must be considered.

- *Sight impairments* These are visual limitations ranging from blindness to other severe sight restrictions such as retinitis pigmentosa. Sight impairments can be doubly restrictive in that they can cause both a visual disability and a reduction in freedom of mobility. Vision limitations affect the impact of print media's graphics and typography elements, but the audio portion of television and radio strengthens communications with consumers who are blind.

- *Speech impairments* These are limitations of intelligible speech resulting from many causes, such as congenital deafness to childhood illness to psychologically induced stuttering. Here, too, a linkage might be noticed, such as a speech impairment resulting from a hearing disability. Telemarketing or customer follow-up efforts would limit response among those buyers who cannot use a standard telephone.

A great many more examples could be cited, but you get the picture. This physiographic method of organizing your customer profiles into these four major health conditions can be quantified to produce population sizes which in turn can determine many market development premises. This strategy can be extended to product or service modifications, user motivations, advertising design and media delivery, and packaging sensitivity and distribution, with a very important prospect or user reaction—the ability to order or respond. Suggestions about "after the sale" customer service or ongoing customer contact are equally vital, as we realize how much more efficient it is to sell to current customers, rather than continually expending larger budgets to recruit new customers.

A thorough explanation of disabilities communications will be applied to the four resources of the promotional mix: advertising, sales promotion, public relations and personal selling. Each of these promotional tools can be greatly strengthened by adjusting to the *abilities* of purchasers with physical or sensory impairments. Initiating the process of disabilities marketing can open the door much wider for disabled customers; maintaining the standards of disabilities marketing will produce long-term and mutually beneficial relationships for marketers and their markets with disabilities.

A WHIRLWIND OF ENVIRONMENTAL FORCES

Look around and I think you'll agree, a transformation is taking place, one that is blending social, economic, legal, technological, and political forces. Slow in synthesis, snapshots of individuals and groups of people are coming into clearer focus. And what we see emerging is a belated consciousness that these people *are* people and should be recognized as consumers with disabilities. Or customers with disabilities. Maybe patrons or investors or clients with disabilities, or even shareholders or regulators with disabilities. These are diverse consumer segments that can be served by most any marketer's product or service. And if well served, they will remain loyal to the firm or brand.

Pressed by the Americans with Disabilities Act legislation (familiarly called the ADA), strategic marketing planning can meld new opportunities—for both the prospect with disabilities and the marketer. On one side, the value and attractiveness of markets with disabilities have long been ignored. On the other side, marketers now have more accurate segmentation tools, more pliant product design and availability, more flexibility in delivery methods.

As a disabled consumer and marketer, I believe the missing linkage between the disabled individual and the marketer is found in the communications channels: marketing departments have failed to recognize "physiographic" characteristics, the physical inabilities or limitations that a disabled customer might experience in learning about or using everyday products or services. Becoming aware of the physiographic capabilities and limitations of segments with disabilities helps the marketer to narrow or close the communications gap by using simple methods to categorize, prioritize, and adjust media vehicles, depending on the marketing environments. Equally important is the marketer's dedication to facilitate "feedback" or response, as in supplying additional product or service information, initiating sales, offering reordering convenience, and furnishing exceptional customer service. Sensitivities and attitudes are crucial in understanding the benefits of parallel media, package access, universal design, and other "disabilities-friendly" techniques.

Having dealt in the advertising communications industry for 20 years, I know what level of commitment to disabilities marketing is needed in effort and empathy; I also know that the return could be an ever-expanding network of mutually beneficial and long-term relationships for both the customer and the marketer.

Myriad forces are bringing the disabled population into the mainstream, and the effects jump out at us daily. Television commercials feature people in wheelchairs; AT&T produces a completely silent spot to introduce its Telecommunications Devices for the Deaf (TDD). Wheelchair athletes with sponsors' logos proudly displayed lead off in marathon races, a deaf tackle plays for the Kansas City Chiefs in the National Football League, and a speechless quadriplegic lectures and holds the Newton chair for physics at Cambridge University. A popular television series has a plaintiff's attorney who is blind unfold his cane, rise, and walk to the jury to deliver his final argument. The Olympics creates a special games, the Paralympics, a showcase for athletes with disabilities. In fact, an archer with a disability launched the flaming arrow that ignited the Olympic torch in the XXV Games in Barcelona. These diverse achievements and events provide outstanding opportunities for innovative companies in contemporary marketing strategy.

While the ADA is a timely issue for human resources consideration, the message of this book is broader than a briefing on legal compliance. I am writing this book to assist marketers, ad managers, advertising agencies, and the news media as well, by isolating real situations and presenting marketing strategies for better serving consumers with disabilities. This goal can be accomplished by "mainstreaming" the marketing process, to allow disabled consumers the ability to access and enjoy the pleasures and products equally with nondisabled persons. Communications with and an understanding of the needs and motivations of populations with disabilities are the underlying themes of this text. Knowledge and comprehension of the capabilities of the disabled will produce a win-win relationship in the marketplace for *both* sides.

CHAPTER ONE

THE AMERICANS WITH DISABILITIES ACT

THE BACKGROUND OF THE AMERICANS WITH DISABILITIES ACT

The enactment of the ADA was long overdue. Largely unnoticed for more than a quarter century, disabilities groups have waged a fight to extend equal rights and opportunities protection to millions and millions of Americans with disabilities. At 10:26 a.m., July 26, 1990, President George Bush signed landmark legislation into law. Called the Americans with Disabilities Act of 1990, this principle represents an unprecedented opportunity to eliminate barriers for the independence and productivity of persons with disabilities. At the same time, managers should be cognizant of the legal and moral impacts of the equilibrating ADA to employment policies and accommodations and accessibilities of public and commercial facilities throughout our nation.

Written to afford equal opportunities and access in employment, public accommodations, transportation, government services, and tele-communications, the ADA has generated considerable attention. To ensure a smoother transition and compliance to workplace policies, business managers should have a general understanding of the law and its ramifications.

Viewpoint 1.1—The real spirit behind ADA

"Suddenly the right to a seat on the bus, the old, first cause of civil rights, is once again vital. Once the struggle was not to be forced to sit in the back of the bus; now the struggle is to get on the bus, period."

Excerpt from former Attorney General Dick Thornburgh's address to the *Business Week* Annual Symposium of Chief Executive Officers on the Americans with Disabilities Act (delivered in Washington on October 12, 1990).

THE PURPOSE OF THE AMERICANS WITH DISABILITIES ACT

The Civil Rights Act of 1964 rightfully restructured opportunities in business, government, and society for many Americans. However, in terms of the basic right of access and employment, persons with disabilities were left outside the law. To correct these oversights, the ADA gives civil rights protections to individuals with disabilities similar to those provided to individuals on the basis of race, sex, national origin, and religion. Specifically, it guarantees equal opportunity for individuals in dealings with public and private sector employment, accommodations, transportation, telecommunications, and state and local government services. Within the marketing context, Title III of the ADA provides for equality of customer or prospect access to the private (as opposed to government services) entity; imaginative compliance actions can set your company apart from the competition. We'll return to the marketing process after an overview of ADA issues is presented.

HOW ARE "DISABILITIES" DEFINED UNDER THE ACT?

The term **disability** covers a wider array of conditions than an easily spotted physical limitation. People who are also considered disabled under the Act are those individuals with physical or mental impairments that substantially limit one or more of the major activities of life, such as walking, talking, caring for oneself, or working. The term also applies to people with a record of an impairment, such as someone recovering from cancer or with a history of lower back problems, as well as people who are "regarded" as having a disability, such as a person with a disfiguring injury such as a burn or scar, even though the individual has no physical limitations.

Many physical conditions are not considered disabilities if the condition, such as a broken arm or leg, are short term in nature. But if an uncorrectable physical limitation results from an injury, this long-term limitation, such as a limp or an atrophied limb, might then qualify the individual as disabled.

Other physical conditions not considered as a "qualified disability" include:

- Physical characteristics, such as blue eyes or red hair
- Personality traits, such as a quick temper
- Pregnancy
- Obesity
- Current alcohol abuse
- Current illegal use of drugs
- Age

Employment practices must observe certain qualifications, though. As an example, former drug or alcohol abusers who are presently participating in rehabilitation programs are covered by the Act. While the law is clear on the included or excluded conditions, a responsible manager will check with the company's legal counsel before taking action.

WHAT SIZE ORGANIZATIONS ARE COVERED BY THE ACT?

For the first two years after July 26, 1992 (the date when the employment provisions of the ADA became effective), only organizations or businesses with 25 or more employees are covered, that is, may not discriminate against qualified individuals with disabilities. Then two years afterward in 1994, businesses with 15 or more employees may not discriminate knowingly against qualified individuals with disabilities.

During the testimony in developing the Americans with Disabilities Act, the small business lobby generally opposed it, worrying that alterations needed to comply with the law would prove too expensive. But since enactment, many business owners and managers have found the adaptions relatively inexpensive and less cumbersome than feared. A *Wall Street Journal* Enterprise column on April 20, 1992, noted:

> Small businesses are finding it less costly to accommodate disabled customers and employees than they had feared. [Since] public accommodations provisions mostly became effective in January [1992] . . . many small businesses are discovering that compliance isn't so burdensome after all. "Small business owners are recognizing that the law is actually making their businesses more accessible," says Todd Harvey, a partner of Design ADA, a New York architectural consulting firm. Compliance "is helping rather than hurting, and it's well worth the cost," he says."

EMPLOYMENT DISCRIMINATION ISSUES

By now marketers should be well versed in ADA policy because these are "people" issues. The ADA prohibits discrimination against qualified disabled individuals and contains specific requirements related to reasonable accommodation, qualifications standards, and other labor management issues such as discrimination in hiring or promotion, or denying opportunity to anyone in a relationship with a disabled person (such as the working parent of a disabled child or spouse). Within the law, employers must make "reasonable accommodation" to disabled workers or applicants, such as physical changes to the office or factory or through job restructuring, for example. The accommodation need not be elaborate, expensive, or burdensome. Remember, reasonable accommodation for a disabled person *should not in any way alter* the standard of performance expected of the employee with disabilities.

WHAT TYPES OF BUSINESSES ARE REGULATED?

This matter is of great importance to the marketer. The ADA guarantees the opportunity of persons with disabilities to participate in the "full and equal enjoyment of the goods, services, facilities, privileges and advantages of any public place." Regardless of staff size or retail square footage or sales volume, facilities catering to the public fall into this "coverage."

■ Other private establishments considered "public accommodations" are restaurants, hotels, retail establishments, shopping centers or malls, office buildings, pharmacies, theaters, museums, libraries, parks, private schools, and day care centers.

■ These establishments may not refuse to serve people with disabilities.

■ Private businesses must remove barriers at existing facilities if possible without "undue burden."

■ Businesses must make any new or renovated facilities accessible to disabled persons; in the future managers must take this provision into account when building, expanding, or refurbishing commercial space.

The ADA also affects public services, such as the telecommunications industry and public transportation provided by state and local government (although commercial airlines are exempted from this law), to improve access in equipment, offer facilities comparable to fixed route systems, and to modify existing facilities to assure access and inter-city and commuter rail accessibility improvements. The deadlines for telecommunications and public transportation are much longer.

ENFORCEMENT OF THE ADA

Managers will be wise to heed the provisions of the ADA for both economic and altruistic reasons. This federal legislation has put teeth into enforcement of equal employment practices concerning persons with disabilities; running afoul of these government regulations can result in fines, or even the closing down of the business. Managers should know that employment discrimination complaints may be filed with the Equal Employment Opportunity Commission and available remedies include back pay and court orders to stop discrimination, not to mention the possibility of embarrassing negative publicity.

In public accommodations issues (such as physical accessibility of the premises from which services are rendered), individuals may bring private lawsuits to obtain court orders to stop discrimination, but the law contains no provision for awarding money damages to the individual. However, individuals can also file complaints with the Attorney General, who may file lawsuits to stop discrimination and obtain money damages and penalties.

Realize that the intent of the ADA is not to punish organizations monetarily. The ADA mandate is to provide an equality of opportunity. People with disabilities don't expect special treatment; they just want *equal treatment*. Capitalizing on legal forces, marketers will be wise to understand the workings and intent of the ADA, and to adapt their products and services to serve consumers with disabilities. The law says it's the right thing to do; the stakes for the marketer are high.

MORE THAN "DE MINIMIS" COMPLIANCE

Marketing managers can make the influence of the ADA work to their advantage as well as to the customers'. While the attention of many marketing managers to disabilities matters has been focused on the employment and accommodations aspects of Title I of the ADA, the deadline for complying with its legal requirements—July 1992—has now passed. Interviewing, hiring, promotion, and job accommodations practices should be in place according to compliance guidelines. Many managers have been charged with completing an *internal* evaluation on human resources practices, giving little thought as to how the influence of the Americans with Disabilities Act could be expanded into appropriate *external* marketing programs.

This inward focus is even more understandable if you have held a marketing management position and remember the crush and concentration on short-term issues like today's key account problem or tomorrow's sales meeting or the day after tomorrow's appointment with the finance committee. Taking secondary importance, tasks such as new markets development, human resources training, or less visible compliance issues such as updating job descriptions are frequently postponed to an unset agenda some time next quarter. But now is the time for savvy marketers to take notice.

Regardless of a manager's time preference, the Americans with Disabilities Act has been legislated as federal law to command attention: The ADA rightfully prevents discrimination toward persons with disabilities. Organizations large and small should be recognizing and addressing the intent and enforcement issues of the employment practices and public access and accommodation. Realistically, though, managers, marketing people included, should extend their understanding of the ADA beyond "de minimis" legal standards to anticipate the practical consequences and economic benefits of bringing consumer markets of diverse disabilities productively together.

What is meant by practical implementation? This civil rights law defines in great detail *what* is to be done: there are written guidelines for physical standards, such as measurements for corridor or door widths, turning radii for wheelchair maneuvering or obligations for installing emergency alarms, both for hearing- and sight-impaired workers, plus many other access and accommodations criteria that, when implemented, provide equality of opportunity for customers with disabilities. These accommodations help currently employed disabled workers perform their job functions as well.

But the practical application, *how* ADA compliance is to be achieved, remains vague. The ADA states the intent of the legislation, to deny discrimination in hiring, promotion, access, and accommodation toward persons with disabilities, but allows supervisors, administrators, or owners to initiate their own training or other processes to bring the organization into compliance during 1992 for most "covered" entities, those enterprises subject to the five ADA titles (Title I, Employment Discrimination; Title II, Government Responsibilities; Title III, Private Entities Access; Title IV, Telecommunications Responsibilities; and Title V, Miscellaneous Provisions). As part of this process, it's incumbent for the supervisor to think beyond the legal requirements, on through the "people portion" of the ADA quotient, to the consequences of workplace interactions, and to expanding the sensitivities and attitudes of employees at all company levels. And if the ADA affects internal practices, wouldn't it be wise to consider external consequences in customer markets? By employing some common sense to the internal and external compliance efforts, the marketing manager can address the practical side of the civil rights law, to the point of a product or service differentiation strategy.

A proactive manager can isolate ADA-impacted audiences and formulate a situation analysis of what has been done *and* what needs to be done. Stop here for a minute to think about opportunities that can evolve to serve new customers or clients with disabilities.

THE ADA AS A MARKETING TOOL

Once a marketer has gathered attitudes that affect populations with disabilities (an assignment we'll talk about shortly), what should be done? So many times people armed with new and innovative marketing initiatives charge off full of steam but gradually lose momentum because of management's lack of interest or imperative. The need for ADA compliance should not only focus the human resources professionals on the legal aspects of hiring, promotion, and accommodations, but should also sharpen marketers to push for marketing practices and policies to become "disabilities-friendly." Besides taking actions to be good corporate citizens, marketers can investigate opportunities that engage product design and segmentation strategies based on "disabilities-friendly" marketing techniques. And to deal more effectively with populations with disabilities, marketing or advertising managers (and human resources people, too) should become adept at "disabilities communications," the method we have discussed to locate or double-check key components of the marketing communications system such as media vehicles that can deliver messages to groups or individuals with diverse disabilities. Likewise, boosting the ability to respond, order, or buy is an important aspect of disabilities communications. Further, the marketing manager should recognize that different disabilities have different needs in information processing. Acquiring sensitivity to segments with disabilities is a wonderful starting point for marketing assessment.

Viewpoint 1.2—Daily newspapers as a source of information

"In a media-influenced society, such as ours, the press can exert an enormous impact on our knowledge, attitudes, and public policies regarding a variety of issues. No better example of this exists than the manner in which the press portrays individuals with disabling conditions. There is evidence [though] that people themselves with disabilities think that the media does not provide information they deem important. Respondents in a national survey of disability issues found the press's coverage of services, benefits, and programs that affect their lives to be insufficient. Also [separate research] surveyed people with disabilities about their satisfaction with a variety of sources of information, including newspapers. About one-third of the respondents found the national newspapers (*The New York Times*, *The Wall Street Journal*, and *USA Today*), and about one-fourth found local newspapers virtually useless as sources of information."

"The Coverage of Persons with Disabilities in American Newspapers," *The Journal of Special Education*, Vol. 24, No. 3, 1990, p. 271.

On intuitive issues the insightful marketer already has an awareness to persons with disabilities' needs in reading larger typefaces or interests in ordering via a voice response menu. The bottom line is that the marketing manager understands that it's his or her job to provide easier access for any consumer, disabled or otherwise, to obtain the company's products or services. Disabilities communications allows the audience an easy response mechanism, whether it be a toll-free telephone number for requesting a catalog or interactive television to take the "pulse" of the market.

But let's slow down a minute. First the priority of disabilities communications must be decided; is the objective to attract external groups as buyer prospects or customer service follow-up? Or are messages to be directed to internal audiences, such as employees or job applicants? If the internal audience is the target, what existing communications channels are presently used? Should new channels be added to provide complementary coverage to workers with specific disabilities (such as large print, Braille, or audio cassette materials for company newsletters or training items; *or* TDD access or hard-copy transcripts of speeches or other oral presentations; *or* for mobility impaired employees who might be working at home, access via computer videotext of memos, company policies, or other office correspondence)?

The variations are countless, but the common denominator is to ask who is the audience and what channels are in place or need to be established to complete the communications loop. Can external customers, some of whom probably already have (or will acquire) a physical disability, order products or services though your existing communications systems?

This awareness and process of disabilities communications serves marketing strategy and implementation well. Also by adapting this method of specialized communications, the marketing manager can embrace a two-pronged commitment to improve marketing productivity (internally driven) *and* marketing efficiency (externally driven) in daily business dealings with persons with disabilities. We'll talk about these strategies shortly.

THE LEGAL AND PRACTICAL ELEMENTS

Each of the stakeholder groups is affected by the ADA in different ways. The chief executive must be concerned with legal compliance, to follow the letter of the law throughout the company's hiring and employment practices. The marketing manager, acting as a first-line leader, must understand legal and practical issues of the ADA that result in balancing efficiency and fairness. And not of least importance is how the company's facilities, services, or products are received by the customer or client with disabilities. Properly enacted ADA practices should make working, shopping, or accessing products easier for the marketer or consumer alike. Elegantly simple, right?

WHY DOES MARKETING HAVE TO KNOW ABOUT AN HR ISSUE?

First of all, the ADA is *not* solely in the realm of human resources; the ADA is a federal law governing our country. Following the ADA should be a company commitment to equal opportunity within and without the organization. Compliance is everyone's job, not just the marketing staff or the training department or the microwave production team.

The better the marketing manager understands the intentions of ADA legislation, the better the match of motivations of markets with disabilities can be to properly tailor products and services. The more knowledgeable the designer, the writer, the media specialist, or the packaging specialist, the better the potential for success. The ADA is a legal document, no doubt about it, but the spirit of the ADA is not about limitations. The spirit is about expansive opportunity and resourceful marketing playing a magnificent role in igniting the flame of imagination for better communications with previously ignored consumers.

The ADA encourages business management and workers alike to understand and respect the diversity of disabilities; more knowledge and exposure to populations with disabilities equates to confidence and a better comfort level for all these business and government publics.

This book is written primarily for the benefit of marketing specialists. In the largest corporations, the marketing director will manage the marketing function and responsibilities; in smaller firms, an owner or high-ranking officer may be charged with these duties. Some firms may entrust marketing planning to an advertising manager, or a public relations chief or a communications manager. Some smaller companies might have only one manager who oversees marketing procedures, while national concerns may employ hundreds at the marketing staff rank.

Regardless of job title, the ADA affects most of America's businesses, and state and local government operations. For example, small businesses may have 25 or fewer employees, yet if the enterprise produces a product or service consumed by the public such as a restaurant, dry cleaner, or shopping mall, your organization is a "covered entity," subject to ADA provisions.

Anticipation of ADA compliance issues is smart business because marketplace interactions occur every day. While some managers can empathize or visualize possible accommodations (after all, who hasn't had his or her mobility impaired by a sprained or broken ankle or wrist?), the best experience is hands-on experience, produced from real-life examples of contemporary activities. Examples within this book are based on actual marketing or communications assignments; they illustrate how nondisabled managers can more effectively anticipate the viewpoints of their customers with disabilities.

EXECUTIVE OVERVIEW OF MARKET FORCES

For more than 200 years, persons with disabilities were outside of the law of equal opportunity. Saluted as the most significant federal civil rights legislation since 1964, the Americans with Disabilities Act is bringing attention and recognition of the employment, accommodations, and accessibility opportunities which are vital to the lives of persons with disabilities. These special populations, as a whole, number more than 43 million people, larger than the entire populations of California and Florida. The potential size and talents to be tapped make a powerful case for attracting and embracing the customer with disabilities. Timing is favorable; the sooner the marketer initiates a disabilities marketing effort, the better, because consumer loyalties are still up for grabs.

The ADA legal compliance deadline brought this fact into focus; moreover, turning compliance into opportunity should be the attitude of the proactive marketing manager. Let's explore the interwoven forces that are bringing groups with disabilities into the spotlight for:

■ Expanding consumer market development

■ Evaluating existing customer satisfaction

■ Accepting a social mandate for corporate responsibility

The best scenario for organizations of all kinds results in a win-win conclusion in which all players, regardless of the size of their role, work together to communicate more effectively, whether your firm adheres to bottom-up or top-down networks. To fully understand the potential of the ADA toward fueling marketing efforts, the marketing manager should be briefed on the intention and scope of the law.

CHAPTER TWO

THE DEMOGRAPHICS OF DISABILITIES

HAVE THE MILLIONS APPEARED OVERNIGHT?

Where have all these persons with disabilities come from? In large part, disabled citizens have always populated our society but as an "underground" group, shamefully hidden away. Yet in the last 10 years, the social stigma of an apparent physical disability has been slowly melting away. The comfort level of working or mingling with disabled people has risen, possibly because of familiarity with a disabling condition of an acquaintance or a relative. Underline this inarguable fact that America is growing older; an older population will possess more and more physical impairments.

Medical technology has made profound advancements, particularly in saving the lives of persons with spinal cord injuries. Recovery, though, results many times in a life-long disability. America is creating more citizens with disabilities, merely through the longevity of the baby boom generation. What is the impact of the expanding ranks with disabilities?

Trends are not difficult to foretell. Look first at future labor requirements. Demographers agree: America is facing an employment dearth, a shortage of entry-level workers, resulting from the low birth rates of the 1960s and 1970s. But what types of job skills are going to be needed, entry-level or otherwise, at the turn of the century? And how do persons with disabilities demonstrate their number as an emerging economic force?

To have influence as an economic force, employment must equate to buying power. How do persons with disabilities fit into the employment pool? According to the U.S. Bureau of Labor Statistics, more than 90 percent of the net new job openings through the year 2000 will be in information-intensive and service-intensive occupations. In these positions brain power, not physical dexterity or sensory acuity, will be the prime requirement.

But that's tomorrow. What about employment rates today? Workers with disabilities are available for employment duties right now. Among men ages 16 to 64, only 36 percent are currently in the labor force. Among women, only 28 percent are employed. This nonemployment statistic is higher than any other demographic group, including the employment rate of young black males, long considered the hardest-to-employ group. According to an International Center for the Disabled study:[1]

> "[we found] 'not working' is the truest definition of what it means to be disabled in the United States today. Two-thirds of the working aged disabled persons are not working. Of these 12.4 million people, 8.2 million want to."

Unlike many immigrant populations, persons with disabilities already have the English language and educational skills that are in demand by service industries. Education levels compare favorably among working ages 16 to 64 years; for those 7.5 million Americans without severe disabilities, 40 percent finish high school with another 30 percent going on to college. Educational levels are telling though, throughout the working and nonworking population, because education is highly inversely associated with work disability. While 22.4 percent with less than a high school education report being unable to work, the percent

---

1   Taylor, Humphrey, Michael R. Kagay, and Stuart Leichenko, *The ICD Survey of Disabled Americans* (New York, NY: Louis Harris and Associates, 1986) 4.

drops to 1.9 percent for persons who complete college, a relative ratio of about 12 to 1.

CONSIDER THE MARKETING IMPLICATIONS

Many of the issues discussed so far have touched the territory of human resources or training and development professionals. What interest or involvement would you expect the marketing department to have? Well, a natural curiosity at the minimum. As human resources staffs see many more applicants with disabilities becoming a larger portion of the selection process, their marketing counterparts in large or small companies should be clamoring to investigate the role of disabilities groups as growing consumer markets. But let's suppose that these two corporate "fiefdoms" have little cross-disciplinary contact, that one hand does not know (or possibly care) what the other hand is doing. Let's furnish the marketing group with additional demographic and psychographic trends of persons with disabilities.

Long considered an "invisible," and thereby an overlooked segment, consumers with disabilities are becoming economic powers now being courted. As the nation's population growth flattens out, many marketers are desperately searching for new customer groups to target as potential buyers. Market investigations are launched weekly by national packaged goods manufacturers and service providers; their market researchers are armed with sophisticated demographic and psychographic analysis tools, and by testing variables they continuously reap data on new market combinations. But researchers will hit walls if they employ traditional means of sample selection from random telephone or mail surveys; no commercial list house has a tape full of persons with orthopedic impairments or total hearing loss.

Do you quit here? No, the market identification process just requires more understanding and will take longer. Briefly, the marketer will be making adjustments in the customer profiling method, which of course is affected by markets with disabilities. Key components in this search among disabilities segments are "common threads" of interest levels that many like-minded consumers hold; health or injury conditions could be the denominator to bring market groups together for both regional and national marketing efforts. National brands can address mainstream messages to their nondisabled markets, then introduce disabilities-friendly messages according to populations sizes and frequencies of health conditions. Targeted communications programs, products and services designed to benefit the disabled consumer, can work to create very loyal customer relationships among the users and referrals and recommendations among family members and friends.

NEEDS WILL BE SHAPED BY NATURE

Marketing managers should recognize the demographic trends that are at work within their customer base. Regardless of whether customers with disabilities have ever been courted, most companies have an excellent chance of "inheriting" buyers who will become disabled through injury or illness at some time in the immediate future; in fact, one in six Americans experience a disabling activity limitation during his or her life.

Even when discounting injury, as age increases the proportion of people with disabilities likewise increases. Forty-five is the age when chronic conditions like arthritis, hearing impairment, and heart disease become prevalent. Baby boomers will swell the ranks of retired and presumably disabled populations through the year 2010. The Bureau of Census has documented a relationship between age and functional limitations; as age increases, disabilities relative to age steadily increase (see Table 2.1):

Table 2.1—As age increases, so do functional limitations.

Age	% with Functional Limitations	% with Severe Limitations
15 to 24 years	5.2%	0.7%
25 to 34 years	7.5%	1.2%
35 to 44 years	13.4%	2.9%
45 to 54 years	23.0%	6.4%
55 to 64 years	34.2%	12.4%
65 to 74 years	49.8%	20.7%
75 years plus	72.5%	41.2%

Source: Bureau of the Census, 1986. Percentage of persons 15 years plus, nationwide.

The ADA is now law, and the number of persons with disabilities increases as we all age. Perhaps group marketing efforts, called affinity marketing, could be appealing; affinity groups are attracted by membership into sponsoring organizations. This sponsorship could focus around college or other special interests such as using a Notre Dame Visa card or a Miami Dolphins Mastercard. The membership potential would continue to grow as baby boomers fill the over-50 ranks. Baby boomers have long been famous for their penchant for purchasing convenience, and as more face the reality of mobility, sight, or hearing impairments, they will "vote their wallets" toward the retailer, manufacturer, or supplier who caters to them. The winning marketers will be those who take the merchandise or services to the consumers with disabilities, rather than making them come to it.

Today's marketing manager also has the tools to assemble more and more efficient message-targeting capabilities, thus directing sales efforts to smaller and smaller like-minded customer groups through sophisticated data base management. Both local and national retailers and services vendors have realized the value in keeping the names, addresses, and preferences of their customers. This contact base has budgetary significance as marketers learn how efficient selling to current clients is, rather than selling to a moving parade of prospects. Improved mailing techniques, electronic ordering, and interactive response media are sharpening delivery efficiency for retailers (and wholesalers) who sell a variety of goods, from lower-priced machine parts to expensive computer peripherals. What took six weeks to process and ship five years ago now can be delivered in 48 hours. Many marketers consider custom processing and speed of delivery to be valuable tools for competitive edge; watch for more speed and convenience in the future.

DIFFERENT DISABILITIES, DIFFERENT ABILITIES

One in seven Americans has an activity limitation,[2] a disability that can result from a variety of conditions. The disability might be a functional limitation such as a missing arm or leg, or loss of sight or hearing. This functional limitation results in the individual's inability to perform a major activity of life[3], such as walking, talking, keeping house, shopping, or working. The disability might be related to a health condition, such as hypertension or arthritis or muscular dystrophy. It might be

---

2   Kraus, Lewis E. and Susan Stoddard, *Chartbook on Disability in the United States* (Washington, D.C.: U.S. National Institute on Disability and Rehabilitation Research, 1989), 2.

3   LaPlante, Mitchell P., *Data on Disability from the National Health Interview Survey, 1983–1985* (Washington, D.C.: U.S. National Institute on Disability and Rehabilitation Research, 1988), 4.

readily seen because of braces or crutches, or it might be physically invisible such as circulatory conditions, hearing or speech impairments.

Recognize the first sensitivity of all, that *disabilities are diverse*, therefore, different disabilities dictate totally different marketing approaches. This tenet will appear over and over as the practice of disabilities marketing unfolds. To emphasize the diversity, let's review the most difficult barrier in life that a person with a disability sees before him or herself. In 1986 a Louis Harris and Associates survey screened 12,500 American households to identify a sample of 1,000 disabled Americans of working ages; this sample was then asked a variety of questions about their everyday life. A diversity of self-perceptions was reported[4] (see Table 2.2).

Table 2.2—What is the most difficult barrier that you have faced in connection with your disability or health problem over the years?

Limitation	Most Difficult Barrier
Limited/lack of mobility	10%
Unable to walk/stand/run/climb stairs	10%
Unable to work due to disability	7%
All aspects of life limited	4%
Pain	4%
Hearing problems in groups	4%
Unable to do housework	3%
Need to depend on others	3%
Peoples' reaction to me	3%
Unable to participate in sports	3%
Can't see well enough to drive	2%
Lack of strength	2%

Source: Louis Harris and Associates, 1986

---

4 Taylor, Humphrey, Michael R. Kagay, and Stuart Leichenko, *The ICD Survey of Disabled Americans*, iii.

These 12 most common responses were followed by 37 less frequent barriers, a total of 49 barriers related by the 1,000-person disabled sample screened from a random population of 12,000. It would be difficult for a marketer to satisfy all 49 obstacles; learning to organize and prioritize opportunities to serve disabled people is only one advantage of disabilities marketing.

WHAT IS THE DEFINITION OF A "DISABILITY"?

A disability can simply be defined as "a limitation in a person's ability to perform a major activity"; governmental statistics recognize a variety of disabilities from annoyances such as sinusitis to debilitating conditions such as rheumatoid arthritis, blindness, or paralysis. Disabilities may also follow accidental injuries or result from chronic (or long-term) health conditions.

Disabilities may be slight, such as hay fever, or they may be severe, such as paralysis or sensory impairments. These more serious conditions limit the mobility or the type or amount of activities an individual can engage in. These limitations to major activities are descriptive, and usually grouped by age, such as the following:

- Working or keeping house, ages 18 to 69 years

- Capacity for self-care, ages 60 plus

- Limitations on nonmajor activity (example, an ability to keep house but inability to work full-time)

While segmenting disabilities produces smaller prospect groups, these prospect groupings can still be quite large. More than 20 percent of all noninstitutionalized civilians over 15 years of age report a *physical* functional limitation. This population is estimated at 37.3 million persons (the government estimation of 43 million includes mental disorders, which are not considered physical limitations). Marketers would agree that working with such huge numbers is difficult, but there are segmentation strategies that could make segmentation decisions easier for marketing or advertising managers.

DEFINING THE POTENTIAL AND THE POPULATIONS

This marketing opportunity is not a regional or spot market phenomenon; disabilities affect Americans throughout the nation. Can we organize and reduce this "universe" into more manageable segments?

We can create smaller clusters of customers with disabilities at a more local or regional level. Since most consumer-oriented retail businesses typically serve a state or regional area, a more manageable projection of various disabilities can be estimated. Marketing is a practical process, and depending on the product's availability, quantifying segment sizes is a handy tool. An overview for the potential population sizes can be determined on a national, state, or regional basis from U.S. government statistics; Table 2.3 divides selected health conditions into segments for national, state (Florida) and regional (Tampa Bay) areas for population projections.

Reports from the National Institute on Disability and Rehabilitation Research (1985) and the Bureau of Economic and Business Research (1989) at the University of Florida documents prevalent and activity-limiting disabilities:

Table 2.3—Prevalent and activity-limiting disabilities can be estimated by incidence rates per 1,000 persons, projected by geographic areas.

Condition	Rate per 1,000 pers	Segment Size		
		U.S.	Florida	Tampa Bay
Hypertension	123.5	28,405,000	1,574,630	319,333
Rheumatoid arthritis	5.6	1,288,000	71,400	15,883
(Plus Osteoarthritis/ other arthropathies)	131.0	30,130,000	1,657,500	366,800
Deaf in both ears	7.5	1,725,000	95,630	21,000
(Plus other impairments)	90.8	20,884,000	1,157,700	254,240
Blind in both eyes	1.6	368,000	20,400	4,480
(Plus other visual impairments)	38.5	8,855,000	490,880	107,800
Speech impairments	10.2	2,346,000	130,050	28,560
Impairment of lower extremities	45.2	10,396,000	567,300	126,560
Impairments of upper extremities	13.5	3,105,000	172,130	37,800

Source: Data on Disability from NHIS, 1983–85

In 1985 the United States' population was estimated at 230,000,000 and in 1989 Florida's population was estimated at 12,750,000 with the

Tampa Bay area's population estimated at 2,836,300 for Hillsborough, Pinellas, Pasco, Polk, Manatee, and Sarasota counties. Multipliers used were 230, 12.75, and 2.8, respectively for national, state, and regional populations.

This narrower focus is helpful. Several disabilities groups, such as persons with hypertension or arthritis, include over a quarter million people at the regional level. These segment estimates are still quite large. Can any health condition information be overlaid to provide a description of characteristics of disabilities? Yes, let's rank activity limitations, such as mobility impairments, by the most restrictive health conditions (see Table 2.4).

Table 2.4—Which health conditions cause activity limitations most often?

Chronic condition	Percent with condition who are limited in activity
Multiple sclerosis	77.0
Paralysis of extremities	65.7
Emphysema	48.2
Intervertebral disk disorders	45.9
Epilepsy	42.8
Pneumoconiosis	41.9
Cerebrovascular disease	41.2
Osteomyelitis and other bone diseases	34.3
Diabetes	32.1
Deformities or other orthopedic impairments	31.6
Heart conditions	31.4
Phlebitis and thrombophlebitis	27.3
Cystic fibrosis	27.3
Asthma	21.3
Arthritis	20.8
Absence of extremities	18.2

Source: Chartbook of Disabilities, 1989

The implication is clear: Demographic forces are expanding the number of persons with disabilities. Can marketers read more than numbers to appreciate and anticipate the influences that are both fragmenting and enlarging the best interests of disabled consumers?

SOCIAL FORCES ENHANCED BY THE MEDIA

When did consumers with disabilities begin to recognize their potential influence? A closer look at social influences starts with the phenomena of media intrusion. In a 1982 edition of *Rehabilitation Literature*, the article "Media and Disability," reported that:

> studied extensively the depictions [of disabilities] on televi-
> sion. In the study on prime-time television shows of the three
> major networks, demographic, dramatic and personal profiles
> were created from the examination of characters depicted as
> having various disabilities. The conclusion of this study was
> evident: Television does stigmatize people with disabilities. Of
> the disabled characters portrayed, 40 percent were children,
> and none were over the age of 65. They came from predomi-
> nately lower classes of society and were unemployed. If they
> did have employment, it was characterized by a low status of
> occupation. They were excluded from important family roles,
> and generally were in schools and institutions. Two-thirds
> were depicted as being single. Almost one-half of the portray-
> als were recipients of abuse, both verbal and physical. Heroic
> status was generally denied, and villain roles were minimal.
> However, story endings were more positive than those with
> nondisabled characters, in that most disabled characters expe-
> rienced a miracle cure at the end of the program. One-half of
> the disabled characters were either included and/or excluded
> from the group. Two-thirds were depicted as being succored,
> and three-quarters were depicted as submissive. Personality
> traits surveyed revealed most were portrayed as being dull,
> impotent, selfish, defensive, and uncultured. They were re-
> garded as objects of pity and care. Overall, they were consid-
> ered not quite human, and virtually immobile in society.[5]

In the last 10 years, though, the existence of disabilities has been recognized as a natural state of life. The news and entertainment media have increased awareness and helped to change attitudes on disabilities issues; portrayals now depict inspirations, not limitations, to tell the story. A few examples are telling:

---

5 Elliot, Timothy R. and E. Keith Byrd, "Media and Disability," *Rehabilitation Literature* (Vol. 43, 1982), 348.

Figure 2.1—A Corporate Salute to Disabilities' Abilities

Anything You Can Do They Can Do, Too

While you flex your muscles in front of your morning mirror and congratulate yourself on your nimble brain, consider this: The light over your mirror was perfected by a deaf man. While your morning radio plays, remember the hunchback who helped invent it. If you listen to contemporary music, you may hear an artist who is blind. If you prefer classical, you may enjoy a symphony written by a composer who couldn't hear. The President who set an unbeatable American political record could hardly walk. A woman born unable to see, speak or hear stands as a great achiever in American history. The handicapped can enrich our lives. Let's enrich theirs.

A message as published in the *Wall Street Journal* by United Technologies Corporation, Hartford, Connecticut 06101

In 1979, United Technologies launched a series of *Wall Street Journal* messages written around the theme "performance as individuals will determine how we perform as a nation." An example of these simple yet powerful full page ads focused on unrenowned accomplishments by disabled scientists, artists and politicians; premiering in May 1980, the salute was a decade ahead of popular corporate efforts. United Technologies received 3,400 letters from readers and mailed 52,700 reprints of the ad. The U.S. Senate Subcommittee on the Handicapped requested multiple copies for its use. The news media noticed as with the *Manchester Union Leader* writing, "We should all do so well to reflect on the following message from United Technologies."

(Used with permission of United Technologies Corporation)

■ In 1987 Marlee Matlin, an actress who is deaf, won an Oscar for her role in the movie, *Children of a Lesser God*; in 1991 she starred in a prime time television series, *Reasonable Doubts*.

■ In 1990 the best picture was awarded to the movie, *My Left Foot*, the story of Christy Brown, an Irish artist who learns to deal with a severe disability, cerebral palsy.

■ Television's Emmy recognized Larry Drake's role as the mentally impaired clerk, Benny, on *L.A. Law*, while the *Life Goes On* series employed actor Chris Burke, who has Down's syndrome.

Viewpoint 2.1—DuPont reports on Bill Demby's comeback

For Bill Demby, the difference means getting another shot.

When Bill Demby was in Vietnam, he used to dream of coming home and playing a little basketball with the guys.

A dream that all but died when he lost both legs to a Viet Cong rocket.

But then, a group of researchers discovered that a remarkable Du-Pont plastic could help make artificial limbs that were more resilient, more flexible, more like life itself.

Thanks to these efforts, Bill Demby is back. And some say, he hasn't lost a step.

At DuPont, we make the things that make a difference.

(Reprinted with permission of E. I. duPont de Nemours and Company)

■ Powerful advertising messages from global companies include the following: a wheelchair user wearing Levi's; basketball player Bill

Demby's prosthesis made with DuPont materials; Budweiser's wheelchair marathon man; McDonald's developmentally impaired employee, Mike Sewell; and Pepsi endorsed by Ray Charles on television.

TECHNOLOGICAL ADVANCEMENTS ABOUND

The outpouring of new technology has meant freedom for many persons with disabilities. Office automation now negates many previously limiting geographical obstacles, particularly for the person with a mobility or sight impairment who has great difficulty in getting to the office every day.

Modems, faxes, hands-free applications, in general the rapid emergence of computer technology is *the* assistive tool in everyone's getting the work done:

■ Look at the explosion of affordable personal computers as a communications tool for the individual in his or her home office or the company workplace; adaptions of keyboards to accept voice or optical character recognition, "eye blink," "sip and puff," and other innovative input methods that allow mobility or sight impaired users to "link to the loop."

■ Depending on the disability, technological advances are astounding. Computerized output devices can read printed materials aloud, voice recognition work stations enable blind persons to access data banks, and computerized electronic matrices attached to video cameras translate eye movements into speech.

■ Major computer companies have established departments and other resources dedicated solely to assisting the public with disabilities technology. Both IBM and Apple staff toll-free telephone numbers for distributing information on its assistive equipment available to persons with disabilities.

■ Costs to eliminate physical barriers or to purchase assistive equipment such as computer peripherals or telephone instruments can qualify for disability access tax credits under the Omnibus Budget Reconciliation Act of 1990.

The marketing departments of many companies, such as Travelers, are recognizing the contributions of workers, whether it be the technician, the marketing representative or the writer with disabilities. Progressive companies are embracing "telecommuting," by allowing the employee to work off site, most commonly at home. The employer can make assignments to employees working at home; on completion of the assignment, the employee with disabilities can transmit via fax or modem back to the central office. The employer saves on overhead, too, through reduced office space, furnishings, and support personnel needed as the home-based employee works more independently. The new password is efficiency, and both the employer and employee are pulling together to be more productive.

A GENERATIONAL SHIFT CALLED "BABY BUSTERS"

As the nation approaches the year 2000, demographic forces will make populations with disabilities an attractive work resource. Another economic factor should be considered, and that is the generation shift called baby busters, those born after 1970.[6] Baby busters is the first generation in American history to be smaller than the proceeding generation. During the 1990s they will slow the rate of household growth, constrict the flow of young workers, and dampen demand for youth-oriented products. Workers with disabilities could fill employment gaps as an attractive labor pool with proven high marks for their work attitudes, attendance, and productivity. With an employment rate of less than 35 percent, there are many willing workers. Their educational level is generally competitive.

CHOOSING A SEGMENTATION STRATEGY

There are several segmentation strategies available through disabilities marketing practices. As explained in the previous chapter, a classification by physiographics uses mobility or sensory limitations as descriptors, and specifies that functional limitations be divided into four groups: mobility impairments, hearing impairments, sight impairments, and speech impairments. Sorting further, individual physiographic groupings such as mobility conditions might range from "little to no limitation" to "severely disabled" or from upper body to lower body limitations or combinations of multiple conditions such as diabetes and sight impairments. As an example, the marketer might introduce an

---

6 Edmundson, Brad, "Meet the Baby Bust," *American Demographics* (Ithaca, NY: American Demographics, February, 1992), 2.

electric clock with easy-to-set alarm buttons for which promotions are aimed at the moderately to severely mobility-impaired population. For a different product, the marketer may regroup the health conditions to emphasize lower body abilities.

Rankings can also be quantified within a group, such as the number of persons most (or least) restricted.

Viewpoint 2.2—Types of functional limitations vary

Different disabilities modify consumer activities in different ways. Some severely disabled consumers face difficulty moving within their homes; larger populations are less restricted in movement but still encounter exertional limits, such as distance walked or weight carried. Understanding how activities limitations such as walking or speaking affect prospect populations from nondisabled customers is critical in marketing program planning.

Activity Limitation	Millions of People
Getting around in the home	2.5
Having one's speech understood	2.5
Getting around outside the home	6.0
Hearing normal conversations	7.7
Seeing words and letters in newsprint	12.8
Going up a flight of stairs	18.1
Lifting or carrying a 10 lb. bag	18.2
Walking a quarter of a mile	19.2

Source: Chartbook of Disabilities, 1989

Depending on the benefits of the product, a marketer can define one of several relevant markets and target to the abilities and the characteristics of the consumer groups on a college campus, for example, such as students or faculty who might appreciate carrying lightweight book backpacks with Velcro fasteners. The marketer segments the potential buyers into smaller buying groups and quickly learns that each target group receives a different benefit for using the backpack:

■ Limited in activity due to mobility impairments (easy to close the fastener to assist poor finger and hand movement)

■ Limited in movement due to sight impairments (Besides easy closure, there are many interior pockets for organizing, which facilitates memorizing the placement of materials.)

■ Limited in activity due to chronic health conditions (the book bag is made of lightweight fabric to reduce exertion)

Larger markets can be drawn from each of the health conditions, and market development potential can be estimated from one of several demographic tables prepared by the Department of Education and the Bureau of Census (see Table 2.5).

Table 2.5—Prevalence of activity limitation due to chronic conditions among males, by main cause of condition

Different conditions have different prevalence at various ages; in this table, various health conditions are stated by age and by how often the condition occurs. The first number is the number of conditions in thousands and the second is percent distribution.

Condition	All Ages		Under 18		18 – 44		45 – 69	
Coronary heart dis	1,090	7.2	1	0.0	62	1.5	788	12.2
Imp of lower extrem	1,028	6.8	74	3.9	524	12.4	322	5.0
Osteoarthritis	1,024	0.9	5	0.3	150	3.5	595	9.2
Other imp of back	1,020	6.7	11	0.6	506	11.9	450	7.0
Invert disk disord	741	4.9	2	0.1	354	8.4	354	5.5
Other heart dis	709	4.7	30	1.6	52	1.2	419	6.5
Asthma	657	4.3	343	18.1	183	4.3	104	1.6
Emphysema	466	3.1	–	–	10	0.2	299	4.6
Other eye disord	461	3.0	49	2.6	175	4.1	137	2.1
Hypertension	406	2.7	5	0.3	52	1.2	270	4.2

Source: Prevalence of activity limitation, Males; *Data on Disability from NHIS, 1983–85.*

This ranking is ordered by the size of the groups of "All Adults" category as the 10 most limiting conditions. The marketer must carefully review the conditions selected, the frequency of the condition, and the age group for more accurate forecasting. Notice the most prevalent age group for osteoarthritis is 45–69 years. But for asthma conditions, the age group under 18 years has a higher distribution.

As a marketer gains familiarity with these health conditions, segmentation by physiographic characteristics becomes much easier.

BIG COMPANIES OR SMALL FIRMS CAN PROFIT

Disabilities marketing can be applied to the efforts of the largest of corporations serving millions of customers, or to marketing the smallest of organizations catering to a retail clientele. Whether the marketer oversees one restaurant or manages national product lines or brands requiring separate marketing plans, disabilities marketing can be adjusted according to customer preferences. Disabilities marketing can be implemented selectively at only one shopping mall or worked into national marketing, advertising, and sales promotion plans for a 350-restaurant chain stretching from Phoenix to Pittsburgh. Or it can be used by a solitary marketing manager wearing several hats or embraced by regional marketing managers wanting to standardize various marketing approaches, disabilities marketing being only one of several marketing programs.

FLEXIBILITY AND SIZE

Each of the past examples demonstrated different scenarios requiring flexibility, depending on product lines or sales geography, as well as supporting corporate or sole proprietor's marketing strategies. Whether it is engaged as a niche or a national program, disabilities marketing actions can be tailored to the desires and demands of consumers with disabilities.

Aside from flexibility, judging the size of potential markets is a significant consequence of embracing the disabilities marketing strategy. Demonstrating that some disabled populations number into the millions should open the eyes of marketing organizations. Managers can fast embark on a hurried test of selling to disabled persons—and fail. Or marketers can investigate the numbers and populations with disabilities, select a segment well-matched to the product or service, and initiate a program that melds disabilities marketing into each step of the process—and produce a winner. The same amount of effort perhaps, sometimes much more, but disabilities marketing will yield long-term benefits.

ASSESSING YOUR ORGANIZATION

SHAPING ATTITUDES AND OPPORTUNITIES

It's a good idea for marketers to put their own house in order before they attempt to attract new customers through disabilities marketing. As they increase their organization's sensitivity to disabled populations, marketers begin to think in new—and potentially profitable—ways about the disabled market niche. It is also good to recognize that persons with disabilities fill many roles, such as employees, managers, politicians, teachers, suppliers, or regulators. They can be customers or account holders who could make or break your product or service introduction. In many cases it is only the restrictive attitudes of others that keep persons with disabilities from achieving their full potential; training and education are shaping attitudes within the work force.

31

HUMAN RESOURCES ENCOURAGE UNDERSTANDING

Employee sensitivity training, to encourage better understanding of the diversity of disabilities, between fellow workers and also in serving disabled customers, is proving to be a most worthwhile endeavor. Effort is being directed to ADA training among managers and line workers; innovative programs are being designed to eliminate the fears, biases, and myths that create barriers in hiring and working with persons with disabilities. Many training modules consist of exercises that pertain to the everyday work world. The result of these upbeat training programs helps managers feel more confident in supervising disabled workers as the employment rates of hiring disabilities increases.

PRODUCT DESIGN WE ALL CAN USE

Sensitivity as to how products and services produce benefits for their users is an important beginning for customer satisfaction, and many manufacturers have found that all their customers gain, including the disabled ones, from conscious design of products and services that are easier to use. Product design and testing is an important service of groups such as the Electronic Industries Foundation in Washington and the Institute for Technology Development in Oxford, Mississippi; both counsel the trades and government on ways to improve the products and services that are available to the disabilities populations.

TAX INCENTIVES FOR THE COMPANY

The federal government has lightened the cost of necessary renovation and assistive equipment to facilitate persons with disabilities through tax incentives available to the employer. There are three specific incentives to be aware of:

- The **Architectural and Transportation Barrier Removal Deduction** states that, under Section 190 of the Internal Revenue Code, all businesses may claim up to a $15,000 tax deduction for removing architectural, transportation, and communications barriers from their facilities.

- The **Disabled Access Credit** allows small businesses with 30 or fewer full-time employees and with sales grossing less than $1 million annually a tax credit to cover making reasonable accommodations to facilities and programs. The maximum credit is one-half of the costs related to ADA compliance, up to $5,000.

■ The **Targeted Jobs Tax Credit** allows employers to obtain a credit of 40 percent of the first year's wages (up to $6,000) per new employee hired from one of nine targeted groups, including persons with disabilities.

IMPROVED CORPORATE COMMUNICATIONS OPPORTUNITIES

Does one vehicle, such as a company newsletter, reach all your constituents, disabled or nondisabled? Probably not. So corporate communications departments should recognize there are gaps or blind spots that limit coverage of existing communications vehicles, directed to the staff or distributor or franchisee, or to the customer or client. Voice mail might be the most efficient interoffice tool since carbon paper, but how effective is the system to the hearing or speech impaired worker? A communications audit of internal and external needs and present delivery channels can uncover areas that exclude workers with disabilities from the corporate network or that prohibit customers with disabilities from ordering or accessing customer service over the telephone.

A change in attitudes is essential if anything more than superficial compliance to the law is to be accomplished. If cursory or patronizing attitudes are prevalent within the company, there is little chance of long-term success in marketing to customers with disabilities. Disabled people are not stupid. They can tell when they are not welcome or being barely tolerated or made to feel exploited.

Knowing how attitudes affect the marketing process is crucial. In every case, first-hand understanding improves marketing communications among all your "publics"—customers, employees, or stockholders, to name a few. The better a marketer understands the motivations of disabled individuals, the more complete and realistic marketing assessments can be.

For managers, previous experience in working with persons with disabilities is very helpful. From these work experiences, most marketers learn that there is little difference in performance between disabled and nondisabled workers. Disabled people make positive contributions and are recognized for their skills, not for their limitations. In interviews with managers who have supervised disabled workers, most managers are quick to assert that the employee's disability caused little if any problem in getting the work done. In fact, several managers working together at a defense plant could not remember what disability their associate had, when in fact the man was blind.

Another point of support can be found in the age of the company's work force. The older the worker, the better the chance the employee or a close acquaintance has experienced a disability of his or her own. Older work forces are more tolerant and less intimidated by disabled persons; perhaps the younger marketing crackerjack hasn't confronted his or her own mortality or the possibility of physical limitation related to aging.

Regardless of the environment, it should be stated that persons with disabilities do not want *special* treatment; they just want *equal* treatment in employment opportunities or in accessing goods and services. Marketers should be open minded about the need for this "different but equal" footing. The understanding that emerges is an empathy (for both sides) for points of view, commonality of solutions, and a foundation for future ideas and accommodations. Let's discuss the intrapersonal dynamics that form our perceptions and attitudes as they relate to the marketing environment.

START WITH SENSITIVITIES

An axiom of basic marketing is the admonition to "know your market." If you've never been exposed to a physical disability, how can you, as a marketer, identify with the needs and wants of consumers with disabilities? The ADA provides enforcement guidelines and legal remedies for employment, access, and accommodations of disabilities populations, yet standards for work or social conduct are ignored within this law. Proactive marketing managers can appreciate the importance and intent of the ADA, to provide equal rights to individuals with disabilities. Before grand schemes are hatched for public consumption, ask your organization about their beliefs and attitudes experiences toward disabled customers.

In shaping attitudes, attention should be given to uncovering those presently held before mapping out future marketing directions. Getting a handle on these opinions should take more effort than a possibly biased "gut-feel" reaction. The marketer should refrain from guessing what management or staff might say. It's best to build attitudes on realistic expectations and the marketer must ask, not guess, how the company feels about serving customers with disabilities.

"Where we are" might vary from one business or industry to the next; businesses whose workers possess higher levels of education produce the greatest support for mainstreaming and marketing to consumers with disabilities. The most efficient process to gauge present opinions and beliefs is to initiate an audit—an anonymous, unintimidating questionnaire that seeks honest reactions from the work force. How comfortable are our customer service people when they encounter consumers with disabilities? How do account holders who are deaf contact the billing department to request a credit for returned merchandise? This audit process will uncover more than a spectrum of attitudes. It will also uncover many service or access gaps. Better to unearth these shortcomings yourself than to have customers or regulators discover the missing ramp or too narrow door widths.

It's rare to find companies that have conducted opinions or needs surveys on a regular basis. Companies that have surveyed their employees on disabilities attitudes are usually industry leaders holding stakeholder benefit and social responsibility in high regard. Consistently administered audits keep managers in touch with reality; organizations of all sizes can gain by taking the company pulse. These audits also provide good benchmarks against which to measure future attitudes or program results.

Several questionnaires that managers can implement themselves will be discussed; these self-evaluations are checklists that focus attention on many fundamental marketing decisions. A natural starting point could be to probe disabilities awareness by employees or to audit your organization's marketing communications systems. A different starting point might use a self-evaluation perspective on programs and policies that comply with the Americans with Disabilities Act. Usually the survey is in written form; occasionally individual or group interviews are held if anonymity is unnecessary. Or rather than self-evaluations, management might bring in an outside consultant if speed or objectivity is in question.

The point is to know where attitude or marketing performance stands *before* any new programs are developed. Let's review several areas of opportunity in which marketing communications can be cultivated.

ATTITUDES AND COMMUNICATIONS CONCEPTS

Why should attitudes or language be considered now? Just read the text on page 35,549 of the *Federal Register*, Part III rules and regulations, July 26, 1991:

> The use of the term "disability" instead of "handicap" and the
> term "individual with a disability" instead of "individual with

handicaps" represents an effort by the Congress to make use
of up-to-date, currently accepted terminology. The terminology applied to individuals with disabilities is a very significant and sensitive issue. As with racial and ethnic terms, the
choice of words to describe a person with a disability is overlaid with stereotypes, patronizing attitudes and other emotional considerations. Congress has recognized this shift in
terminology, e.g., by changing the name of the National
Council on the Handicapped to the National Council on Disability.

In keeping with the government's spirit to use up-to-date, current
terminology, let's begin with a few basic concepts to add sensitivity to
the marketing manager's vocabulary and language. These language and
attitudinal suggestions are not "silver bullets" nor magic solutions, but
they do demonstrate empathetic insight rarely encountered 10 years
ago:

■ Discard the word "handicap"—derived from the beggar's practice
  of asking "cap in hand"—when referring to a person. Use in its
  place "person with disabilities." Toss out old-fashioned words like
  "cripple" or "shut-ins." Just think about a word like "invalid"; the
  converse is "valid" or "of value."

■ Recognize the distinction between **disability** (a condition
  caused by accident, trauma, genetics, or disease that might limit a
  person's vision, speech, mental function, or mobility) and a
  handicap (a physical or attitudinal constraint imposed upon a
  person regardless of whether that person has a disability). A
  handicap equates to a disadvantage. Some people with disabilities
  use a wheelchair; stairs, cobblestones, or narrow doors are handicaps imposed upon people with disabilities who use wheelchairs.

■ Focus on the *person* before the disability; put the person first: a
  person who is blind, rather than a blind person; executives with
  disabilities; populations with disabilities; one who is deaf. In this
  text, I may occasionally use "disabled person(s)" for brevity's
  sake, but the preferred expression is "person(s) with disabilities."
  Harsh phrases like "the disabled" or "the blind" or the "emotion-
  ally disturbed" should be avoided since they are impersonal labels. Thoughtless categorizations such as "an epileptic" or "the
  crippled" are sorely stigmatizing.

■ Focus on the *abilities* of person, not on limitations or disabilities.
  Allow the applicant or the worker with disabilities to decide what

he or she is capable of doing; don't allow the employer to make this decision.

■ Beware of "substitutions," bringing back the old stereotypes. If you think to yourself it's a job a disabled person could do very well; be careful. This attitude is patronizing and condescending. And if it sounds bad, it's probably distasteful.

■ Refer to persons who have no disabilities as nondisabled persons. This may sound stilted or awkward, but it is a neutral description rather than frequently used but objectionable labels such as "enabled" or "healthy" or "normal."

■ Also avoid "value loading" your descriptions of conditions of persons with disabilities. Be careful of negative phrases like "suffering from," or "a victim of," or "being confined to" or "restricted to"; use factual depictions such as "wheelchair user" or "sight impaired."

■ Strike out the euphemisms. Masking the condition does not change the fact. Most persons with disabilities find casual characterizations like "mentally challenged" or "special abilities" to be condescending and distasteful.

■ Don't worry about the word gaffes like asking a person who is blind to "see here" or a person who is mobility impaired to "stand up and be counted" or telling one with a hearing impairment to "listen up." These figures of speech are familiar and used by all to get the meaning across. This can be a source of humor for the individual with a disability, particularly if the wheelchair user is considered a "roll model."

■ Understand too, it is permissible to ask about the disability (other than in the formal interview and hiring process) because it shows you are interested in the individual. The person with the disability may choose to talk at length of his or her condition and how he or she copes with the inconveniences, or may choose not to talk about it at all.

■ Don't be embarrassed, for yourself or for the person with disabilities. We're all trying to play the best hand (and probably the only one) dealt to us. We're all more alike than different.

Some of these thoughts may seem simple to sophisticated marketers, but over the years, much has been left unsaid about the conditions and emotions of persons with disabilities. Rather than groping for or guessing about opinions, use the preceding information as a foundation on which realistic dialogue can be built. Displaying a sensitivity to today's attitudes and language is not fad or fashion, but a meaningful recognition of the contributions and roles that populations with disabilities are making. This change to embrace the individual with a disability has been long overdue.

MENTAL DISORDERS AND APPREHENSION

Our discussion has focused on physical disabilities; are mental disabilities subject to marketing efforts? In most cases physical disabilities (those involving mobility, hearing, sight, or speech impairments) are "acceptable" conditions, while mental disorders are not. Mentally based disorders have a certain degree of mystique that is uncomfortable to the public. Perhaps this is because the field of psychology is relatively young; for instance, the American Psychological Association celebrated its 100th anniversary in 1992. And many of the psychoanalytic practices have gained wider exposure only during the last 50 years. Perhaps the public is more comfortable with its knowledge of the causes and predictable course of physical disabilities, while many psychologically based disorders remain a quandary to both mental health practitioners and researchers.

Like physical disabilities, there are myriad mental disorders. *The Diagnostic and Statistical Manual of Mental Disorders* published by the American Psychiatric Association lists over 200 different types. These disorders are quite varied, and include such categories as eating disorders, attention deficit disorders, organic brain disorders, affective disorders, psychotic disorders, psychosexual disorders, and adjustment disorders. These disorders often have mixed features, further complicating the psychiatric diagnosis. To say the least, mental disorders are complex even to the trained practitioner; simply put, lay people generally are unable to understand and differentiate among types of disorders.

These misunderstandings often lead to stereotypes. For instance, the term "schizophrenic" is often incorrectly used to mean multiple personalities. Likewise, the term "posttraumatic stress disorder" often conjures up the image of war veterans who often experience flashbacks, and sometimes act in an inappropriate and violent manner. However, many people are unaware that this diagnosis is often given to individuals who have experienced injuries (such as an amputation), or a catastrophic life event (such as surviving a tornado). These examples illustrate how a stereotype can lead to incorrect attributions of associated behavior of a mental disorder.

Because society often has a misunderstanding of mentally based disorders, many people, including marketers and sales staff, are apprehensive about dealing with consumers with mental disorders. Since they do not understand mental disorders and since they often perceive people with mental disorders to be unpredictable and uncontrollable, they choose to avoid contact and interpersonal relationships with persons with mental disabilities.

Because of these mental health complexities, the strategy of disabilities marketing will develop applications to engage consumers with physical and sensory disabilities, by far the majority of disabled Americans. These conditions are more favorable for gaining the interest of disabled customers and the support of marketing management. As diverse as physical disabilities are, putting mental disabilities aside can expedite the marketing process.

THE ADA IS ONLY THE FIRST STEP

Social and media forces complement the legal catalyst of the ADA, and marketers should be looking ahead, not behind. These language and attitude tips can be used in all manners of communication—from personal to mass media—and for various methods of the marketing mix—advertising, sales promotion, public relations, and personal selling. Above all the strategies, though, there must be an honest commitment to getting to know the disabled account holder better. If there is no commitment, there can be no success. Marketing to populations with disabilities is no casual effort; it can take years to build a substantial customer and referral bank. But with enthusiastic support and participation by top management, disabilities communications can build a following of highly loyal customers, plus earn the appreciation and patronage of their relatives and friends.

The suggested language is intended to buttress an evolving relationship between the consumer and the supplier; persons with disabilities take notice as more and more media advertisers recruit and portray photographic models with "their" disability. The emphasis on language and attitudes also works to strengthen verbal skills and etiquette when sales representatives serve customers with disabilities. So many marketing programs fail at the personal selling level, when the disabled consumer comes face to face with the insurance agent or the retail clerk or the auto salesperson. By anticipating how customers with disabilities will interact with your marketing process, the marketer commands an advantage if the sales force has been trained on improving disabilities communications.

Apart from business, the marketer adds his or her understanding of disabilities issues such as equality of access or participation in social agendas for family, education, or other community matters. Persons with disabilities play the same parts as do nondisabled people; if tolerance and knowledge have already been established in the civic structure, then more time can be spent solving the pressing problems, rather than sorting through interpersonal motivations. Let's look toward these motivations; what perceptions do disabled people have about themselves?

UNDERSTAND HOW PERSONS WITH DISABILITIES PERCEIVE THEMSELVES

Let's return to the 1986 Harris poll presented in Chapter 2. The survey screened 12,500 American households to identify a sample of 1,000 disabled Americans of working age. This sample was then asked a variety of questions about their everyday life. One question asked respondents to describe the way most people react after learning the individual has a disability. Happily, 56 percent of the respondents noted that other people treated them "as equals" after learning of their disability. Unhappily, the other 44 percent experienced negative attitudes, such as "acted sorry for you" (11%), and "shied away from further contact" (7%). It's the 44 percent of the population which has negative perceptions of disabled populations to which training and education should be directed.

The Harris survey disclosed key comparisons between working and nonworking disabled persons aged 16 to 64; simply put, working makes a vast quantitative difference in attitudes. Those who work are better educated, and have much more money. They are also more satisfied with life, much less likely to consider themselves disabled, and much less likely to say that their disability has prevented them from reaching their full abilities as a person:

- About four times as many working disabled persons as those who do not work have a four-year college education. And almost twice as many nonworking disabled persons (43%) as working disabled persons (22%) did not finish school.

- Over twice as many working disabled persons report a 1984 household income of $25,000 or more (44%) as do those who don't work (21%).

■ Eighty percent of those who work are at least somewhat satisfied with life, compared to 62 percent of those who don't work.

■ Only one-quarter (26%) of those who work consider themselves a disabled person. Among those who don't, a 59 percent majority consider themselves disabled.

■ Less than half (47%) of those who work say their disabilities have prevented them from reaching their full abilities as a person. Six out of ten nonworking disabled persons believe that their disability has had this effect.

Viewpoint 3.1—A profile of the sample of 1,000 disabled Americans by key measures of disability

BASE	**1,000**	
Self-Reported Condition*	%	
Physical Disability		**44**
Nonparalytic orthopedic impairments	29	
Neuromotor/neuromuscular disorder	8	
Brain dysfunction/memory loss/senility	6	
Other physical disabilities	2	
Sensory Impairment		**13**
Blind/visual impairments	7	
Hearing, speech, language	6	
Mental Disability		**6**
Mental retardation/developmental disorders	3	
Mental illness	3	
Other Serious Health Impairment		**32**
Heart disease/blood or blood vessel disease	16	
Respiratory or pulmonary disease	5	
Cancer/diabetes/kidney disease/other	11	
Not sure/refused	4	
	Approximating	**100%**
Multiple Disabilities		
Multiple Disabilities	32	
Not Multiple Disabilities	68	

Onset of Disability

Birth to adolescence	20
Young adult	25
Middle age	23
After age 55	31

Onset of Limitation

Birth to adolescence	13
Young adult	21
Middle age	22
After age 55	37

Severity of Disability

Slight	14
Moderate	31
Somewhat severe	28
Very severe	24

* Most limiting condition or single condition

Source: Louis Harris and Associates, 1986

As we construct a "typical" disabled consumer profile, we are immediately in violation of the fact that disability conditions are diverse and that each condition should receive special consideration before being returned to a larger market segment of "like" prospects. With this caveat in mind, we could "characterize" a theoretical disabled person as

- Most likely to experience a mobility impairment (44%) that is the result of several chronic causes, although heart, lung, and internal diseases account for 32 percent of the conditions

- Single disabilities constitute two-thirds of the conditions

- Forty-eight percent encountered a disability between the ages of 25 to 55 years; this group relates well to employment/career opportunities.

- The onset of the limitation occurred later in life though, with 59 percent of the adults 40 years plus reporting physical limitations.

- Physical limitations are not slight. Most (73%) answered that limitations were either "moderate," "somewhat severe," or "very severe."

Let's draw no tighter a demographic depiction than this unrealistic description. There is no better way for us to lose sight of disabilities' diversity than using as a homogenizing process demographic "averaging."

To make disabilities marketing work, training and educating of the marketer's sales or customer service staff is critical. The marketer must "enable" the staff to buy in and support the premise. How best can you enlighten the work force to honestly adapt attitudes of equality for employees or applicants with disabilities?

CONSIDERATIONS FOR THE WORKPLACE

Is conduct appropriate for the workplace any different than that practiced at home or in social circumstances? Not in the least! But remember that the ADA has been enacted to prevent discrimination in employment, hiring, and promotion practices among private and public entities as well as to give disabled citizens a chance to participate in or benefit from improved access and accommodation to goods, services, or facilities; private lives are not covered by the ADA titles. But the attitudes learned from ADA training will benefit the marketer and his or her staff in *all* encounters with disabled friends, relatives or clients, regardless of the circumstances, in personal dealings or company-related events, in public and private situations, for local or national markets.

Attitudes toward disabled people permeate the whole of the company; it's more than the territory of marketing or human resources. Marketers should support training that draws a positive picture of the actions and consequences of ADA practices. In fact, personal interactions are easiest to understand since many employees have had an exposure to a disability within their family. By integrating these personal experiences and feelings, employees help to build a consensus within each department to work with and embrace persons with disabilities as co-workers or customers, or to answer to them as stockholders, or cooperate with them as suppliers. Most readers should agree this issue is not a "bleeding heart" sympathy campaign. It's well to know that the ADA's enforcement provisions have been given real teeth via law suits and fines for noncompliers. But penalties are not the issue; the issue is the opportunity for persons with disabilities to contribute to economic or social environments.

These contributing roles that persons with disabilities can play extend throughout an organization. Opportunities abound in the marketing function to improve product or service design, distribution efficiency, marketing training or employee relations, customer communications, or government relations, to name a few. As a bonus, many manufacturers have found that alterations made to accommodate users with disabilities also make the products and services more "user-friendly" to all customer groups, disabled and nondisabled alike. Who, with grocery bags occupying both arms, wouldn't appreciate a lever-type door opener in place of a dead bolt lock and key?

SETTING THE EXAMPLE

A marketing manager should avoid making the assumption that all disabilities are alike. Are all consumers alike? Disabilities are numerous, and needs or skills of customers or employees with disabilities are diverse. Further supporting the diversity of disabilities, a second study by the National Institute on Disability and Rehabilitation Research documents that 38 percent of the disabled people of working age possess physical disabilities; another 13 percent have sensory impairments (such as sight, hearing, or speech impairments). An estimated 32 percent have encountered activity-limiting conditions (such as heart or respiratory disease), while 12 percent experience a mental disorder. Given this disparity, it's a good practice to review the marketing opportunity (and ensuing assignment if justified) with objectivity, taking care to avoid generalities about the diversity of disabilities.

TAKING STOCK OF ATTITUDES

Learn what familiarity your present staff has with persons with disabilities; don't assume you know. Employee knowledge can be gathered through a self-evaluation questionnaire called a disabilities awareness survey. This survey is designed to be administered internally, and its purpose should be explained to employees. A sample questionnaire is provided at the end of this chapter.

If your staff has a concern about anonymity, ask an outside supplier, such as a market research firm or accounting firm or advertising agency, to conduct a written survey for you. Uncovering honest opinions is the reason for making this baseline effort; take the time to consider the questions and consequences carefully. Many well-intentioned opinion surveys have created havoc because employees were not informed as to the purpose or use of the survey answers. Second guessing, defensive responses, and incomplete information made the survey results virtually worthless, as well as creating a state of uneasiness among the employees. So take the time to explain why and how the opinions and tabulations are going to be used.

The results may surprise you. Recently a Fortune 500 industrial company administered this disabilities awareness survey and learned that more than 70 percent of its supervisory force had firsthand knowledge of a disability (as in caring for a relative or close friend). Twenty-five percent of the supervisors had personally experienced a disability, most frequently noting "back problems" as the disabling condition. This higher than expected disabilities familiarity allowed the trainers to adjust the focus and schedule of the attitudes/etiquette training and concentrate on the legal aspects of the ADA, the employment rules of Title I.

PUTTING WORDS INTO ACTION

After these attitudes are gathered, marketing managers will find differing levels of awareness, uncertainty, or fear concerning exposure to persons with disabilities and their potential participation. Work forces in some organizations will be very enlightened and in others very suspicious.

Once attitudes are surveyed, the results will point to the areas in which disabilities awareness is warranted. Are company facilities accessible for customers or workers with disabilities? Could new markets be established with buyers with disabilities? Could customer relations channels or procedures be improved to offer better services to policy holders with disabilities? Each of these questions suggests worthwhile pursuits that could benefit both the company and the individual with a disability.

Regardless of expectations, the marketer should consolidate these varying responses into action programs that top management can bless and lead. For low levels of familiarity, sensitivity training on broad issues such as disabilities types or limitations may educate the marketing force most effectively. Or if acquaintance is higher, perhaps personal selling strategies or prospect interviewing techniques could be instituted. In some cases the training and development department will set the training agenda. In other organizations the marketing department or the sales department might lead the training. In smaller companies, an outside specialist might be called upon for evaluation and training skills.

SHARE THE EXPERIENCE

Consider spending some time experiencing a disability in a meaningful way. Perhaps a marketer could test drive a wheelchair for half a day, thereby gaining a better understanding of how placement of furniture or office equipment can complicate its use. Xerox, for example, has introduced a side-loading copier that a wheelchair user can operate more easily than top-loading models. Test driving a wheelchair could provide proof that a deep pile carpet and pad restricts a wheelchair user almost like beach sand.

To experience a hearing impairment, put on earphones (but don't plug them in) for a half day; to approximate a speech impairment, muffle your voice with eight or ten marshmallows, then try to use the telephone. Or secure one arm behind your back, then wrap a present, tie a bow, cover it in brown paper and finish the job with shipping twine. Two-handed actions or full mobility takes on a new level of importance.

TREATING ETIQUETTE PROPERLY

Some marketers have little or no experience in interacting with disabled populations, so anticipating a sales interview with a disabled customer might be awkward. Are there "right" things to do or obvious statements or subjects to avoid? Can you make small talk about sports, or is this offensive to mobility-impaired persons? Are there different "rules" for different disabilities? Should women with disabilities be treated differently from men? These are all great questions, and marshalling the sensitivity to contemplate them is an excellent lesson in building awareness about physical disabilities. To improve communications and interaction, here are a few tips to make learning a bit more comfortable. As the marketer gains experience in dealing with consumers with various disabilities, he or she will have many more insights on verbal and nonverbal communications.

Finding Your Place of Business

As a routine, instruct the receptionist to ask if directions to your store or office are needed. Many people will not need the information, but this courtesy gives the person with a disability the opening to ask about possible barriers that most nondisabled persons dismiss. This "mapping" is very helpful to people with severe sight impairments since many pace or count steps from location to location. Make sure the receptionist is accurate in approximate distance and direction from the parking area, and where the nearest "disabled parking" spaces are and the nearest wheelchair accessible bathroom is located.

Greeting the Disabled Person

First of all, be yourself. Relax, be comfortable, and you'll start off on the right foot. Allow the disabled person to lead the introduction; follow the lead. Don't rush. If the right arm is missing, the disabled person may be more comfortable extending his or her left hand. But shake whatever is extended, stump or prosthesis. Or return the smile if the traditional handshake is replaced with a hearty grin and a nod of the head. Let the disabled person get comfortable, preferably seated and set up with necessary materials, before jumping into business.

If the visitor uses a wheelchair and the meeting is held in a conference room, pull the chair closest to the entry door away from the table. Or in a smaller office make room for the visitor by moving a chair from in front of your desk. The desk top provides space for organizing the meeting materials to keep the executive from having to work out of his or her lap.

Ask her or him if any refreshments (or other courtesies extended to other visitors) are desired.

Treat the person with a disability as an adult. Call a person by his or her first name only when extending the familiarity to everyone present.

Before starting any meeting with one who is disabled, prepare yourself to listen. Compose yourself, adopt an attitude of interest, and lean back and listen.

When talking to a person who has a disability, look at and speak directly to that person, not to a companion, interpreter or guide who might be along. Particularly in the job interview process, interview the applicant. Don't direct questions to the companion; he or she is not the job seeker.

Respect for the Person

Unless you're familiar with the person with a disability, don't touch her or him to demonstrate respect. We all need our private space; give a disabled person the same room.

When (and if) to Lend Help

Always, always ask permission to physically assist a disabled person; don't grab the chair or cane because this unexpected force usually causes a worse imbalance. Help with doors is appreciated, but let the person know what you're going to do. A mobility-impaired person might expect to lean into a door only to find no resistance as someone opens it from the other side.

Few nondisabled people are adept in guiding a wheelchair accurately, and little is more embarrassing in a crowded room or elevator than for a "helper" to run over an innocent bystander's feet or up his heels with the chair's footrests. Hold your enthusiasm and wait for instructions. Like the physician's oath, "First do no harm."

If you ask permission to help, don't be offended if you're turned down. She's dealt with her disability for a long time and usually has a pattern or solution of her own to rely on.

The key to lending help is to keep talking so that you both understand who's to do what. Particularly for visually impaired persons, your voice helps them to judge distances and locations.

Conversing with a Wheelchair User

A most annoying thing for a wheelchair user is having to converse for a lengthy period, perhaps for more than a minute, with someone's belt buckle. If you're standing in the office, pull up a chair and get eye to eye with the disabled person. If you meet in a hallway or lobby, move to the closest seating area and sit down, even for a three- or four-minute chat.

If you're outside, kneel or squat down. This shows your sensitivity and concern for face-to-face communications; it also reduces possible glare and neck strain for the wheelchair user. You'll hear one another better, reducing the times questions or answers have to be repeated.

Never patronize someone in a wheelchair by patting him or her on the head. Also never lean on the person's wheelchair; the chair is part of the "personal space" that belongs to the person who uses it.

Don't be surprised if a helper dog accompanies the wheelchair user who is not blind. The helper dog has been trained to retrieve or carry objects for persons with mobility impairments.

Conversing with One Who Is Blind

When greeting the person with severe sight impairments, always identify yourself and others who might be with you. Say for example, "On my left is Bill Jones." When conversing in a group, give a verbal cue by announcing the name of the person to whom you are speaking.

Again, maintaining a normal conversational tone is best when speaking with a person who is blind. Face him or her as you speak since turning your head changes the "triangulation" of your voice to the listener. Keep talking if you're moving about the room. Also be sensitive to background noises (loud music, traffic, and construction sounds, for example); reducing this distraction is important so that no words or understandings are lost. There is no need to speak louder; a blind person will tell you if he or she is also hard of hearing.

Allow the person with a visual impairment to take your arm (at the elbow). This will enable you to guide, rather than push or lead the person.

Don't offer to retrieve a dropped cane or crutches unless the individual requests otherwise. Many people are fiercely independent and do not wish to accept assistance at virtually any cost. If help is desired, the person who is blind will ask.

Don't pet or distract a guide dog from its duty; even when at rest, the dog is "working."

While not a point of etiquette but of safety, remember that as maintenance is performed in the office or in a store's remodeling, make the employee who is blind aware of the dates and scope of the construction. This applies to any change in the physical layout of the office floor plan (such as temporary tables set up for coffee and pastries for an afternoon's open house, or a painter's drop cloth in the hallway). Many people who are blind or possess severe sight impairments memorize an office's furnishings and step-count to locate offices, restrooms or turns in halls, to find the stairs or elevator. Anything out of place constitutes a danger over which to trip and fall, so be sure to think ahead of department relocations, renovations, or other changes in the common walkway areas. Tell workers who are blind about the changes before they happen.

Conversing with One Who Is Hearing Impaired

Understand that **deafness** is a condition of total hearing loss; **hard of hearing** refers to partial or impaired hearing ability. Since a hearing impairment is usually a "hidden" disability, the hard of hearing person will usually bring up how best to communicate. One woman I met wore a button that read, "Face me when you speak." Persons with hearing impairments or who are deaf may be lip-readers and if they can't see your mouth, they can't lip-read. So don't turn your back and continue to talk, particularly as you walk single file in your office or conference room.

Position yourself within the visual distance of the listener: usually three to six feet is best. Few persons lip-read, but there is another reason to face the person with hearing impairments. Looking at the listener reduces problems in the directions in which sound travels. Simply put, it's easier to hear if the person looks at you.

Use short sentences. Be persistent; keep talking until you both understand one another.

Many persons who are deaf will use sign language as well as lip-reading. In business conferences consider the need for a signing interpreter
who stands by the speaker and signs the content of the speech.

Most hearing impaired persons don't lip-read or sign; they merely
adjust to the hearing environment. Those with hearing aids will be
concerned about noise levels in general. Hearing aids simply amplify *all*
sounds. So what is loud to you will be even more annoying to an
individual with a hearing aid.

To get the attention of a person with a hearing impairment, tap the
person on the shoulder or wave your hand. As with sight impairments,
be sensitive to background noises as you converse if the listener uses a
hearing aid. Music, intercoms, impact printers, copy machines all add to
the cacophony of the office environment; traffic, air conditioning com-
pressors, or airplane noise can be equally obscuring in outdoor meetings.

Direction and distance of sound are also important since turned
heads don't enunciate crisp consonants such as "pin, fin, win, sin."

Likewise, be sensitive to proper lighting in retail or office environments. When you speak, make sure your face, and certainly your
mouth, is in full light, not in shadows. Try not to move all over the
room as you speak; following your movements and following your
mouth can be difficult. Be careful to keep your hands or other obstacles
(the telephone receiver or a memo) from blocking a clear sight of your
mouth. Likewise, keep cigarettes or food away from your mouth as you
speak. Take the chewing gum out of your mouth for the duration of the
conversation. Why? All these hindrances can slur speech, making discussion more difficult.

Speak in an even, distinct tone; slow down and enunciate. Don't
shout; shouting contorts the facial features and confuses the lip-reader.

If you're attending an educational conference or seminar with a hearing impaired person, offer her or him a copy of your notes if the presen-
tation will be mainly verbal. Check to see if loud speakers are positioned
throughout the room, not merely at the front. Ask that front row seating be reserved for persons with hearing impairments; the farther the
distance sound has to travel from the lecturer, the harder it is to hear (or
lip-read) the speaker's comments. Consider having tapes or transcripts
of the speeches available for the hearing impaired attendees to order.

As with the vision impaired person, a cue may be helpful when
conversing in a group. Here a visual sign might be appropriate to facilitate conversation.

Conversing with One Who Is Speech Impaired

Patience is key here. The impairment may be physical (deafness, or congenitally or injury induced), or it may be psychological (such as stuttering or other impediments); it may be slight or profound. The point is that verbal communication is difficult and can be made more painful if the listener is impatient or acts annoyed. Don't finish sentences for the speaker; how do you know what she's thinking? Be encouraging, but don't correct. When appropriate, ask short questions that require short answers or a nod or shake of the head. Be ready to adjust eye contact if necessary; some persons with speech impairments will look away to show discomfort. Others will tenaciously stare you down until the point is made. Be willing to repeat your questions. But don't agree with the impaired speaker unless you really understand. Don't pretend. Keep talking until you both really understand, or resort to written notes to get the points across. Repeat what you understand, or incorporate his statements into questions you might have. That person's reactions will give you a clue toward comprehension and guide you toward an understanding.

Mild to Severe Impairments

Recognize that the degree of ability ranges from mild conditions, such as partial hearing impairment, to severe, such as quadriplegia or language dysfunction. Be sure to understand what or how assistance is needed. In mild cases the individual may need little assistance, but in severe cases, more assistance will be required. A sensitive representative should ask what tools or routines can be provided to make sales meetings or other marketing tasks more accommodating.

Think to Include the Whole Team

Consciously include the *whole* staff in accessible meeting places (on location and off); be sure to scout the meeting room beforehand to be sure of its access. This goes for employee functions and for marketing events in which customers are brought together. An inaccessible meeting room where new products are being introduced would certainly be a disaster if steps or narrow doors were encountered by trade media, distributors, or salespersons with disabilities.

Review your internal communication systems so that all employees, regardless of ability or disability, are included in appropriate memoranda or correspondence, and recognize you may need to institute a redundant information system such as newsletters or memos for hearing impaired persons, audiotext for sight impaired employees, or e-mail for the worker at home.

Hands-Free Isn't Rude

Don't take offense at conversing through a "hollow" sounding speaker phone since, for many people who are blind or have arm or hand impairments, a hands-free phone is the only access to telephone communications. Most users will advise you of the presence of the speaker phone connection, so be tolerant of this vital communications accommodation. If privacy is a requirement of the call, an appointment time for the call can be set to avoid interruptions, or easier yet, the hands-free caller just closes his or her office door. These phones have volume control, so there's no fear of "broadcasting" the conversation throughout the department.

Don't Ignore Lunch

An important instance of office communications is the daily lunch ritual. Many inner-office decisions are discussed and finalized at the corner luncheonette or sandwich shop. It's an easy habit to fall into, but think to include (or at least invite) a disabled colleague to lunch. Falling out of touch with informal communications networks, like the lunch bunch, can readily be avoided. Or bring lunch in once or twice a month.

Training for Everyone

Also remember to invite and include all staff to training or educational sessions; if information needs to be maintained consistently, make sure everyone participates in the educational actions. Again, are there any employees with special needs who might require large-print text or audio cassettes of training materials? Is lighting adequate for following written texts? Has front row seating been offered to trainees with hearing or sight impairments?

Travel Can Present Special Problems

Before you decide that your disabled employees would not be interested in traveling to a convention or workshop, ask them about it. While airplane travel can be uncomfortable and overnight stays might require special accommodations, most persons with disabilities will want to put out the effort. Trade shows, conventions, or conferences are valuable to everyone's career, including persons with disabilities. Preparing for a trip just takes more time.

Here's an example of "the earlier, the better" preparation. For persons with mobility impairments, flying involves being loaded on a narrow cart that is squeezed down a narrow aisle. The earlier the traveler can book the flight, the better the chance of securing one of two aisle seats in which the seat arm swings up and out of the way. Otherwise, the disabled traveler is lifted higher (over the fixed arm) and dropped farther into the seat. Uncomfortable, yes, but an inconvenience most will accept, if need be, to participate in worthwhile conferences or conventions.

As you are planning for staff travel, ask well in advance if any special needs should be met. A checklist might include wheelchair accessible baths, dietary requirements, TDD service, signing interpreters for conference speeches, and Braille or audio tape equipment.

A Social Environment to Match the Work Environment

In social gatherings among customers, clients, or co-workers, keep the facility uncluttered and refreshments easy to handle. Rotate the responsibility for party planning among all staff members; those with disabilities can decline if they want to. Much of the fun in planning the festivities is in the anticipation of the party, and it's no different for social committee members with disabilities. Don't assume they will automatically turn the invitation down.

ACCOMMODATIONS AS THE MARKET REQUIRES

This text deals primarily with the marketing environment, and it's the role of the marketing manager to be proactive by seeking out and correcting conditions that could possibly limit the performance of marketing efforts. Again, knowledge and foresight arm the marketer with accurate guidelines to follow and to implement needed accommodations.

- A great victory in accommodations solutions is for the marketing department to recognize that there *are* obstacles which could affect the potential or performance of programs targeted to consumers with disabilities; recognizing the problem is more than half the battle.

- Anticipating the appropriate accommodation in a retailing environment might entail an external (as in outside the store) as well as an internal check of these commonplace amenities:

- Availability and use of parking and an unobstructed path of access to the facility's approach

- Entry and use of the facility

- Access and use of bathrooms and water fountains

- Availability of text telephones for hearing impaired persons to use in emergencies

- Access to other public and common areas

- Accessibility for obtaining goods, services, programs, facilities, accommodations, uncluttered sales areas, and equipment

- Alternative customer service methods or delivery systems

Let's take a short audit of a commercial business, using as an example a financial institution that welcomes customers daily. A quick 15-point checklist can reveal how barrier-free the business is, or can identify which impediments must be eliminated:

1. Are there reserved parking spaces for disabled customers, marked by signage, near the front doors?

2. Are there curb cuts and sloped walkways into the building?

3. Is the business entry flat or gently sloped?

4. Are the front doors easy to open, preferably with an electronic-eye opener? If not, are the doors in the line of vision of an attended desk?

5. Is the floor tiled or covered with a low-pile or similar "hard" surface?

6. Are aisles or desk clearances at least 36" wide?

7. Are banking forms stored at an accessible height?

8. Is at least one counter or teller window low enough for wheel-chair users? If not, is a lap desk kept available to use as a writing surface?

9. Do the tellers face and speak directly to all customers?

10. Are tellers aware of the need to hand transactions to sight or mobility impaired customers, rather than wait to have them reach awkwardly?

11. Do tellers ask for permission to assist, rather than grab an arm or wheelchair uninvited?

12. Are tellers familiar with the law concerning guide or support dogs?

13. Is someone available to assist those who have difficulty writing?

14. Are international access symbols displayed to help in entering or exiting the building, especially in emergencies?

15. Do elevators reach all floors?

Yes, some of these accommodations are required by law, but other points on the checklist, while not exhaustive, will make an office into a more attractive place for disabled persons to do business, and a more easily accessible place, which the disabled individual will tell his or her family and friends about, as a referral endorsement.

These same points could be checked by a fashion retailer with hundreds of outlets in 10 states or an optical shop occupying only 1,500 square feet of sales area. Accessibility according to the ADA standards have a cause-and-effect relationship in store design; in most cases, the more standardized the design, the easier it is for the shopper with a disability to plan his or her purchases.

PUT FEELINGS INTO ACTIONS

Business managers who embrace persons with disabilities as employees and as customers face win-win consequences if the firm is aware of disabilities opportunities and then moves in an affirmative direction to tap this resource. Whether national or local in scale, retail or business focused, producing niche or multi-product lines, disabilities marketing can build enduring, loyal user groups. For once, the good of the community and the company can be inseparable and mutually beneficial. What marketers could ask for more?

QUESTIONNAIRE

As a responsible partner in our community, (Company name) is conducting a survey on employee attitudes toward co-workers with disabilities. Your opinions are important to us. As in all our surveys, neither your name or organizational affiliation will be released, and the study's findings will be reported in aggregate form to protect confidentiality.

1. In which office/city are you employed?

2. In which department do you work?

3. What is your job title?

4. Would you say that a strong emphasis on social and community responsibilities is an important part of our corporate culture, or not?

   Yes, very important   ( )
   No, not important   ( )
   Not sure   ( )

5. Concerning persons with disabilities (persons who have physical, sight, hearing, or speech impairments; emotional or mental disabilities; or long-term health problems), have you had any personal experience?

   Yes   ( )
   No   ( )
   Not sure   ( )

6. If you answered yes, what is (was) your relationship to that person?

   Your spouse   ( )
   Your parents or in-laws   ( )
   Your children   ( )
   Your relatives (aunts, uncles, cousins)   ( )
   A close friend   ( )
   A co-worker   ( )
   A neighbor   ( )

7. What was his or her physical condition or limitation? (If more than one, please list all of them.)

   #1 _____

   #2 _____

   #3 _____

   Not sure   ( )

8. Was the condition the result of an injury (such as an auto, motorcycle, sports, or work accident)?

   Yes   ( )
   No   ( )
   Not sure   ( )

9. Was the condition long term (happening before you first met this person)?

   Yes, long term   ( )
   No, a recent condition   ( )
   Not sure   ( )

10. Have you ever given care to or assisted a person with a disability?

    Yes   ( )
    No   ( )
    Not sure   ( )

11. Have you ever worked with (or for) a person with a disability?

    Yes   ( )
    No   ( )
    Not sure   ( )

12. If Yes, how would you say *your* job performance was affected by the disabled worker's presence?

    Better   ( )
    Worse   ( )
    No difference   ( )
    Not sure   ( )

13. How would you rate disabled workers to nondisabled workers you've known?

	Better	Worse	About Same	Doesn't Apply	Not Sure
a. Formal education					
b. Job skills					
c. Leadership abilities					
d. Communications skills					
e. Dependability					

14. Would you say that a disabled worker if qualified should be promoted at about the same rate as most other employees, or at a faster or slower rate?

Get promoted at the same rate ( )
At a slower rate ( )
At a faster rate ( )
It depends ( )
Not applicable ( )
Not sure ( )

15. Would you encourage a disabled relative or friend to apply for a job with our company?

Yes ( )
No ( )
Not sure ( )

16. Here are some statements concerning disabled workers. Please make a check mark on each row according to how you feel about each statement.

	Agree Strongly	Agree Somewhat	Disagree Somewhat	Disagree Strongly	Not Sure
a. Special privileges must be made for disabled workers.					
b. Disabled workers have fewer accidents on the job than do nondisabled workers.					

   c. Disabled people just
      don't fit in with
      most nondisabled
      employees.

   d. Disabled workers are
      harder to supervise
      than nondisabled workers.

17. Do you feel that disabled workers or job applicants often encounter job discrimination from employers?

Yes	( )
No	( )
Not aware of discrimination	( )
Not sure	( )

18. Are you aware of any efforts or programs our company has made or programs our company has established to promote the hiring of persons with disabilities?

Yes	( )
No	( )

19. Are you aware of any programs or literature that helps our employees learn to work with disabled persons?

Yes	( )
No	( )

20. Have you yourself ever experienced a disability?

Yes	( )
No	( )
Not sure	( )

21. If yes, did the disability affect your work performance?

Yes	( )
No	( )
Not applicable	( )
Not sure	( )

22. What is (was) the disability?

Sight impairment	( )	Hearing impairment	( )
Speech impairment	( )	Heart/cardiovascular	( )
Paralysis	( )	Emphysema	( )
Neck/back disorders	( )	Epilepsy	( )
Diabetes	( )	Orthopedic impairment	( )
Arthritis	( )	Hypertension	( )
Amputation	( )	Neuromuscular disease	( )
Mental disorder	( )	Emotional disorder	( )
Osteomyelitis-Bone disease	( )		
Other			
Not sure	( )		

23. How long have you worked for our company?

Thank you for sharing your opinions.

CHAPTER FOUR

EXPANDING COMMUNICATIONS OF DISABILITIES MARKETING

SELECTIVITY WILL BE THE KEY

The situations and communications described thus far have dealt with personal interactions and observations of many diverse yet common disabilities. Attention has been directed toward learning more about conditions of disabilities and how marketers can better relate to people with disabilities. Just as a marketer who doesn't know his product will meet failure, so will a marketer who doesn't know how to communicate with her prospective market.

Attempts to court segments with disabilities will be unsuccessful if the marketing efforts are shallow or makeshift. Buyers with disabilities will see right through superficial motions. We are building relationships, and so far, marketers should have a better idea as to the expectations of disabled customers. Let's move on, toward creating a more structured process based on how the disabilities marketing strategy can be applied. Marketing communications plays important roles in message, segmentation, media, and distribution decisions; if poorly planned or executed, marketing repercussions can be damning to future performance aimed at disabled consumers.

STEPPING BACK TWO HUNDRED YEARS

Marketing communications has traveled the full circle in its facility to speak directly to the consumer, regardless of ability or disability. In the early 1800s peddlers took products to the market, from door to door and town to town. Personal selling acted as the major channel of distribution and face-to-face presentations were just about the only communications arrow in the manufacturers' quiver.

The country continued to expand westward, and the population began to disburse itself into fledgling regions that became states and into thriving settlements that grew into towns and cities. By the 1850s the itinerant merchant could no longer personally cover his territory efficiently, and manufacturers enlisted city newspapers and national or regional magazines to begin tapping "mass" markets.

One size fit all, and the marketing strength swung to the producer who, experiencing little competition, expected the consumer to take it or leave it. The odds were in favor of the manufacturer since many newspaper or magazine messages were falling on eager doorsteps. Mass media offerings were further fortified with regional and national radio and television networks, and mass messages, with the presumed ability to move herds of consumers to the manufacturer's product and away from the competition, reached their zenith during the late 1970s.

An increase in education, expectations, and disposable income caused consumers to rethink what they wanted; no longer predictable, they were instead discretionary. Some were even described as fickle and aloof. Marketers found this independent attitude unsettling; moreover, costly marketing communications programs had to be initiated to court the consumer. Unfamiliar as it was, market power shifted back to the consumer. They purchased what they liked, and many producer products and services failed for lack of satisfying any buyer group.

Not only did the consumer have many choices of similar products, choices in advertising media mushroomed. In addition to mass media, the ability to deliver messages to smaller, more selective media audiences became available. In the late 1970s cable television, personalized magazine advertising, and direct marketing grew more pervasive and sophisticated. Distribution capabilities expanded with direct to the consumer distribution allowing a new, timely, and economical "personal" channel. Now messages customized to smaller markets, personalized service based on computer data banks, and convenient doorstep delivery seem in vogue, just like "relationship" merchandising 150 years ago. What other trends should be recognized in markets and media forces?

WHO'S LOOKING AND LISTENING TODAY?

A trend toward matching products with appropriate buyers is proving to be a most effective targeting, or segmenting, strategy. Segmentation is the marketing practice of breaking wholes into smaller parts, with the expectation of increasing effectiveness (more qualified buyers) at a cost to efficiency (probably at a higher cost-per-thousand rate). During the last decade, marketers began to demand more and more targeted delivery of advertising messages to special interest groups, such as gardening enthusiasts, health-conscious senior consumers, or buyers of gold jewelry; this winnowing process could be an opportunity for media segmentation. But mass advertising vehicles have been slow to recognize the value that this segmentation capability holds to marketers, or have been unable to segment markets because of technology or production limitations, such as broadcast television's wasted viewership.

Today's mass media has been described as "effective as a colander for holding sand at the beach." Messages to "particle markets"—those market groups that grow more defined in characteristics and more focused in interests—appear to be falling through the mass media net. This spotty delivery pattern, resulting from efficient but ineffective reach of broad media vehicles, has not been an overnight phenomenon; savvy marketers have recognized this tendency throughout the 1980s.

THE SHRINKAGE CONTINUES

Mass media, because of its inherent extensive nature, will prove to be less efficient in supporting marketing programs directed toward disabled consumers. Cost efficiencies are dropping in general because the numbers of viewers and readers are dwindling. Broadcast television is a good example. In 1982 viewers of the three major networks accounted for 90 percent of households watching TV, but by 1990 the networks' viewership had dropped to a 65 percent HUT (households using television) level. Some media experts predict HUT levels dropping to the 50s by the turn of the century, the result of cable television penetration, video rentals, and changes in lifestyles as more women work outside the home.

Daily newspapers have also experienced a slippage in household penetration, as measured by a Newspaper Advertising Bureau index of copies per household. In 1946 American households were delivered 133 daily papers for every 100 homes, thanks to the competitive forces of two or three newspaper cities. By 1970 the index had fallen to 98 papers per 100 households, and in 1991 the Newspaper Advertising Bureau index estimated 67 papers were delivered to each 100 households in the United States.

So looking ahead, as the battle for consumers' (both disabled and nondisabled) attention becomes more competitive, will these traditional vehicles of television and newspaper—the ones marketers have relied on in the past—produce acceptable, accountable results?

BLENDING MARKET AND MEDIA ACTIVITY

New media capabilities will be required in planning disabilities marketing strategies. Not only must advertising media be evaluated by comparing costs, but also on effectiveness, such as access to the medium, convenience, and ease of use by the disabled consumer. Message delivery also continues to be a critical determinant for marketing success in the immediate future. And in sorting out these new parameters, marketers should be alerted to base disabilities communications efforts on the unique characteristic of **media interactivity**, in which the medium provides a complete loop allowing the disabled consumer to respond directly to the product or service provider. Further, the message receiver can respond with minimal effort or time. Response does not have to be instantaneous; a postage-paid reply card can be mailed to complete the order process. However, the quicker, the better, and that's what most people remember.

Consider the comparison that interactive media be a *three-way* street to the customer. First, the marketer sends the message to the consumer; second, the consumer receives the message and has the interactive capability to order quickly and easily. Third, the return path tracks an accurate, hopefully no more than overnight, delivery to the consumer. New accounts or reorders from existing accounts should receive the same speed and attention.

Many account holders with disabilities have functional limitations that make the simplest effort difficult, such as driving to the post office or catching the bus to the mall. The marketing issue for disabled segments is to be able to promise doorstep delivery convenience to the prospect, whether that mandates paying by credit card over the telephone, delivery to the doorstep by UPS, or providing toll-free telephone numbers for customer services, or providing postage to the mobility impaired individual to eliminate the need to visit the post office to buy stamps.

Besides interactivity, attention should be given to alternative media vehicles that possess abilities to segment demographically, target geographically, or project a unique personality. These characteristics go against the grain of mass media; the marketer should look to limiting television or radio to demographic niches, or buying newspaper or magazine media to exacting geographic areas. Are we asking too much of mass media? Could narrower media delivery be of value to the other consumer segments you serve?

Media strategy should be rethought to form a new perspective, one that pursues and balances audience interest and cost of delivery, rather than being based solely on cost-per-thousand criterion. Product and service potential abounds when focusing on markets with disabilities, and marrying the goals of cost efficiency and selectivity is the most realistic approach to assuring media value as a marketing weapon in the 1990s.

REPLACING THE MAINSTREAM WITH THE NONTRADITIONAL

Good advice to marketers is to approach media selection creatively; this search should include an investigation of nontraditional areas of new technology for applications to media interactivity. Some considerations for unique delivery to disabled population targets in the future might include extensions of communications presently in use today. Yes, print advertising could turn over a new leaf, to offer house-by-house or reader-by-reader selectivity. But media innovations will probably come from electronic vehicles. So marketers should be on the alert for video and audio applications that weren't even around 10 years ago, particularly those media that permit communications direct to the consumer, unburdened by several layers of distributors, wholesalers, or retailers. More control of the buying relationship with fewer pockets to siphon the pricing pool, these are factors marketers should be searching for and testing.

FIT MEDIA DYNAMICS TO THE MARKETS' DEMANDS

There are three criteria—time, place, and convenience—that marketers must keep in mind. Marketing efforts are devoted to being "disabilities-friendly," a descriptive term that will continue to pop up in all areas of disabilities communications strategy. This concept is even more important to media success because if the media isn't "easy to receive," the product or service message is ignored. The marketing paradigms of time, place, and convenience deserve a closer examination. The time element is simple; the medium must be flexible enough to work 24 hours a day.

The advertising vehicle must also be ubiquitous, to have the ability to deliver the message virtually everywhere. There are many ways to carve geography—by zip codes, area codes, and by state, county, and city limits. Regardless of the geographical depth, the advertising vehicle must cut *through*.

Finally, to build on interactivity, convenience is necessary. If the market isn't "coming to the message," the media can take the message to the market.

SIGHT, SOUND, AND SELECTIVITY

Interactive TV, which gives individual households the opportunity to electronically order, vote for, or choose from a variety of preferences, provides the ultimate in market targeting and customer service. An example can be found in Video Jukebox Network, Inc., a Miami-based entertainment cable channel that interacts with its audience. For a $2 to $3 fee (charged to the caller's phone bill), viewers call in to request the music video they wish to see from a library of 450 current titles.

Launched in 1989, Video Jukebox has grown to 12 million subscribers in 135 locations. While pop music is this medium's specialty, channel programming for various interests, entertainment, information, and education paralleling this over-the-counter company are more than possible.

WHAT HATH MEDIA TECHNOLOGY WROUGHT?

Open minds and new technology have unfolded many new avenues of communications that can pinpoint the interests or needs of persons with disabilities. Some use the computer, but all will need to use creativity to be successfully deployed. Let's review several media applications that are presently available to marketers.

Viewpoint 4.1—Interactive TV Starts to Come into Focus

Interactive television may be starting to live up to its long-heralded promise. Most interactive systems have been limited in scope or required more than basic TV equipment to use. But GTE is test marketing a cable channel that works simply and offers a range of services.

The system, called Main Street, Is funnelled into homes through standard cable wires. It lets subscribers use their TVs to shop, bank, trade stocks, and call up library reference materials, among other services. When tuning to the channel, subscribers see a menu, make a selection, and enter other data via their remote controls. The data is transmitted from the home through the user's regular telephone line, plugged into the cable converter box.

Interactive games for sports and trivia buffs, programmed by NTN Communications, a small interactive-television company in Carlsbad, Calif., are also offered through the channel. Through the on-screen display, the games test users' football play-calling abilities, among other things, and then rank them by points at the end.

It isn't yet clear whether consumers will accept the service. GTE, testing Main Street in Cerritos, Calif., and in Newton, Mass., won't give any figures on how the service is doing, but plans to expand it to the San Diego area by year end. One drawback: When in use, the system ties up a phone line.

Main Street carries a price of $10 a month, on top of a subscriber's basic cable fee, but it could get more costly. Though the individual services are free for now, GTE and other companies involved say they may impose additional charges in the future.

Wall Street Journal, August 3, 1992

Selectivity Is Intrinsic

Computer applications are seemingly endless when videotext, usually a private network of information presented in text form, is employed; just pick up any weekly news magazine and you'll see advertisements for up-to-the-minute information services like investment data and selection, news, sports, even lottery updates, and much more. Presently, national networks like CompuServ, Nexus, and Prodigy, all pay-for-use memberships, provide desired information to home computer users as on-screen typewritten messages called videotext.

User networks of special interest groups are being created every day. These common interests span all ages and affluence levels. Videotext networks might link retired first grade teachers, football card collectors, or Mozart concerto enthusiasts. Each member of the network joins voluntarily to gain videotext information. Given this common desire, opportunities to deliver information to the computer user with disabilities could be plentiful.

SeniorNet, headquartered in San Francisco, is a good example of special interest bundling. This is a nonprofit organization whose goal is to build an international community of computer-using older adults. Since 1986 SeniorNet has established more than 35 SeniorNet sites throughout the United States and Canada that serve to teach seniors computer skills and information access to enhance their lives. An optional membership service is the SeniorNet online network, a place to "meet" other members from around the country and discuss many issues, such as news and legislation from Washington. According to SeniorNet literature,

> We offer Special Interest Groups (SIGs) on subjects such as "getting into computers," writing and "electronic citizenship." If you are interested in another topic that you think will be of interest to other members, such as gardening, genealogy or financial management programs, please let us know . . . maybe you can start your own SIG!

This working model parallels what could be organized for disabilities interests. The communications tool is the personal computer with modem; SeniorNet is a wonderful example of bringing the outside world with all its curiosities indoors, regardless of geographical boundaries. The immediate implication could be a network of computer users with disabilities, easily segmented by interests and needs according to the user's choice.

Target by the Spoken Word

What videotext is to the eye, audiotext is to the ear. Audiotext, most likely a prerecorded message but in some cases, a live operator or counselor on the line, was developed in the late 1980s as computer-driven telephone switching and enhanced automation drove costs down and capabilities up. Presently audiotext advertising is a nascent industry of advertisers using toll-free 800 telephone numbers, with no charge as a convenience, or pay-per-call 900 numbers, with a charge for timeliness, to encourage direct response from special interest consumers.

Audiotext applications like *Fortune* magazine's "Fortune InvestorLink" or Dow Jones' "Journal Phone" are readily dialed using only a touch-tone telephone. No special equipment is required. While the 800 number is free to the caller, the 900 number is charged by the minute to the caller's phone line; charges range from $0.95 per minute for stock quotes, sports, or joke lines to more than $35 per minute for accounting, legal, or other specialty information. Ordering products or accessing information by telephone is very attractive to mobility impaired or sight impaired consumers; the inconvenience of distance can be eliminated by toll-free calls. Since this medium is new, many questions are rightfully circulating on its proper role as a self-regulating communications vehicle.

Interactivity and Direct Mail

Direct mail's selectivity by age, income, and other demo-psychographic characteristics has proven stalwart during the last 20 years as marketers pumped specialized products and services via the post office. While direct mail has demonstrated cost effectiveness, it produces a monologue directed at the prospect, allowing no means of feedback, also termed "interactivity," from the customer. This is the problem that Gift of Gold Marketing, Inc., of Dublin, Ohio, recognized and solved.

Targeted to senior consumers, Gift of Gold packages samples of products and services in an attractive gold "hatbox," delivers the package to demographically selected households, and requests the recipient to answer usage questions about the products contained in the box. In one test surveys were returned by 70 percent of the sample, and 60 percent advised they were favorably impressed with the products to consider repurchase. Planned expansion began with delivery to 24,000 senior households in selected Florida markets in 1990; by 1993 Gift of Gold was expecting to sample more than 300,000 households in five regions of the United States. Unbiased feedback on packaged goods and services is critical in the consumer communications linkage; this response capability sets the Gift of Gold system apart.

Stake Out Your Zone of Influence

But maybe the marketer is interested in store-specific promotion to influence the customer when they visit the retail outlet. A pinpoint delivery of media messages could give a powerful competitive edge to marketers battling at the store level. This strategy can presently be employed through a recently commercialized low-powered radio frequency (RF) band like electronic shelf-tag systems. Using spread spectrum, a broad band RF transmission system (previously reserved only for highly secure government communications), a transceiver "broadcasts" price information to individual shelf-mounted price tags. Changes and special offers can be made instantly by entering the new price information, which is then transmitted to each product label. This is a productive way to feature special promotions, keep prices accurate, and reduce labor and materials cost, yet is flexible to make even hourly price adjustments.

Maybe the company enterprise is large, covering several acres or more; investigate the possibility of operating a low-powered AM radio station that "broadcasts" exclusive messages to a limited geographic area. This medium might be encountered while driving to Walt Disney World, international airports, or regional medical centers. Each coordinates parking, traffic, or hours of operation information through low-powered AM transmissions. Retailers, community developers, or manufacturers could well benefit from straight talk to the consumer as they drive in and around "your" boundaries of commerce.

Or retailers could take a lesson from Madame Tussaud's "Rock Circus" in London, where spectators don wireless headsets and walk through musical salutes (complete with vocals, hence the headsets) to famous entertainers of the 1960s, 70s, and 80s. This audio system could easily assist blind or sight impaired persons in learning more about a product line or specifications at a trade show exhibit.

SPECIALTY PRINT CAN TARGET, TOO

Special interest publications including magazines and newsletters can deliver to narrow consumer profiles; look at the success that *Modern Maturity*, with its 22 million-plus circulation mailed to members of the

American Association of Retired Persons, has achieved or at *Entrepreneur*'s circulation growth, up 28 percent in 1989 alone, encompassing more than 340,000 eager start-up subscribers. As strong as *Entrepreneur*, "America's small business authority," is today, the publication has humble roots; it began as a newsletter in 1973. These specialty publications are read for a reason, to gain quality information on products, activities, and trends on special interests that serve special consumers. Magazine publications that target various disabilities markets are currently available; among these are *Sports 'n Spokes*, *Paraplegia News*, or *Spinal Network*.

ELECTRONIC WRITING ON THE WALL

After reviewing this intriguing list of alternative media, the marketer should realized that, while media can be used to segment different consumer groups with disabilities, attention must be given to the receivers' ability to access and manipulate the message. Think how sight impairments would make direct mail virtually useless as an advertising vehicle, or how upper body impairments would exclude magazine ad readership. Further recognize that few of these electronic media were in use a mere 10 years ago. Audiotext, videotext, interactive cable TV, and broad band RF transmission all have applications as disabled and senior consumer communication vehicles in the 1990s, and a marketer would be wise to familiarize himself or herself with these technologies.

THE FUTURE

Accept the fact that this rapid deployment of media segmentation tools will progress in geometric proportion. Barriers in electronic loads, complexity, costs, speed, and interactivity are broken every day as many new applications are created. So plan for huge leaps in message delivery efficiency.

With this delivery advantage in mind, marketers must get to know the customer better—those likes, dislikes, shopping habits, packaging, and payment preferences—to investigate all the choices that could set a marketer's product or service apart. Then ask, "If we can deliver our messages to individual households, what do we say?" The reality is that soon the marketer can be standing on the customer's front doorstep, and he or she had best be prepared to carry on a conversation.

Viewpoint 4.2—Dell Computer to Slip a Superstore in America's Mailbox

Are Americans, famous for kicking tires and squeezing toilet paper, ready for a computer superstore-by-mail?

Dell Computer Corp. is about to find out. The computer mail-order pioneer is planning a vast expansion of its product line in a direct challenge to the industry's booming new retail superstores. The Dell move, expected to be announced later this month, is being pitched to suppliers as sort of a mailbox superstore, offering all the selection of the retail giants without the hassles of parking or salespeople.

So far, industry executives say dozens of the nation's largest software suppliers, computer equipment vendors, and high-tech game makers have signed on for the new venture, which would mark the biggest expansion of Dell's product mix since the Austin, Texas, company went public four years ago.

But the move comes loaded with risks. Others have dabbled with the concept before, unsuccessfully. Analysts worry that the expansion could jeopardize Dell's reputation for top-notch customer service, since the plan calls for Dell to resell products it doesn't make or guarantee.

Wall Street Journal, September 10, 1992

CHAPTER FIVE

SETTING MARKETING DIRECTIONS

THE SITUATION ASSESSMENT

Yes, marketing possibilities to individuals or groups with disabilities are endless, which is why managers might have a difficult time deciding where to start. With most marketing communications programs, an excellent starting point is the **situation assessment,** which helps to organize and evaluate various environments in which the marketer will compete. It is beneficial for marketers to survey past activities, current programs, and future objectives before initiating new actions.

Among the environments to weigh are economic issues, demographic trends, and competitive opportunities, the uncontrollable forces that buffet the marketing mix. A review of the controllable elements, those the marketer can adjust in the marketing mix, be it product design, price, distribution or promotion, exposes or reinforces the shortcomings or acceptability to markets with disabilities. These decision factors, the internal strengths and weaknesses and external opportunities and threats, will set the foundation for disabilities-directed marketing efforts.

Flexibility in marketing planning is critical during evaluation stages. Approach the planning process as if it were a blank sheet of paper. Why? Because traditional rules change as marketers attempt to attract consumers with disabilities. Take a retailer's crown jewel, the department store, as an example.

BIGGER IS BETTER, ISN'T IT?

Retail store sizes are expanding, some doubling or tripling in square footage. Wal-Mart and K mart, for example, are experimenting with "hyperstore" designs in the 240,000 to 300,000 square feet ranges. More space benefits the customers, right?

But think what the consequences are for some previously obscure market segments, now correctly referred to as persons with disabilities. As we have previously discussed, the federal legislation, the Americans with Disabilities Act, addresses accessibility and accommodations for a wide variety of private businesses, from rinks to restaurants to retailers, on behalf of disabled persons. The ADA encompasses regulations for retail store design and operation; in recent years, commercial building codes have specified access standards for retail establishments. Architectural firms and building contractors know to work within these guidelines. But who specifically are these disabled people, and what limitations would they face in activities as all-American as shopping at the hometown K mart or eating at McDonald's?

To narrow the disability discussion, let's select one example of a prevalent health condition and track the consequences of the ensuing disability. One large category is cardiovascular diseases (CVD); one in four Americans suffer from CVD in one form or another. CVD includes conditions like hypertension and atherosclerosis, which can result in coronary heart disease and strokes. Hypertension, for example, reduces strength and endurance, which could directly influence the ease or difficulty in mobility functions such as walking, shopping, or carrying items.

Viewpoint 5.1—The effects of hypertension

Condition: *Hypertension* (high blood pressure) affects 61,870,000 Americans over the age of six; additionally *Coronary heart disease* affects 6,080,000 persons; *Stroke* affects 2,930,000 persons; *Rheumatic heart disease* affects 1,290,000 more.

Physical limitation: Shortness of breath, fatigue, mobility impairment

Consequences: Limitation in ability to walk distances, to climb stairs, to lift or carry heavy items such as bags of groceries or other merchandise.

WHAT IS THE SIZE OF THE MARKETS OF CHRONICALLY IMPAIRED PERSONS?

We spoke briefly in the second chapter about the numbers of consumers within disabilities segments. Activity impairments resulting from many long-term conditions affect many people; National Health Interview Surveys (*Data Book*, 1989) put the noninstitutionalized population at 231.5 million adults aged 18 and over. Concerning activity limitations, NHIS research reports that

- 19.2 million are restricted to walking a quarter mile or less

- 18.2 million are restricted to carrying or lifting a bag no heavier than 10 pounds

- 13.5 million are severely limited in physical functions (as needing assistance to perform physical activities such as seeing, hearing, lifting or carrying, speaking or working).

It seems reasonable that a mobility impaired person, one of the 19 million who can walk no farther than a quarter mile, could become fatigued in a "hyperstore" because of its physical size. What are retailers doing to make their establishments disabilities-friendly? None of the retailers or their design firms surveyed were aware of research commissioned to measure the sales impact of disabled consumers or even of demographic profiles of them. McDonald's Corporation did mention that drive-throughs are used frequently by mobility impaired customers and that drive-throughs now contribute half of all units' sales. One-half of McDonald's sales is no small number.

LOGICAL ACCESSIBILITY ADAPTIONS

Wal-Mart design consultants BSW Group of Tulsa stated that all retail store design is of course subject to building codes and accessibilities standards, for example, for door and aisle widths, and turning areas. But Wal-Mart nevertheless recognized that the increased store size (from the store format of 40,000 to 60,000 square feet expanded to their "Super Center" size of 110,000 to 180,000 square feet) might intimidate some shoppers, including those with disabilities. Architect Bob Workman of BSW Group noted that the length of shoppers' journeys was carefully studied with constantly changing merchandise plans. One key finding resulted in moving customer service desks, bathrooms, and refreshments up front for easier access. Seating and benches are strategically placed to help flagging shoppers complete their rounds.

K mart Corporation also has committed to making its stores more disabilities-friendly. In 1990 K mart went on record to rededicate the corporation to a $2.3 billion "renewal" of all its sales outlets by the end of 1995; this included refurbishing 2,500 stores with modernizing features including wider aisles and electronic doors. In large K marts over 86,000 square feet, 1,300 electric carts became a standard store amenity. The testing of electric carts is spilling over to the three new American Fare stores, mammoth in scale from 146,000 square feet to 244,000 square feet—these vehicles are parked at the entry of each store. Expansion and refurbishing changes merchandising plans, and K mart managers are charged to produce new "store maps" that guide customers through the new merchandise arrangements. These maps are available for several months after each store reopens.

Combining the forces of barrier-free design standards and building codes, the new civil rights law and the potential of disabled consumers as an economic force, retailers are slowly making their stores and warehouses easier to patronize. As baby boomers continue to age, disabilities will be more common and will cause the retailer to be more creative and inventive in service and facilities delivery, not only to comply with ADA requirements but to provide a competitive edge.

THE MARKETING AUDIT

The disabilities marketing strategy is a new evaluation process that classifies prospects by physical characteristics. A marketing manager can then anticipate and approximate the market development potential for serving an array of populations with disabilities. On a step-by-step basis, a marketer can sort out the relevant questions to ask of selected customers with disabilities. For either new or existing products, a marketing or advertising manager can determine what marketing tasks have been accomplished and what further tasks are yet to be addressed.

The disabilities marketing strategy helps by setting direction amid the elements of the marketing function, such as the buyer target, the prospect's needs, media and distribution channels available, and monitoring sales performance of the product or service. This evaluation is a marketing audit. It begins simply enough, in checklist form, asking questions such as who is our market and how many people potentially comprise this group? This method can work downward to levels of detail such as response card stock recommendations or sales display widths and heights. It's the marketer's call to define the amount of detail required for making communications decisions.

To initiate a marketing audit, you may need to quantify the various disabilities markets. As with any grouping, begin with the broadest measures of prospect data and work toward the narrowest information salient to your product or service. What information would marketers want to test opportunities or interests among certain consumers with disabilities? Most would want to determine the sizes of segments and demand projections from population and user research. A key resource in disabilities marketing analysis is specialized demographic statistics that are arranged by health condition and are prepared by federal government offices, such as the Department of Education's National Health Interviews Survey (NHIS) prepared by the National Institute on Disability and Rehabilitation Research (NIDRR), or the National Rehabilitation Information Center (NARIC). Research resources are listed in Appendix B.

CLUSTERING AROUND COMMONALITIES

Any segmentation strategy seeks to bring together like groups, which is precisely the logic for applying disabilities marketing to your overall marketing plan. The largest categories of persons with disabilities can be identified by the impairment, as either sensory (sight, hearing, or speech) or motor (injury, orthopedic, or neurological conditions for example).[1] Accounting for approximately 44 percent of activity limitations, motor impairments restrict movement, whether the impairment involves upper body limitations such as missing limbs or paralysis of the hand or arm, or lower body limitations, such as missing limbs or paralysis of the foot or leg. As a percentage of conditions, mobility impairments comprise the greatest number of functional disabilities. Sensory impairments comprise 13 percent of activity limitations.

From these two major populations, marketers can continue the segmentation process, narrowing the fields by distinguishing between four broad chronic health condition categories:[2]

- *Mobility impairments* of the upper, lower, or whole body. The five chronic conditions most frequently reported as activity limiters are:

  - Arthritis (12.3% of all persons with activity limitations)

  - Heart disease (11.5%)

  - Spinal curvature and other back impairments (7.8%)

  - Impairments of lower extremities (6.1%)

  - Intervertebral disk disorders (4.4%)

- *Sight impairments*, including blindness and impaired vision, totaling 67 conditions per 1,000 persons or about 7 percent of activity limitations.

- *Hearing impairments*, including deafness (inability to hear any sound) and being hard of hearing (ability to hear some sound).

- *Speech and language impairments* account for 101 conditions per 1,000 persons, but only 6 percent of activity limitations since these disabilities have little effect on the ability to move about.

These are quite distinctive health conditions; each could produce a unique set of physical limitations. Using physical limitations alone, let's devise a marketing strategy that targets a selected disabled segment that matches well a product or service's benefits. The first step is to gauge the economics.

---

1   ICD Survey I, 13.

2   Data Book, 60.

ESTIMATIONS OF THE MARKETS' POTENTIAL

National markets. Regional markets. Local markets. Here we can use population statistics to quantify the market size depending on the marketer's choice of geographic coverage. Fashion retailers with multiple locations might need data of a different scale than would a neighborhood men's shop. Obviously there will be certain industry formulas or numbers that some marketers must meet before proceeding toward a decision to test market a new concept. Extending this audit process, many marketing managers will recognize familiar and meaningful quantitative and qualitative checks and measures that they regularly use in new product development or market expansion decisions. From the appropriate research sources, let's initiate a market audit in the form of a marketing checklist. Tailor the checklist according to your industry, product or service.

Checklist 5.1—Economic Analysis Outline

I.   Population(s) size(s)

    A.   National total (This total can be factored by incident rates per 1,000 persons as cited by knowledgeable sources such as *Chartbook on Disability in the United States* (1989) compiled by the National Institute on Disability and Rehabilitation Research or nonprofit health organizations such as Muscular Dystrophy Association or National Multiple Sclerosis Society. See Appendix A for extensive health condition information).

    B.   State population total (Again using the condition rate per 1,000 persons, factor a state population according to those considered to be your relevant market. States may have conducted a census of populations by health conditions as set by the appropriate state government offices, such as Department of Health and Rehabilitative Services, or other statewide nonprofit health groups.)

    C.   Regional, county, or city estimates (Again drawing on national incident rates, define local government or nonprofit health groups' population or client estimates.)

II. Distribution of population

    A.   Age groupings (if appropriate)

B.   Number of households (if appropriate)

C.   Urban versus rural concentration (if appropriate)

D.   Sex (if appropriate)

III.   Economic profile(s)

A.   Labor force participation

B.   Personal income per capita

C.   Disposable income (annual)

D.   Percentage of income spent on health care

E.   Percentage of income spent on transportation

F.   Amount of supplementary income provided by government transfer payments or private disability insurance

G.   Average family income (if appropriate)

IV.   Level of technology applied to marketing process

A.   Current technology in place

B.   Impending assisting technology

C.   Technological skills of target market(s)

V.   Channels of distribution

A.   Direct distribution (to consumer)

1.   Proprietary channels

2.   Cooperative channels

B.   Retailers

1.   Number of potential retailers (national, state, or regional)

2.   Specialized merchandise or mainstream products?

3.   Size of retailer (large or small)

4.   Type of operation (cash, credit, third-party payment)

5.   Opportunity for stocking by chain stores

6.   Need for any specialized sales training? Displays that might be viewed negatively by retailer?

C.   Wholesalers

1.   Number of potential wholesalers (national, state, or regional)

2.   Size or number of products carried by wholesalers

3.   Method of payment (cash or credit)

D.   Penetration of geographical market

       1.   Share of market percentages (estimated number of consumers served by each competitor divided by target market size)

       2.   Ranking order of competitors

E.   Order process potential

       1.   Alternative methods evaluation

          a.   Personal (face-to-face) selling

          b.   Telemarketing

             i.   Buyer-initiated (first order)

             ii.   Seller-initiated (reorder)

          c.   Direct response

             i.   Buyer-initiated (first order)

             ii.   Seller-initiated (reorder)

          d.   Electronic ordering (modem link)

             i.   Buyer-initiated (first order)

             ii.   Seller-initiated (reorder)

          e.   Doorstep delivery

          f.   Policy for returns/credits

          g.   Customer service policy

F.   Availability of credit

       1.   Cash only

       2.   Buying club (affinity group/membership only)

       3.   Bank/credit union credit card

       4.   Bank/credit union debit card

       5.   Private credit plan offered by retailer

       6.   Approvals procedure for third-party pay

       7.   Government transfer payment (Medicare or Medicaid)

G.   Opportunity to coventure with established partner

       1.   Market test with compatible/complementary product

       2.   Ongoing program as part of a co-op package

H.   Packaging considerations

       1.   Sensitivity toward disabilities-friendly easy-opening or easy-to-handle packaging

       2.   Simplicity in instructions and graphics legibility

       3.   Emphasis on environmentally friendly package materials

I.   Availability of trade shows or consumer exhibitions

      1.   Identify most prestigious trade show to attend for product information and for competitive intelligence

      2.   Participate in the most popular consumer exhibition in the local market

VI. Media review and coverage patterns

    A.   Availability of disability-specific print media (such as *MDA Newsmagazine, Paraplegia News* or *Sports 'n Spokes*)

    B.   Appropriateness of general newspaper or magazine media

    C.   Availability of disability-specific electronic media (such as closed-caption, community access cable TV, closed circuit systems available at many hospitals, or talk/news radio stations)

    D.   Appropriateness of broadcast television or radio media

    E.   Direct mail (to build as prospect/customer bank)

    F.   Electronic data networks (such as Prodigy or CompuServ)

    G.   Mass transit advertising (if available)

    H.   Outdoor/signage (if appropriate)

VII. Nonpaid media review

    A.   Health organization newsletters (local and national)

    B.   Appropriateness of general newspaper or magazine publicity

    C.   Possible qualification as public service announcement material

---

The disabilities marketing strategy focuses on the working aged civilian population, defined by government records as 16 to 64 years, who are not institutionalized, meaning persons who live at or make their own home; NHIS estimates put this universe at approximately 231 million Americans.

Much additional health data are found in the *Data Book*; tables specify demographic data such adult, male, or female conditions, prevalence of activity limitation due to condition by age and by race or ethnicity, and incomes or work limitations, among other characteristics.

Drawing upon available data, segment sizes for appropriately targeted products or services can be established. (Data sources are listed in Appendix A.) Consider working through this question or task list as you contemplate the product's appeal to users with disabilities. Marketers know their target markets very well, and it would not be surprising if you were to expand this cursory checklist tenfold to better describe your relevant markets.

Viewpoint 5.2—Segmentation by males

National Health Interview Surveys, 1983-1985 (three-year average) is a definitive resource for a variety of segmentation information. For example, here is one excerpt of a record on males, in various age groups:

(Number of conditions in thousands and rate per 1,000 persons)

Chronic condition	Under 45		45–69		70–84	
Osteoarthritis	1,891	23.7	5,787	230.4	2,407	391.4
Impair of upper ext	3,168	39.6	1,754	70.3	367	59.7
Speech impairment	1,138	14.2	301	12.0	91	14.8
Hypertension	3,268	40.9	6,740	268.3	1,977	321.6
Migraine headache	1,467	18.4	492	19.6	49	8.0

PRODUCT AUDIT

As with any marketing task, an audit of where the company stands *today* is the best start for gauging customer satisfaction levels or launching new programs. The systems presently in place may serve disabilities marketing efforts well, or a new marketing mix might be required to best serve customers with disabilities. Let's create a fictional product, a glycerine patch, that fits the needs of a huge population with hypertension, a common heart ailment. Statistics have established that hypertension affects one in four Americans. This number sounds enormous, but before the marketer begins to line his or her pockets with receivables, let's ask several questions to evaluate the competitive environment.

An excellent checkpoint is the product's attributes and benefits. Does the product-form presently exist, or must you create a new product category? Different marketing strategies will be required if you're entering an existing category, as a competitor with no brand loyalties. But if you have a new and unknown product category, changing consumer education and habits entails different actions. Let's ask more situation assessment questions through the product performance viewpoint (see Checklist 5.3).

Checklist 5.3—Product Audit

I. The proposed product
   A. Compare the proposed product as a "new entrant," which a specific disability group should recognize as "needed"; what benefit(s) should be selected for promotion?
      1. Superior performance or relative advantage
      2. Familiarity of use or application
      3. Convenience of use
      4. Speed of application or use
      5. Comparative cost
      6. Other qualities (Simplicity of steps, simplicity of packaging, improved strength or purity, storage ease, extended shelf life, more cosmetic appearance, and so forth)
   B. Comparison for negative perceptions or consequences (Not all products' usages can be considered positively, particularly in health care or similar commodity or "institutionalized" applications; a realistic evaluation is very important in this beginning stage.)
      1. Relative disadvantages
      2. Unfamiliar use (requiring consumer education)
      3. Complexity in use or application directions
      4. Slower application or slower results of use
      5. Higher cost of use
      6. Other disadvantages (such as awkward packaging, short shelf life, few distributors, and so forth)
      7. Competitor disadvantages (How did they or could they overcome the disadvantage?)
II. Evaluate the markets to which the proposed product will be sold (These market evaluations can take several forms, and the marketer must look from several directions to confirm the proposed market need.)
   A. Geographic market areas (Define numbers of potential users in smaller and larger parameters.)

      1. Local area

      2. Regional area

      3. National market

      4. International market (This audit may prove very complex depending on the cultural fabric of the host country; Northern European countries react much differently than Asian cultures when relating to disabilities. Also the ADA is the legal imperative only for the United States and its possessions.)

B. Consumer purchase patterns (Refer to the product evaluation highlights, Checklist 5.2.1.A)

      1. Product features/use preferences

      2. Existing product use patterns

      3. Size of order/purchase

      4. Frequency of purchase patterns

      5. Shopping habits

      6. Warranty expectations

C. Distribution patterns

      1. Purchaser preferences

      2. Order/purchase patterns

      3. Reorder preferences

      4. Direct-Retail-Wholesale patterns

      5. Delivery preferences

D. Customer service preferences

      1. Initial purchase follow-up

      2. Complaint resolution procedures

      3. Ongoing contact

E. Promotional mix applications

      1. Advertising message and media selection

      2. Sales promotion techniques

          a. Trade directed (push strategy)

          b. Consumer directed (pull strategy)

      3. Public relations programs

          a. Trade directed media

          b. Consumer directed media

      4. Personal selling programs

F. Communications channels

1. Existing channels
2. Preferred channels
3. One-way or two-way channels (degree of interactivity)
4. Targetable or broad channels
5. Message life (short life or long)
6. Periodicity (frequency of publication or transmission)
7. Level of redundancy (for various health conditions)
8. Expendability (ability to carry complementary products)

G. Pricing strategy (Define how the pricing structure is to be applied to the proposed product or service.)
1. Retail pricing
2. Wholesale/quantity discount
3. Other trade or merchandise discounts
4. Direct marketing pricing
5. Broker/agent pricing (if applicable)
6. Affinity group pricing (working through affinity organizations, such as AARP or special interest health groups)

ANTICIPATE THE COMPETITION

So far we've looked at the product potential. If we are investigating this potential, won't the competitors also be looking in the same places? Of course they will. So let's make our own analysis of external competitors (see Checklist 5.4).

Checklist 5.4—Competitive environment audit

I.   List and evaluate uniquenesses of major competitors.
   A.   Major product advantage(s) enjoyed by each competitor
   B.   Major product disadvantage(s) attached to each competitor
   C.   Geographic opportunities or threats
   D.   Distribution opportunities or threats
   E.   Customer service opportunities or threats
   F.   Promotional mix opportunities or threats
   G.   Communications channels opportunities or threats

H.   Pricing opportunities or threats

I.   Warranty opportunities or threats

II.   Market size versus competitors (How large or small are the competitors your product will be facing?)

A.   Estimation of industry sales per year

1.   Estimation of competitors' sales per year

2.   Estimation of company sales per year

B.   Summary of salient trends in the marketplace

C.   Statement tying proposed product to marketing strategy specifying:

1.   Prospects with disabilities

2.   Acceptable pricing

3.   Targeted promotional mix

4.   Appropriate distribution

D.   Bibliography of sources

Given a careful review of the marketing process potentials, each of the marketing variables will be discussed at some length. Most practitioners and business students recognize the "five P's" of marketing: product, prospect, promotional mix, price, and place (the channels of distribution). These are the controllable aspects the marketer assesses, eliminates, and reshapes to his or her advantage. Which is most important?

Logically, without a product or service a marketer has nothing to sell, so let's examine the product or service nuances as applied to markets with disabilities.

EVALUATING PRODUCT/SERVICE DESIGN

Marketers and manufacturers are probing usage patterns by various groups with disabilities to determine how well products or services fit their needs. Some products might be easier to use than others; studying daily usage of products removes the guesswork about the habits of consumers with disabilities. Over the last few years, two major industrial design concepts have emerged: "universal design" and "adaptive design."

Universal Design

Universal design considers the abilities of all users, from 5 to 95, to develop solutions that make handling or applying a product easier for everyone, including persons with disabilities. The leading proponent, Patricia Moore of Moore Design Associates in Phoenix, suggests that "disabilities are basically defined by *products* and *architecture*, not by age or health." With ergonomic-designed products, "elderly or disabled people should be able to continue using the telephone, kitchen utensils or other ordinary items, even at advanced ages or with severely limiting physical conditions." The *Business Week* article chronicled Ms. Moore's collaboration in creating a line of cooking utensils:

> [The client] consulted Moore and came up with a three-part solution. [First] simply enlarging the handle would improve leverage and spread the squeezing pressure over the entire palm, eliminating cramping of the fingers. [Second] using a rubbery material instead of a slippery plastic would make gripping much easier, especially when knives and spoons are wet. Lastly, adding a few fins for fun made people want to pick up and use the products.[3]

The big-handled line, named "Good Grips," is a marvelous study on unifying users' needs, which, incidentally, incorporates disabilities-friendly features. The name chosen for the line is also appealing because it avoids patronizing or narrowing references to "handicap helpers" or other excluding labels. The design concept doesn't hang labels on any single user group such as the elderly or those with disabilities. Moore sums up the appropriateness of universal design as "allowing business to widen the consumer market for all products."[4] (See Viewpoint 5.3.)

Universal design principles are also found in office environments; again the issue is expanding the "usability umbrella" for making business products and systems as functional as possible. Hands-free speaker phones, large-sized number keys, voice-activated keyboards all are assistive, whether the operator is sight or mobility impaired.

---

3 Nussbaum, Bruce, "What works for one works for all," *Business Week* (New York, NY: April 20, 1992), 112–113.

4 *Ibid.*

Viewpoint 5.3—Disability is a common occurrence

Universal design does benefit everyone, says June Isaacson Kailes, a disability policy consultant from Playa del Rey, CA, because "disability is a predictable and universally common occurrence of the human condition. It is common to think about disability in the narrowest sense, that is, a person who uses a wheelchair or crutches, but the reality is that most families are touched by such disabilities as hearing and visual impairments, arthritis, epilepsy, heart disease, lack of endurance, trouble walking, joint pain and stiffness."

There is an 80 percent chance of having to use a wheelchair sometime in a lifetime, she added, and there is a 95 percent chance of experiencing temporary mobility impairment such as a broken leg, sprained ankle or twisted knee.

"More Homes Designed with Disabilities in Mind," *Los Angeles Times*, 9/19/92

Adaptive Design

Adaptive design, another approach that is receiving attention from manufacturers and industrial designers, is frequently used on existing products and services, to accommodate customers with disabilities. Marketers reconfigure product specifications, package weights, sizes or opening/closure methods, and delivery or customer service systems to simplify use for the person with disabilities.

An example of adaptive design (and good public relations) is Procter & Gamble's decision to switch to a retractable plastic pouring spout on its Tide laundry detergent. The heavy gauge cardboard made opening a box of Tide difficult for many persons with mobility impairments. With this plastic opener/spout adaption, the Arthritis Foundation endorsed the new closure, allowing P&G to place its certification on the front of the Tide box.[5]

---

5 Broderson, Linda, "User-friendly Product Design," *Arthritis Today* (Atlanta, GA: Arthritis Foundation, May-June, 1989), 16–19.

Adaptive design applies to services, too, notably financial systems such as Merrill Lynch, many banks, and even the Internal Revenue Service, which provide Telecommunications Devices for the Deaf (TDDs) as a means of accessing customer account information. This system provides a user-friendly, convenient way to inquire about checking or savings accounts, portfolio information, and other financial matters 24 hours a day.

The adaptive design process begins with the marketer recognizing the opportunity to be of greater service to "special" populations, specifically groups with disabilities. It takes a conscious effort to be on the alert—by keeping sensitivities close by—to how a product can be changed to offer improved benefits to disabled users.

MARKETING INTELLIGENCE-GATHERING LISTENING SKILLS ARE CRITICAL

Tapping into the opinions and experiences of consumers with disabilities is an important task-setting marketing direction, and it pays to be a good listener. Several proactive "intelligence-gathering" methods can be initiated. A marketer's information needs might best be served through a formal assignment of marketing research methods, such as focus group interviews or user surveys.

Usually an independent research company is engaged to recruit and conduct **focus groups** also known as **focus panels**, small gatherings of 8 to 12 individuals who are led through a discussion of their general attitudes or experiences in product or service use. The focus group leader usually is a trained professional who, from experience, knows how to guide the group through the relevant questions and to keep individual members from dominating the group discussion. Most times the products and clients paying for the research are not identified; this anonymity reduces bias among respondents.

The focus group research tool is best used early in the marketing planning process, to assist in direction-setting efforts. Focus panel findings are qualitative in nature, summarizing attitudes and opinions held by prospective market groups. The questions are general in form, such as "When you bought your home, what were the two most important considerations?" or "What features would you find attractive?" and the moderator guides the dialogue for an hour or two. The transcribed responses set opinion parameters for marketers, such as identifying price or convenience or dependability as the product or service benefits that the chosen market segments hold most dear and would be willing to pay for. It takes an experienced talent to lead and interpret focus group opinions. Since only the largest companies maintain in-house research departments, most marketing managers call upon independent marketing research firms or large advertising agencies to conduct consumer research studies.

A second formal method to consider once marketing directions are a bit more set, but not yet carved in stone, is **survey research**, which can quantify and further define the subject market's habits or usage rates. Marketers might ask about product preferences; purchase influencers, such as personal referrals or media channels; or payment methods. A survey with closed-ended questions (the respondent must select from a provided list of answers) might ask a sample with disabilities about frequency of use or other "percentage of population" questions, such as brand preferences or market penetration. Another form of survey questionnaires could ask open-ended questions, such as "What kind of atomizer did you last purchase and why?" The method is unwieldy, though, when large numbers of respondents are surveyed because so many different (and possibly illegible responses in written questionnaires) answers might have to be tabulated.

SURVEY SELECTION DEPENDS ON SEVERAL FACTORS

Surveys can be conducted through the mail or over the telephone: cost, sample size, geographic coverage, and depth or technicality of information usually dictate the form of a survey. Telephone surveys can sample all parts of the nation.

Surveys can be conducted face-to-face, such as personal in-store interviews (this is a popular method for checking customer service or product satisfaction) or by mall intercept interviews in which shoppers are randomly stopped and asked to answer survey questions. This technique works well when the marketer has well defined the prospect's demographic profile (the quantifying characteristics, such as age, income, or educational levels) or psychographic profiles (lifestyle or interests, among others). A disadvantage of face-to-face interviews is that samples must be geographically clustered to minimize travel or other field costs.

Compared to face-to-face interviews, telephone interviews are generally less costly and can include more callbacks to contacts. The telephone survey also has an advantage because of the greater opportunity it affords for supervision and quality control. Disadvantages of telephone or mail surveying must be weighed; usually the harder to reach, the wider the area; or the more technical the information, the more costly the research project is.

Less formal methods can be employed and can produce very valuable customer or client insights. Managers (and department staff) should get out of the office and into the field to investigate prospect preferences and experiences by scheduling personal interviews with officials of disabilities or health groups. Examples of these groups are the Heart Association, the Muscular Dystrophy Association, the Multiple Sclerosis Society, and the National Spinal Cord Injury Association; categorize them as serving adults or children to better match the product's user group (see Appendix B for list of organizations). Ask for their expert opinions on how the product or service could best serve members with disabilities. Also ask for permission to participate in a support group meeting to better understand how health conditions affect the lives of persons with disabilities.

By attending such a group meeting, the marketer will learn directly from the potential user and from friends and families of the person with disabilities what they think and what they need or don't need; which topics are discussed and which are taboo. Does the national marketer hear similar opinions voiced in Augusta and in Omaha? If not, why not?

Consider meeting with state or local government officials or health care providers who work in vocational rehabilitation or other human services programs to gain insights into the problems and opportunities facing their constituents. Many physical or occupational therapists have a unique appreciation of how their clients contend daily with disabilities or the consequences resulting from the disabilities and can be very helpful by sharing their knowledge. Picking up tips and know-how, the marketer earns credibility in the eyes of the product users. Respect is earned by deeds, not promises.

TRACKING THE INDUSTRY

One last informal information-gathering method is to make staff assignments to keep up-to-date with "marketing intelligence" that might be applied to improving disabilities marketing programs. One staff member might be alert to tracking new technology in media or assistive computer applications. Another might be assigned to reading industry publications for competitive products or services, or joining a speakers' bureau and keeping track of dates of conventions or meetings for disabilities interests. Staying current is staying competitive, and it takes a conscious effort to establish "listening posts" for tapping into market trends.

Of course the success of any of these marketing research methods assumes the appropriate questions are being probed; before jumping into any research project, managers should ask themselves what the purpose of the research is, just what it is they need to learn.

KEEP IT SIMPLE

The marketing research effort should produce a wealth of information and suggestions to improve the design and use of the marketer's proposed product. Real people using (or being unable to use) the existing or proposed product are the best judges of performance; by carefully listening, the marketer will embrace many of these design suggestions:

- Improve efficiency/effectiveness of the main product or service functions; think through possible utilization problems encountered by the four major groups of disabilities (mobility, sight, hearing, or speech impairments).

- Eliminate unnecessary, trivial, redundant and/or noncontributing secondary functions; in other words, design or manufacture the product to achieve the primary function well before (or possibly eliminate) considering any possible secondary feature.

- Maintain a commitment to function over form, in design and operation. This does not mean that ugly is preferred, but that function is the top priority.

- Reduce the number of steps required to carry out the usage function; be aware of growing resentment among the *whole* population of increasing complex product assembly or operating instructions. Remember, the product was bought to reduce problems, not create them.

- Reduce the human effort (either dexterity or strength) required to operate a product or perform a function.

- Particularly with services, automate functions and systems so they can be accessed 24 hours a day, seven days a week. And keep the operating steps simple.

- For users with sight impairments, consider including tactile uniquenesses in controls differentiation.

■ Keep the mindset that it's the marketer's fault if the product is difficult to use or program. Customers want only the time; they don't want an explanation of how to build a watch.

Here are some ease-of-use examples that marketers have added to existing products; these disability-friendly touches improve value to current or potential customers or clients:

■ Built-in comfort and convenience benefits all your markets segments, both disabled and nondisabled. Where would we all be without

- Cordless telephones for mobility?

- Remote control devices for convenience—garage doors, TVs, and VCRs?

- Automatic timers for coffeemakers, sprinklers, or alarm systems?

■ Concentrate on making products easy to open and close. Eliminate small caps by incorporating the cap as an extension of the bottle or package:

- Product dispensers like pump toothpaste or squeeze catsup, mustard, or salad dressings.

- Snap-open and shut pouring spouts like the Tide detergent example.

- Snap-open or screw-off lids for cans and bottles.

■ Make products easier to handle or dispense:

- Simplify access, such as water and ice through an in-the-door dispenser on refrigerators.

- Consider dexterity problems resulting from having to grasp or turn small or smooth knobs; push or pull levers on plumbing fixtures or entry doors are helpful.

- Recognize that range of motion restrictions affect dexterity too; hard-to-close fasteners, such as buttons or other closures in the back of clothing, can be replaced, as well as lowering light switches or using detachable controls.

- Consider nonskid surfaces for containers, particularly if the contents are refrigerated and the container "sweats" at room temperature.

- Investigate smaller packages for lighter weights.

- Explore many container shapes, with or without handles, grips, or lowered centers of gravity.

- Test smaller bottle necks or openings to slow down spilled contents if the container is overturned.

■ If envelopes are required, reduce the strength or dexterity needed to open them. Can an envelope be designed to be opened with one hand? Think about strength and dexterity for styrofoam packing forms; make sure the fit is snug but not "frozen" in place.

■ If statements are being mailed, are the pages already collated or printed on perforated "tractor-feed" paper so recipients don't have to struggle with unfolding, stacking, or attaching several pages?

■ Insist on easy-to-read, highly visible user-friendly instructions:

- Be sure to test the instructions; call together a focus group of people with various disabilities to read and follow the instructions.

- Consider initiating an 800 information line, staffed with knowledgeable people who can answer product or service questions. This is a great strategy to improve customer satisfaction and also to build customer name and address lists for future product introduction or testing.

■ Weigh safety considerations as well as convenience:

- Nonbreakable bottles and containers (plastic not glass) for kitchen and bathroom use.

- Auditory or tactile warnings around potential dangerous areas (stepdowns, exterior exits, stairs).

- Improved antitampering wraps that allow the user with disabilities an adequate means to break the seal without breaking an arm.

- Inclusion of a "smart chip" (like those music-playing greeting cards) to alert sight-impaired persons to operating instructions or of a toll-free number to call for verbal step-by-step directions for product use.

An exhaustive situation analysis reinforces the marketer's understanding with better information on what the existing or proposed product or service can (or can't) do for segments with disabilities. Universal design or adaptive design principles add value to disabled users in addition to better serving the whole of the market. Armed with these insights, let's look more closely at how the markets can be segmented into smaller, more effective customer groups.

Once the marketing direction has been set, managers should turn their attention toward the segmentation strategy employed by disabilities marketing. We're now ready to consider how disabilities-friendly prospect segmentation can be.

CHAPTER SIX

SELECTING DISABILITIES SEGMENTS

CLASSIFICATION OF VARIOUS DISABILITIES

In this section the disabilities marketing process is examined according to a series of decisions made to classify and target appropriate disabilities groups. The purpose of this process is to identify, quantify, and rank narrower consumer segments which, in turn, allows more effective message delivery and encourages ease-of-use response vehicles. A classification scheme for marketing strategy is logical because the nature of the disability can affect how, or even if, the disabled prospect is likely to use and enjoy the product or service benefits.

Most physical limitations follow from either a chronic health condition or an injury. Injury-caused disabilities (from automobile, diving, or motorcycle accidents, for example) affect an estimated 14.8 million persons. The majority of these injuries result in activity limitations, mainly mobility impairments. Mobility impairments could restrict either (or

97

both) upper or lower body movement, such as reaching, writing, grasping, or walking. Products or services which override mobility restrictions would be welcomed by persons with quadriplegia, paraplegia, or circulatory conditions such as hypertension.

Chronic health conditions form the largest category of disabilities; we have seen them further defined as mobility impairments, hearing impairments, sight impairments, speech impairments, and mental/developmental impairments. Chronic health conditions may be highly apparent, such as paralysis or slurred speech, or the condition may be invisible, such as hypertension or hearing impairments.

In general 14.1 percent of noninstitutionalized American adults (accounting for 32.5 million persons) have an activity limitation; that's one in seven individuals who are limited in a major life activity. There are 37.3 million persons (20.6%) who have a physical (in contrast to a mental) functional limitation; many experience daily limitations such as the following:

- 19.2 million are limited to a quarter-mile walk (82.9 persons per thousand people).

- 18.2 million are limited to lifting or carrying a 10-pound bag (78.6 persons per thousand people).

- 12.8 million are limited in their ability to see words and letters in newsprint (55.2 persons per thousand people).

- 7.7 million are limited in their ability to hear normal conversation (39.3 persons per thousand people).

Of these populations, 7.5 percent, or 13.5 million persons, are severely limited in physical functions (needing assistance to perform physical activities such as seeing, hearing, lifting or carrying, speaking, or working). Recognizing the number of persons in various disabilities classifications and how their disabilities shape their lives is *the* most important information a marketer can gather and use to the benefit of his or her product and customer group. Regardless of the visibility or the severity of health impairment, a marketer should take into consideration the fit of the proposed product or service.

QUANTIFYING THE CONSUMER GROUPS

For years and years, persons with disabilities seemed not to exist, at least where marketing was concerned. However, in the last few decades, several public and nonprofit organizations have initiated survey research to quantify the disabled populations. Most of these surveys were efforts to extract the opinions and self-perceptions of persons with disabilities; many studies were needs assessments of various health organizations such as the Multiple Sclerosis Society or the Muscular Dystrophy Association. None of the investigations was designed to serve as a marketing facilitator. The names and addresses of the disabled persons are privileged and not available through health organizations sources for marketing efforts.

How is a marketer to judge marketing potentials with no consumer base to draw upon? One reliable way to estimate various segment sizes is to use population statistics compiled for the U.S. Department of Education by the National Institute on Disability and Rehabilitation Research from health surveys averaged between 1983 and 1985. Figures for estimating incident rates (the number of individuals affected in a population of 1,000 persons) for a variety of chronic health conditions could establish the customer group sizes which might benefit from a complementary product's use.

Continuing with the glycerine patch example in the previous chapter, let's conclude that our product research department has demonstrated that the patch provides a superior delivery method, eliminates intolerance from oral ingestion and is easy to apply. Which health conditions could be affected by this innovation? Substantial numbers of people encounter many heart ailments such as hypertension and circulatory conditions: 123 of every 1,000 Americans experience hypertension alone. This incidence rate can be projected to national or local levels.

Perhaps your product is not medicinal, perhaps it is accelerator/brake hand controls for an automobile. Which persons with disabilities might be most concerned with assistive devices for driving? Let's investigate those disabilities that are most limiting because of mobility impairments. According to the National Health Interview Surveys, there are many chronic conditions that can cause activity limitations (see Table 6.1).

For a more complete listing of various health conditions, refer to Appendix A.

Some market segments could be further quantified according to the presence of multiple impairments. Suppose the product is a voice-activated telephone answering device that announces and displays incoming messages; persons with visual and hearing impairments could find this machine attractive. Before checking for individual segment sizes, consider whether both impairments might affect the same individual. Statistics from the National Health Interview Surveys report the preva-

Table 6.1—Projecting chronic health conditions that result in the highest incidence level of activity limitation

Populations are estimated at national and regional levels.

Chronic Condition	% Causing Activity Limitation	Rate/M Persons	Segment Size National (230MM)	Tampa Bay (2.8MM)
Multp Sclerosis	77.0%	0.7	161,350	1,985
Paralysis (Comp/Partial)	65.7%	6.1	1,406,050	17,299
Emphysema	48.2%	9.1	2,097,550	25,807
Intervertebral disk disorders	45.9%	17.0	3,918,500	48,212
Epilepsy	42.8%	4.5	1,037,250	12,762
Cerebrovascular disease	41.2%	10.9	2,512,450	30,912
Osteomyelitis- Bone disease	34.3%	12.8	2,950,400	36,300
Diabetes	32.1%	25.6	5,888,000	71,680
Impairment of lower extrem	31.6%	45.2	10,396,000	126,560
Heart conditions	31.4%	93.2	21,436,000	268,960
Asthma	21.3%	37.1	8,533,000	103,880
Arthritis	20.8%	130.0	29,900,000	364,000
Hypertension	18.2%	123.5	28,405,000	345,800
Visual impairts	16.7%	68.5	15,755,000	191,800
Hearing impairts	3.9%	80.0	18,440,000	226,880

Source: Data Book, 1988

lence of multiple conditions causing activity limitations, such as the following:

Multiple eye and/or ear impairments	481,000 persons
Arthritis and hypertension	469,000 persons
Heart disease and hypertension	458,000 persons
Heart disease and arthritis	384,000 persons
Heart disease and diabetes	313,000 persons

Source: Chartbook, 1989

Are some conditions more limiting than others? Yes, some cases of multiple conditions severely reduce the activities of some individuals with disabilities. These are the highest prevalence rates:

Cerebrovascular disease and diabetes	74.5% are limited
Absence/paralysis of extremities and diabetes	69.5% are limited
Mental disorders and arthritis	67.8% are limited
Absence/paralysis of extremities and heart disease	65.7% are limited
Absence/paralysis of extremities and hypertension	65.4% are limited

Source: Chartbook, 1989

Matching the product or service's attributes to the appropriate segment is probably one of the two most difficult tasks in developing a disabilities-directed marketing program. But with proper understanding of the markets' needs and of the voids unrecognized by competitors, a realistic appraisal and strategic plan can be implemented.

UNDERSTANDING THE LIMITATIONS

The abilities to understand and organize are critical factors in effectively collecting the customer lists; an honest comprehension of various disabilities gained by reading newsletters and magazines, talking with prospective users, visiting with support groups, and learning from health organization officials will produce a wealth of experience that will be noticed and appreciated by prospect groups. These organization and segmentation tasks will test a marketer's creativity and flexibility in establishing a smooth path to the doors of customers with disabilities.

The emphasis must be on *taking the time* to understand the ramifications of various disabilities. Designers, engineers, production people, and marketers must see the product in the hands of the customer to know how difficult or easy use is. Usage patterns, such as using clear plastic tubing as a 24-inch beverage straw for persons with upper body paralysis, bring new combinations to the attention of the marketer. Few people can creatively speculate on the unintended applications that serve consumers with disabilities so well. Flexible foam rubber sleeves make forks or spoons easier to grasp; patches of Velcro replace buttons as closure devices; joysticks serve as controllers for wheelchairs, light dimmers, or volume controls for stereo amplifiers. None of these uses were originally intended, but from necessity, new applications were explored and adapted. Careful attention is mandatory; the rewards can be well worth the effort.

SELECTING THE DISABILITIES TARGET

In selecting a customer target, factors of the "go or no go" assessment revolve around three critical marketing decisions over which the marketer has control. The marketer can define the "controllables" by choosing the prospect segment (such as 18- to 34-year-old females); selecting geographic areas (such as southern California); or proposing the price (such as $9.99). "Controllables" can be specified as:

- Segment size of the market(s)

- Geography of the target market(s)

- Price of the product or service

The method used to quantify the segment size has been discussed; is the prospect group (or groups) large enough to provide economies in production or distribution? Or is the number of users so low that each becomes a "custom adaption"? What is the break-even point for your anticipated market effort?

Can the segmentation strategy be approached in a more creative way that looks for new shared attributes or threads that might hold two or more market interests together? The major categories of mobility or sensory impairments might be reexamined as physical limitations to movement; for example, would a combined grouping of lower extremities impairments *and* sight impairments (which many times reduce the ability to freely move about) produce a greater prospect base? Could heart conditions (which can result in lessened stamina) and orthopedic impairments be linked to expand the user group? With thorough research and a sincere interest and understanding of how various disabilities affect peoples' lives, a marketer can adapt his or her goods to better serve markets with disabilities.

ADD GEOGRAPHY TO THE EQUATION

The physical location of the prospects is also important information. What is the incident rate at the city, county, state, regional, or national level? Do wider geographic areas need to be chosen to enlarge the prospect pool? Some health conditions are sufficiently frequent to allow marketing efforts at a county level (such as arthritis at 130 cases per

1,000 persons or hypertension at 123.5 cases per 1,000 persons), while others (such as multiple sclerosis at .7 case per 1,000 persons) may require adding the populations of whole states to produce adequate user bases.

Yet, while the incidence level might be low or obscure (such as amyotrophic lateral sclerosis, estimated at 30,000 to 40,000 cases nationally), understanding the prognosis and the limitations could enable the marketer to expand the grouping to "neuromuscular disorders," thus possibly encompassing sufficient numbers to make the test of the product worthwhile. The depth to which you dig to learn more about groups of physical conditions is entirely up to you. Amount of interest, effort, and success usually go hand in hand.

PRICE AS THE REGULATOR

A decision on price must be made. How much can (or will) the market pay for the proposed goods or services? Research is needed to provide the marketer with a good idea of how much the individual will choose to pay for convenience (such as mail-delivered prescription reorders or dry cleaning delivered to the front door); these are "common goods" that most everyone has had experience buying. Buyers with disabilities are no fools; they are willing to pay for added convenience or easier use only to a point.

It is more difficult to estimate the price or demand for innovative products or services with which this market (or any other segment, disabled or not) has no familiarity. Product trial, usage patterns, price elasticity, and customer satisfaction levels are all unknown, so the most prudent approach to pricing new goods or services is to conduct focus panel evaluations to establish a benchmark for future marketing comparisons. Every pricing analysis must begin at some level, and careful comparison among market groups may dictate how other new products or services might be speeded up or adjusted according to the markets' pricing preference.

CONSIDER TRIAL PERIODS AND STRONG WARRANTIES

For hundreds of years, product manufacturers have whetted customers' appetites with samples or trial opportunities to experience new goods. This "try before you buy" method has proven effective in demonstrating product superiority among innovative entries, from vacuum cleaners to lawn mowers to sporting goods. Recently, Saturn put its own automobile nameplate to the ultimate test, allowing prospects to try the model for 30 days or 1,500 miles and bring it back "no questions asked" if they weren't satisfied. One dealer boasted he had only one taker on the offer, and the returnee became an upgrader to a model with a fancier interior, but still in the Saturn line.

This strategy can work well to calm uncertainties about large dollar purchases by persons with disabilities if the manufacturer has confidence in his or her products. For example, electric wheelchairs cost from $4,000 to more than $8,000; when spending that much, everyone wants to be sure the wheelchair he or she is considering is comfortable to be in for 8 to 12 hours a day, is reliable and mechanically sturdy, and has manageable steering controls. The best proof is a test drive for a few days, after which, either the sale can be completed or a more appropriate substitution can be recommended.

The higher the cost, the more logical a trial period might be. Products such as innovative computer systems with voice-activated or eye-blink input, electronic readers, or services such as signing interpreters or sophisticated data bases could be tested for satisfaction.

The marketer should also recognize the value of warranty promises. Realizing the physical limitations of many persons with disabilities, a strong warranty plan gives peace of mind should problems arise after purchase.

Often a customer-driven warranty can be the strongest marketing weapon a marketer can introduce. Promises of 24-hour access or 24-hour turnaround eliminate many worries about down time of a broken wheelchair, computer system, or other necessities. Build warranty costs into the price, not as an add-on option. Marketers should remember that products and services are bought to solve problems, not to create them. Warranty obligations are the best way to define who is going to rectify the problem, especially if the cost to the consumer is included in the price.

COLLECT AND DOCUMENT THE RESULTS

No marketing program is complete until an evaluation procedure is chosen and records can be kept to document the performance of the media or message. Marketing is a process that organizes controllable and uncontrollable factors, a reoccurring series of steps that begins when the **sender** (the manufacturer or service provider) directs a **message** (the product or service benefit) through a **channel** (a communications vehicle) to a **receiver** (the customer or client) who responds with **feedback** (action, preferably sales or information).

The last step of the marketing process—that of gathering sales input or other important marketing information—measures how well (or poorly) the consumer received the product, how efficiently the media worked, or how effectively the message was received.

These measurements provide information that can be used in designing the next season's or year's program. This marketing cycle can be repeated and improved year after year, with marketers fine-tuning the controllables, such as product, price, distribution channels, and promotion while learning more and more about the uncontrollable elements: the prospect and her or his reactions.

BUILDING PROSPECT BASES

Isolating the prospect is a difficult task. There should be no mistaking the amount of effort and persuasion needed to encourage her or him to become a loyal customer. There are few if any direct mail lists that include the selection choice "physical or emotional disability." In years of searching, I've found only one list purported to contain names of electric scooter purchasers. The list was 18 months old.

Membership or subscriber lists are usually confidential, therefore unavailable. Medical or government files are privileged information. Gatekeepers such as health organizations (for example, the Muscular Dystrophy Association or the Heart Association), rehabilitation centers, or support groups also shield members from unwanted solicitations, and rightfully so. Many injuries and health conditions are difficult enough without having to put up with the distraction of unwanted sales calls.

Unwanted is the key. Appealing or ease-of-use products, or time- or effort-saving services are desirable to consumers with disabilities. It's the responsibility of marketers to offer tempting choices that persons with disabilities and their gatekeepers will *want* to take advantage of. Demonstrating desirability will attract attention to build prospect lists; lists can then be categorized and sorted by a predetermined set of characteristics, such as arranging by mobility, hearing, sight, or speech impairments.

Many marketers will choose to subdivide more narrowly, perhaps dealing solely with mobility impairments but sorting by upper body, lower body, or complete paralysis. These divisions can then be further divided for the lower body, for example, into complete or partial paralysis, absence of toes, foot or leg, orthopedic impairment, spinal or disk impairment, or a dozen other impairments of specific lower sites. For some products, narrower is better (such as shoe or instep accommodations); for others (such as flotation cushions or medicinal salves), broader definitions serve well.

The most interested prospect is one who chooses to be added to a customer list by returning a coupon or warranty card, by telephoning or TDDing a toll-free number for consumer information, by registering for a free membership card and account number, or by writing for the current product catalog.

And what makes someone want to be "added to the list"? The simple desire to have one or more problems solved by an empathetic marketer's goods or services, at the right price with convenient delivery and easy-to-use operation, plus the security of knowing there is a technical support person available on the customer service line.

A RECRUITMENT STRATEGY FOR PROSPECTS

To build a prospect or customer base requires patience, understanding, and creativity because the process is exploratory and long. Patience is needed since awareness of your product or service does not come overnight; in fact, this disabilities marketing strategy is not the answer for products or companies that are looking for a short-term "fix." Continual probing and tweaking is essential, and it might take two or more years to match the marketing components properly.

In addition to patience, the marketer must gain an understanding of how the prospect benefits from and values the product. Is it the only product in its class, or can the customer substitute one or more competitors? Does the marketer understand what limitations face the user with disabilities? What has the marketer done to gain first-hand experience of these limitations? How can the product or service be adapted to be more disabilities friendly?

Creativity is indispensable because the marketer will find many obstacles, each surmountable, strewn in the path of ordinary marketing activities. Identifying the unknowns and the unfamiliars will challenge the marketer to use many new combinations, old strategies blended with new input, to meet the needs of the purchaser with disabilities.

With attention to these qualities, the marketer can embark on an exploration of "concentric influences," a method that places the individual (or like group) with disabilities at the center of outwardly expanding circles. The ranking of these circles depends on the degree of contact, from personal to casual to impersonal. These relationships have different bonds, from the frequent personal contact of a family member to the much looser, more impersonal influence of an insurance company or government agency.

The marketer's job is to stay as close to the center as possible, building relationships throughout this network. Let's suppose the research department has produced a new telephone device that allows for storing voice messages and TDD messages, with installation as simple as plugging this machine into the telephone jack between the phone and the wall. How could the prospects for the improved answering machine be ranked?

Set Sights on the Center

First look to the center of the target, at telephone users with disabilities. The universe of users includes the following persons:

1. Persons with mobility impairments who may be restricted in movement so that calls are missed because of time or distance to the phone. Mobility impairments could include
   A. Absence of lower limb(s)—inability to walk
   B. Paralysis—inability to walk
   C. Orthopedic impairment—inability to walk
   D. Osteoarthritis—reduced ability to walk
   E. Curvature of spine—reduced ability to walk
   F. Hypertension—lack of stamina
   G. Heart disease—lack of stamina
   H. Phlebitis and varicose veins—reduced ability to walk
   I. Emphysema or asthma—reduced ability to walk

2. Persons with hearing impairments who may not be able to hear the telephone so that calls are missed. Hearing impairments could include
   A. Deaf in both ears
   B. Other hearing impairments

3. Family and friends of the person with a mobility or hearing impairment

4. Speech therapists, occupational therapists, physical therapists

5. Vocational rehabilitation and career counselors

6. Client services directors at rehabilitation centers

7. Services directors at health agencies and associations

8. Products managers at home health care suppliers

9. Case workers for government human resources services

The further down the list from the person with the disability, the more diluted the marketing contact will be. As the circles expand, the marketer should consider how the reasons, interests, and benefits differ from group to group and that each group will require different communications strategies. Some groups will be users (those with mobility and/or hearing impairments), while family or friends might seek a better way to keep in touch with their brother, mother, or close friend.

Primary users may recommend the product to their disabled friends; there also is an opportunity for referral (also called word of mouth) recommendations, from health care professionals. It's their responsibility to be familiar with new products in order to do their jobs better, such as speech or occupational therapy. A product or service "blessed" by a trusted health care provider carries great confidence among persons with disabilities. First-hand experience is valuable to the health organizations since these groups can keep their memberships informed and updated on new products and conveniences.

Remember that the structure for "covering" these markets is arranged in outwardly directed concentric circles, with the highest potential for building long-term relationships at the inner-most circle, the "bullseye." Work to cover the center circle as thoroughly as possible before moving outward; many marketers lack the discipline to keep focused on one group before jumping to the next influence ring. This process is not real estate, where the more you have the better you are, but one of relationships, where deeper is better. Resist also the temptation of trying to stretch the budget too far by attempting to court too many with too diluted a message. Trying to talk to everyone results in actually talking with no one. No awareness or impression is made, and the experiment is a conclusive failure.

Rank by the Universe of Users

According to the disabilities marketing strategy, an approximation of primary users (those prospects with disabilities) can be established by consulting the tables of "Prevalence of Selected Impairments and Chronic Conditions" compiled by the U.S. Department of Education, listed in Appendix B. Depending on flexibility, the product or service might find many applications. Let's return to the answering machine with TDD display and begin by ranking its user populations, before giving any consideration to message or communications tasks (see Table 6.2).

Table 6.2—Ranking of health conditions that are the most frequent causes of mobility impairment, by descending frequency of condition per 1,000 persons.

1. Osteoarthritis	125.4/M
2. Hypertension	123.5
3. Other hearing impairments	83.3
4. Various heart diseases	82.5
5. Impairment of lower extremities	45.2
6. Asthma	37.1
7. Phlebitis and varicose veins	34.5
8. Curvature of spine	19.7
9. Arteriosclerosis	13.5
10. Emphysema	9.1
11. Deaf in both ears	7.5
12. Paralysis	6.1
13. Other orthopedic impairment	1.4
14. Absence of lower limb(s)	1.2

Source: Data Book, 1988

This reranking certainly shows an increased frequency of mobility impairments (four of the top five conditions), which suggests stressing the product benefits of convenience and ease of effort—Never miss a call.

A secondary user group is comprised of those who are hard of hearing; the TDD replay capability is a unique benefit to stress, but from a different viewpoint than those with mobility conditions. "Never miss a call" might also be an appropriate message but with body text that highlights an easy-to-read TDD display screen with a memory function. This reranking process establishes a quantifiable foundation for judging how and with what resources various segments with disabilities can be reached.

BUILDING DISABILITIES CONTACT LISTS

The Prevalence of Conditions statistics produces a tidy method to numerically prioritize populations with disabilities; the frequency and size can give the marketer a strong reading for market potentials. But for the hierarchy of influencers, the family, friends, therapists, and so forth, an easy gauge of segment sizes disappears. A marketer could assume that for each condition of disability two or three interested family members or friends exist, but there appears to be no direct channel of communications to them. For the moment, let's disregard the family and friends ring.

What then proves to be the most effective method to organize contact lists of influencers who should produce trustworthy referrals for the new answering machine? Because of medical confidentiality, the marketer cannot directly solicit the name and address or telephone number of the person with a disability. Efforts should be turned toward building banks of names voluntarily offered, resulting from communications programs narrowed to special interests.

Disabilities contact lists can be assembled from three prospecting efforts aimed at (1) individuals with disabilities, (2) groups with disabilities, and (3) relatives, friends, and "gatekeepers." The first and quickest effort encourages an individual to voluntarily add his or her name and address to a list in order to receive information of interest to persons with similar disabilities. To compile such a list, a company could place advertising in a "designated disability" publication, or place notices in health organizations' newsletters. The sponsor of this list-building message (the company) would be identified.

The marketer should be aware that disability-oriented information is highly prized among prospects with disabilities; news of current research, new products, new services, and a calendar of upcoming events are welcome items of interest to these segments. There are many other relevant concerns among persons with disabilities as well. The two of greatest consequence are health care availability and cost, and the opportunity to live and work independently. A marketer must recognize these motivations and strive to incorporate them into the marketing environment.

A second prospecting effort can be directed toward groups with disabilities, from speaking to support (often called self-help) groups to participating in disabilities organizations' "trade shows," such as job fairs, disabilities awareness events, or conventions. The goal here is also to gather prospect lists via registration of names, addresses, and type of disability. Experience has shown this process of list compiling is slower since the schedules and agendas of the disabilities groups are beyond the control of the marketer. He or she must wait until the next monthly, quarterly, or even annual meeting is held. Further, permission may be required from the national office before any contacts can be made among an organization's members.

A third prospecting effort can be directed toward relatives or close friends and through "gatekeepers" such as health groups, government agencies, medical and rehabilitation professionals, insurance professionals, and educational professionals. Publicity of new products and services in local news media is the best contact effort; we will discuss publicity in Chapter 8. These influencers are quite diverse; some have more interest than others in overseeing the well-being of a relative with a disability. Attentive groups will encompass the individual himself or herself, brothers, sisters, children, or other relatives and close friends. By better serving the person with a disability, the marketer is making daily life a bit easier for the caregiver, either family member or friend.

HEALTH CARE PROFESSIONALS SERVE THE CLIENTS' NEEDS

Referrers with lower involvement or interest ("gatekeepers") would be those persons who provide therapy, educational, or other disabilities services but in a more professional, detached manner. Lacking the emotional attachment of the client's family or friends, the professional referrer would look toward helping better serve the person with a disability as an extension of her or his job responsibility. Some will be receptive, while others will dismiss the referral request immediately due to time and staff restraints.

During the last 30 years, large urban hospitals have developed many new services and sources of revenues. One such source is the rehabilitation center providing therapies for head or spinal cord injuries, or health conditions such as strokes. These centers are natural hubs of disabilities activities; a promising way to become part of this community is to sponsor or underwrite a program or a competitive sports team representing the center. The sponsor should get to know individual team members, their spouses, friends, and relatives on a first-name basis; thereafter, names and addresses could easily be compiled.

Media interest often focuses on the unique: What could be more fascinating than covering the "final four" at a quad rugby competition? The good neighbor becomes the good friend as honest and steadfast support is proffered to participants and spectators with disabilities.

MANAGING YOUR DATA BASES

All three contact strategies, the direct, personal "sign-up" and the indirect, "second party" referral from family or from health care professionals are needed to spread the prospect bases for efficient and effective marketing efforts. The national marketing director might enlist regional or local sales representatives to evaluate both direct and indirect strategies and select one or the best of both to join. Comparing notes from activities in different parts of the country could produce some exciting customer service ideas.

As the marketer plans the strategic process of attracting persons with disabilities, an important tactical element, expandable data base management, must be anticipated. Bringing an information systems specialist (as in computer) into early planning decisions is smart. Knowing what the marketer expects as output (highly selective and recombinable name lists, for example) is many times more important than specifying what input is to be entered. Some marketers will want to arrange their contact lists by health condition or by physical limitations, by age or by sex, by mild or by severe impairments, by geographic regions, by zip or area codes, or by occupation or relationship to the disabled person.

This sorting flexibility is very handy, particularly if the marketer is charged with promoting a whole brand or line of goods. Depending on the disability, the product may have several uses. To the manufacturer of foam rubber products, a cylindric sleeve of foam was intended to insulate a one-inch hot water pipe. But the user of a wheelchair recognizes the foam as a way to pad the armrests. And the individual with fine motor impairments sees the foam as an enlarged "handle" in which to slip a pencil or pen for better manipulation and writing.

Efforts to customize data management is not necessarily more difficult for information specialists, provided you outline your expectations before they begin programming. In fact, taking the time to share the past and the future of the marketing task provides an excellent orientation for pathfinding.

IS DISTRIBUTION AFFECTED?

As with all factors in the marketing mix, distribution—or how the target market gains access to goods and services—should be evaluated. Traditional distribution methods, such as shopping at the neighborhood grocery or visiting the local service station for auto repair, may be the most appropriate and familiar manner of utilizing a company's goods or services. It might, though, be a worthwhile endeavor for the marketer to play "what if" scenarios with alternative means of distribution to weigh if one method of allocating goods or services is superior to others. The marketer should start at the end of the marketing process, focusing on the satisfactory delivery of the user benefits; does the choice of distribution channels enhance buyer satisfaction, as one might be greatly preferred over others?

This evaluation might be meaningless if the company's product is immobile, such as those involving elaborate equipment, technical skills, or professional expertise; a hospital or a state court system requires that the market comes to the supplier, rather than the supplier (the doctor or judge) coming to the market. However, in some cases, distribution channels might be equivalent in, say, the ways to deliver medical records from a clinic back to the doctor's office. Choices in delivery could include the U.S. Postal service, Federal Express or DHL services, or intercity courier services. If each performs well, what criterion for choosing could be set?

Viewpoint 6.1—How hard is it for disabled people to learn about services available to them?

The Louis Harris and Associates research company asked a sample of 1,000 disabled Americans this question and recorded the following views:

Almost impossible	7%
Very hard	21
Somewhat hard	25
Not too hard	23
Not hard at all	17
Not sure/refused	8

The response was divided: 53 percent of the people thought learning about services was "almost impossible" to "somewhat hard." Conversely, 40 percent of the sample found learning about services "not too hard" or "not hard at all." Communications access would appear to produce problems for some persons with disabilities. If half of the services are doing it right, what are the other half doing wrong?

Here, it's the marketer's job to learn which manner of distribution the market prefers. What is necessary and what is preferred? Does the market rate ease, cost, speed, or accuracy as meaningful in choosing products or suppliers? Does the target market with disabilities care about the distribution method at all? It's probable that a market with disabilities has preferences and, therefore, would be alert to differentiated products or services. An effective way to make the product well-known among users with disabilities is through the distribution means; the better served the market, the more likely the referral opportunity. So distribution does affect the target markets and promotional mix.

Generally, the shorter the distribution method from the manufacturer to the customer, the better. This direct method eliminates many mistakes in the order entry process and reduces the opportunity for miscommunications among marketing levels. Unless superior sales training or order tracking buttresses the distribution system, a distribution system is prone to miscues. The transfer of information in ordering and the distribution of the product or service from the source is exposed to several potential blunders. Consider the number of possible "turnovers" as more intermediaries are involved: the salesperson, the retailer, the distributor, the wholesaler, and the manufacturer. More complex systems could be conceived, but the important point is to simplify the distribution pattern, which hopefully would result in lower prices, quicker delivery, and deeper relationships with customers with disabilities.

We have discussed how marketers can devise a disabilities marketing strategy that builds on understanding and attracting a critical consumer group. The marketing plan segmented, organized, and ranked categories of disabilities; let's now turn our attention toward marketing implementation of specific communications tools: advertising, sales promotion, public relations, and personal selling.

CHAPTER SEVEN

EXPLORING DISABILITIES COMMUNICATIONS AS AN APPLICATION TO MEDIA ADVERTISING

GLITCHES AND HITCHES IN THE MODEL

Communications are communications; what's to get in the way? From first-hand experiences with disabilities and with marketing communications, we know that what *should* happen in a communications cycle and what *does* happen can be two different things. The traditional five-element communications model of "sender-message-channel-receiver-feedback" does not perform well in practical application because interference can develop in two elements: channel and feedback. But before we discuss the communications gaps, let's examine the communications model as it is intended to function.

115

COMMUNICATIONS INPUTS

Successful marketing involves the transfer of information and the distribution of a product or service for the purpose of satisfying an individual's needs or wants. This sounds simple enough. So what problems can arise in communication with markets with disabilities?

As the first step, the marketer is usually designated as the sender, the party "sponsoring" the message. The sender could also be a product, service, corporation, government, or even a charity. The sender then designates what message is to be sent to a receiver, for purposes of this discussion, the person with a disability. The receiver is expected to respond with "feedback," defined as some reaction, such as a perception, feeling, or action to the message, or to stop doing something, such as quitting smoking or drinking and driving.

In the micro sense, the "controllables" of the marketing process are (a) the sender, (b) the message, and (c) the channel (which could serve either for the media or for the distribution functions). These elements are controllables in that the marketer can purposefully designate and project the identity of the sender; likewise, the message can be selected from thousands of benefits that could appeal to the receiver. Perhaps the message is a new product introduction, or lower prices, or expanded service department facilities. The message selected should emerge from consumer research, hence the deliberate control.

The third controllable is the channel choice; the marketer can deliver the message in many ways, from mass exposure to one-on-one dialogue. Distribution channels can also vary, from private courier to the United States Postal Service.

WRESTLING THE UNCONTROLLABLES

The last two elements of the communications model, the receiver and the feedback, are deemed "uncontrollables," the part of the process that touches the fickle consumer elements. Who knows if or when receivers (potential consumers) are reading, watching, or listening? Who knows if the receiver with disabilities can *access* the media channel, to be able to see, hear, open, or grasp the message? What interference (such as an inability) prevents receivers with disabilities from responding with feedback, be it a marketer's telephone survey to those with hearing impairments or a plastic-wrapped, 64-page, full-color catalogue that can't be opened by those with upper body impairments or an environmental group's newsletter that can't be read by one with a sight impairment?

BRIDGING THE CHASM

Two factors distort the communications model as it applies to consumers with disabilities: access to the media channel and the ability to respond. Here is the basis of bridging the chasm fostered by mass marketing communications:

1. The marketer must recognize that more than one media **channel** must be used to expand exposure among the diverse populations with disabilities. Duplication of channels is necessary, and a choice of channels should be weighed for maximizing closure by making the communication model as complete as possible.

2. More than one manner of **response** should be considered when soliciting feedback from prospects or customers with disabilities. Feedback is the ability to respond to the message, which could include product sales or service memberships, customer service opinions, or orders placed directly with the manufacturer.

The common thread is access: can the prospect or customer learn of the offering the marketer is making? Is the ability to respond, order, or buy denied these consumers? What can a marketer do to eliminate channel or feedback interference? Before grand plans are made, let's audit the communications process to see what steps are currently being followed.

THE COMMUNICATIONS PROGRAM AUDIT

Every consumer goods or services marketer has ongoing communications programs at work. These programs could be targeted to consumers of all types: to build loyalty among current users, to encourage product trial among nonusers, to persuade previous rejecters, or to introduce new line extensions. Given the variety of communications goals, an analysis can evaluate the current consumer communications as the company presently deals with disabled customers. The result of this evaluation will probably show that the company has no records of customers by disability (health care, insurance, or medical supplies companies excepted). How does the company communicate with its disabled constituents? What communications methods do people with disabilities prefer?

An objective method for gathering information about communications habits is to hire a capable research firm. At the outset, the wise marketer should make no assumptions that could introduce bias to the

Figure 7.1—Budweiser taps six lifestyles in its "Heartland" television campaign

(Woman to Jack, as they leave the gym.) "So, how do you feel?"

(Jack to woman) "I know . . . one more, Jack."

(Woman to Jack) "One more for me."

(Woman to viewers) "Jack and I aren't your ordinary couple."

(Woman to Jack, who is lifting weights) "One more, Jack . . . think about tomorrow."

Figure 7.1—Budweiser taps six lifestyles in its "Heartland" television campaign

(Jack in wheelchair) "Ready to rock and roll."

(Jack in race, replaying woman's words in his head.) "One more, Jack."

(Jack wins race.)

(Voiceover) "Only one beer has the taste as genuine as the people who drink it : Budweiser."

(After dinner) "Let's sleep in tomorrow."

In 1992 Anheuser-Busch, Inc.'s Budweiser introduced six new television commercials that appealed to everyday "slice of life" events. Realistic in message and setting, a father and son play basketball while talking about the son's upcoming wedding. Another situation chronicled a young business executive's decision to take up amateur boxing against his friends' advice.

These commercials provided equal footing to a wheelchair marathon man who trains hard, then wins the international race and celebrates the victory. The dominant point in the ad demonstrates that persons with disabilities are like the rest of us, and are affected by emotions of pride, exhilaration, and disappointment. These are mainstream messages that all markets can appreciate.

(Used with permission of Anheuser-Busch, Inc.)

research assignment. The best research tool to probe habits and opinions for setting general marketing directions would be a focus group
that asks consumers directly what preferences or prejudices toward a
product or service they hold. Of greatest value to disabilities marketing
efforts are focus groups comprised of persons representing the major
disabilities groups—mobility, hearing, sight, and speech impairments if
possible. Perhaps the product is of use only to those with mobility
impairments; concentrate recruitment on persons with mobility conditions.

Disabilities are numerous, and one communications accommodation
does not fit all limitations. Use caution to assemble an appropriately
matched focus group (if only one group is interviewed) that reflects the
interests and abilities of the marketer's product. It's wise to convene
more than one focus group if major decisions are to be made from the
research findings. Disabilities are diverse, so a product that better serves
the hearing impaired consumer should be tested by like participants.
Those with mobility impairments could have no empathy with hearing
loss situations. It's likely that research might be asking the right questions but to the wrong market segment.

The focus group research should point to a general approach for
further marketing communications planning, an approach that will integrate the perceptions of the market into the product specifications. An
accomplished moderator could query some of the preferences on communications; not all audiences fit or use each product or service,
though. The marketer should think through those areas about which he
or she has the least audience information. Topics to investigate might
include the following:

- What information sources do persons with disabilities use most
  frequently to learn of new product news?

- What, if any, barriers do consumers with disabilities encounter in
  receiving marketing communications?

- Which information methods does the person with disabilities
  find easiest to use?

- Does the person with disabilities share recommendations or other
  positive product or service experiences with other disabled friends
  or relatives?

- What product/service delivery systems does the person with disabilities find most accessible?

Figure 7.2–Merrill Lynch asks before acting

Merrill Lynch
Deaf/Hard-of-Hearing
Investor Services
P.O. Box 9019
Princeton, NJ 08543-9019

Bulk Rate
U.S. Postage
PAID
Permit #0003
Mid-Fl IMPC FL

Merrill Lynch

Put your financial needs in experienced hands.

Before launching its new Deaf/Hard of Hearing services, Merrill Lynch wisely conducted research on customer attitudes and needs among its hearing impaired clientele. Focus group input from lip-reading and sign language users weighed heavily in Merrill Lynch's development of this direct mail piece, which addresses the communications needs of hearing impaired investors. Closed caption video tapes were also produced to explain these new customer services.

(Used with permission of Merrill Lynch, Pierce, Fenner & Smith, Inc.)

■ Which of the following does the person with disabilities value most in consumer purchases?

- Low price
- High quality
- Assortment
- Speed of order response
- Convenience/ease of ordering
- Convenience/ease of delivery
- Vendor takes insurance consignments

These suggestions are by no means exhaustive. But much consumer information can be gained from asking simple "why" questions. If the marketer is a good listener, an agenda can be identified from the focus group discussions and can easily lead to a conclusion as to whether or not the proposed product or service has the capability of satisfying populations with disabilities, in general.

Since focus group research plays the role of "theory-builder," the marketing process should now be standing on firmer ground, with the prospect "beacon" pointing more steadily to the north or south, for example, rather than spinning aimlessly.

Because the focus research can produce a qualitative communications premise, the next step in the research process should be an attempt to quantify the premise. A prospect or customer survey can act as a "theory-tester," in which the marketer ceases making assumptions and starts listening and recording the market segment's demands, habits, preferences, and views.

Depending on the target segment, a marketer can address areas of survey questioning, such as preferences in media, delivery, or customer service, that might be appropriate for your product or service. Checklist 7.1 is a sample of such a survey.

Checklist 7.1—The Media Usage/Purchase Audit

Preferences/needs profile

1. How would you classify your disability?

Mobility impairment	( )	Hearing impairment	( )
Sight impairment	( )	Speech impairment	( )

2. What is the medical name for your condition?

   _____

3. Do you have multiple disabilities? If yes, list the more limiting first.

   _____ and _____

4. What media do you use to learn about new products or services?

Personal contact	( )	Telephone	( )
Newspaper	( )	Magazine	( )
Television	( )	Radio	( )
Direct mail	( )	Product samples	( )
Advertising inserts	( )	Special offer coupons	( )
In-store displays	( )	Outdoor messages	( )
Other _____			( )

5. Which media do you find easiest to use? Please rank your preferences with #1 as the most preferred.

Personal contact	( )	Telephone	( )
Newspaper	( )	Magazine	( )
Television	( )	Radio	( )
Direct mail	( )	Product samples	( )
Advertising inserts	( )	Special offer coupons	( )
In-store displays	( )	Outdoor messages	( )
Other _____			( )

6. In Question 5, what advantages or benefits do your top three media offer; please rank your first preference as #1.

   #1 _____

   #2 _____

   #3 _____

7. Is mail readily accessible to you (delivered to your door?)

Yes   ( )
No   ( )

8. Do you have telephone service?

Yes   ( )
No   ( )

9. Which of the following do you find to be barriers to media communications (such as advertisements or press articles)? Please
   check all that apply.

Lack of reader for sight impaired persons   ( )
Lack of signing interpreter for hearing impaired persons   ( )
Lack of TDD for hearing or speech impaired persons   ( )
Inability to open mail packages   ( )
Inability to respond to information offers
     (coupon size or return card)   ( )
Inability to request customer service   ( )
Inability to request warranty service   ( )

10. Do you share with other disabled persons your buying, product,
    or service experiences (usually called a referral or word-of-mouth
    recommendation)?

Yes   ( )
No   ( )

Product/service delivery

11. Which shopping methods do you find most accessible? Please
    rank your preferences, with #1 as most preferred.

Shop in store   ( )
Shop by telephone   ( )
Shop by mail   ( )
Shop by television   ( )
Shop by computer link   ( )
Shop by auto drive-throughs   ( )
Other _____   ( )

12. What one physical condition makes retail shopping at (fill in store or company name) less desirable? Please check all that apply.

Only in-store availability of goods or services ( )
Distances to be traveled ( )
From home to mall ( )
From parking area to store ( )
Telephones always busy ( )
Unavailable sales staff ( )
Rude or untrained sales staff ( )
Problems of delivery and installation ( )
Other _____ ( )

Customer service/information gathering

13. Have you ever been contacted to share your opinions in a "customer satisfaction check"?

Yes ( )
No ( )
Don't remember ( )

14. Which method of monitoring service or product satisfaction do you find most convenient? Please check all that apply.

Personal visit by customer service representative ( )
Telephone follow-up ( )
Mail follow-up ( )
In-package "check list" questionnaire ( )
Other _____ ( )

15. What kind of questionnaire form is easiest to respond to?

Check box/blacken lines ( )
Hole punch ( )
Personal interviewer ( )
Telephone interviewer ( )
Fill in blanks ( )
Other _____ ( )

16. Do you require the assistance of another person to complete a questionnaire or survey?

    Yes   ( )
    No   ( )
    Don't know   ( )

17. Do postage-paid response mailers help encourage you to respond to surveys?

    Yes   ( )
    No   ( )
    Don't know   ( )

18. For product or service information, do you use toll-free 800 numbers frequently?

    Always, if they are available   ( )
    Frequently   ( )
    Seldom   ( )
    Never   ( )
    I would not make the call if I were charged for it.   ( )

19. What source of ongoing product or service communications causes you the most inconvenience?

    _____

20. If you are blind, would product or service advertising in Braille be more convenient?

    Yes   ( )
    No   ( )
    Don't know   ( )
    Not applicable   ( )

21. Would you have a more positive feeling for companies which sponsored Braille advertising?

    Why? _____

    _____

22. If you are hearing impaired, would you be interested in commercials with closed captioned messages on broadcast or cable TV?

    Yes   ( )
    No   ( )
    Don't know   ( )
    Not applicable   ( )

23. If you are hearing impaired, would you be interested in TDD service for ordering products or services?

Yes   ( )
No   ( )
Don't know   ( )
Not applicable   ( )

24. Would you have a more positive feeling for companies that sponsor closed caption or TDD services?

Why? _____

_____

_____

Needless to say, the content of the questions can vary, depending on the market's ability to communicate or on the interests or attitudes you are seeking. There are no "magic" questions. What is crucial is a sincere desire to learn more about the customer or prospect's needs.

If the marketer's audience is sight impaired, an audio application, large text, or Braille form of the questionnaire should be circulated. Likewise, those with hearing impairments should not be solicited over the telephone unless the whole sample has TDD equipment for translation.

MEDIA MIX ON A PERSONAL LEVEL

The disabilities communications process now can be examined on a more personal level to obtain information on ways to target messages to narrower physiographic segments. As demographic characteristics are used to quantify population descriptions, and psychographic traits delineate group lifestyle profiles, physiographic segmentation is also a sorting procedure that separates various categories of disabilities into like groups of physical conditions. The marketer can then adjust the mix of media vehicles to compensate for communications gaps that break the channel linking a disability segment.

Why are different media mixes needed? On one hand, think of interests in music, hence the various radio formats (from contemporary to 1960s and 70s oldies to big band to talk stations) or magazine editorial formats (from business to sports to hobby to gossip) that appeal to different demographic groups. On the other hand, think of the various ways music can be physically enjoyed, from live concerts to music videos, from vinyl albums to magnetic tape cassettes, from compact discs to video discs. The equipment you have *does* make a difference; one replay format does not serve all listeners.

Some media vehicles exclude huge populations, yet unless the marketer is aware of the exclusion, the use of that vehicle might continue for years. The exclusion is readily apparent in many cases. It is logical that customers who are blind cannot see newspaper or magazine advertisements. Nor does it take a rocket scientist to realize that a person with a hearing impairment may not listen to the radio. But some marketers may be unaware that persons with upper body impairments may not be able to open direct mail packages because of limited strength or dexterity. Or that television commercials produced as voice-overs *with* superimposed captions are communications-friendly to both the hearing impaired customers who statistically comprise 7 percent of the population *and* sight impaired customers accounting for another 6 percent of potential users. At 13 percent of the population, this customer universe could add a substantial number of prospects, a round estimation of 29.9 million persons.

Here's what can happen when unintentional exclusions pop up. To promote an annual awards banquet sponsored by city government, news releases were mailed to all radio and television stations to invite different disabilities groups and sell dinner tickets. Planning was thorough to accommodate various disabilities groups; a signing interpreter was hired to sign during the speeches and awards announcements. As the banquet started, the interpreter asked for a show of hands of those with hearing impairments. No one raised a hand, and the interpreter sat down to enjoy the program.

The invitations committee had overlooked the deaf community; no pre-event publicity had been obtained from print media. Persons with hearing impairments were left outside the communications loop. And the publicity committee learned what not to overlook the next year and for years to come.

SENSORY VERSUS MOTOR IMPAIRMENTS

Here is another view of segmentation strategy. The International Center for the Disabled (ICD) engaged pollster Louis Harris & Associates to investigate the attitudes of persons with disabilities toward employment. Within the 1,000-person national telephone sample conducted by Harris, physical and sensory impairments were recorded as shown in Table 7.1.

Table 7.1—Types of disabilities by cause, according to research by the International Center for the Disabled

Physical Disability (total <44%)

Nonparalytic orthopedic impairment	29%
Neuromotor/neuromuscular	7
Brain dysfunction/memory loss/senility	6
Other physical disability	2

Sensory Impairment (total <13%)

Blind/visual impairments	7
Hearing, speech, language	6

The ICD/Survey defined a range of "handicaps disabilities and health conditions." Other prevalent disabilities described in the sample profile included mental disabilities (6%), heart disease (16%), respiratory or pulmonary disease (5%), and a catch-all category of cancer/diabetes/kidney/other (11%).

The first decision that marketers must make about disabilities communications is whether messages will be directed to prospect audiences with sensory impairments *or* to those with mobility impairments. Marketers must then decide if their priority is to attract nonbuyer prospects or appeal to current buyers for, say, customer service follow-up. If a current customer audience is the target, marketers must examine what communications channels are presently being used. Can this audience be expanded? Could new channels be added to provide complementary coverage to customers with specific disabilities, such as supplying large print, Braille, or audio cassette materials for special promotions or catalogues for sight impaired customers *or* by adding TDD access ordering by phone or checking account status for those with hearing impairments? For mobility impaired customers who might be ordering from home, investigate access via computer videotext of catalogues, insurance assignment company policies, or other sales correspondence. How can complementary coverage be organized?

PHYSIOGRAPHIC MEDIA MATCHES

The premise that some forms of media are more disabilities friendly holds true. Among persons with upper body impairments such as paralysis or missing limbs, unfolding and flipping pages of a broadsheet newspaper is difficult. Magazines with perfect binding or cover weight advertisements won't remain open. For those persons with lower body impairments such as orthopedic or neuromuscular conditions, walking or even reaching to the mail box can be an obstacle to direct mail messages. What can be done to reduce "channel interference"?

CONSIDER RECEIVER-FRIENDLY MEDIA MIXES

Some media mixes are better suited for communicating with different groups with disabilities than others. A media mix is a combination of two or more complementary media that can be easily accessed by members of a disabilities group, such as persons with mobility impairments or hearing impairments. The marketer can draw upon knowledge of the target market's capabilities and limitations in media use as well as its ability to respond to media offers. Familiarity with each group's strengths and weaknesses in marketing communications is necessary; this knowledge is the key to implementing a media/disabilities differentiation. Through experience and practicality, you can develop your own mix of differing media vehicles to serve consumers with disabilities.

Let's divide disabilities into the four major physiographic groups and define complementary media mixes. According to the disabilities segments, Table 7.2 categorizes appropriate media mixes.

Table 7.2—Four alternatives for media mix strategy, according to physiographic segmentation

Mix	Disability	Capability	Media Components
Mix 1	Mobility	Visual and auditory	Electronic (broadcast TV, radio, cable TV), computer network, telemarketing, print
Mix 2	Hearing imp	Visual	Print, computer network, direct mail
Mix 3	Sight imp	Auditory	Electronic, telemarketing
Mix 4	Speech imp	Visual	Electronic, print, computer network, direct mail

Matching the impairment to the capability is a procedure that cancels the effect of the physical limitation. While readers with mobility impairments may have difficulty holding or paging through the broadsheet newspaper, these prospects have little trouble seeing and listening to broadcast or cable TV or logging onto a computer network from their homes.

For those with a speech impairment, the ability to speak clearly is unnecessary because the visual medium is emphasized as the communications channel. To reach those persons with speech impairments, there are several alternatives from which to choose: electronic, print, computer network, or direct mail could each be considered and selected, depending on the importance of image consistency (TV or print), retention value (print), ability to tell a highly technical story (direct mail or print), or grouping of esoteric interests (computer network) or cost (a vehicle-by-vehicle comparison).

These media-mix strategies can be deployed at national, spot market, or regional market levels. From a control standpoint, those areas in which marketers best know the prospect, presumably at a county or regional level, will provide better cultural, social, or educational similarities among customers of like disabilities. Yes, disabilities are diverse, yet it is a marketer's job to piece together common threads of product use or desire.

A question could be raised about the rationale for using electronic media, specifically broadcast television and cable television, for communicating with persons with visual impairments. The logic for this match results from the audio portion of the communication; many persons who are blind frequently use the TV as a "radio" for listening to popular prime-time series, to weather channels, and to other special interest programming such as historical or geographical documentaries. Certain television programs are content rich in either the video or audio portion of the medium.

WHAT DOES THE MEDIA MIX FORETELL?

The implication of the various media mixes according to disabilities communications is that several disabilities segments will require a distinctive overlap of vehicles to satisfactorily cover the prospect market. Much like Venn diagrams in set theory, the overlap results from necessary duplication, which by some critical minds is less efficient, but essential to overcome exclusionary channel interference.

Take Media Mix 2 in Table 7.2, for example. The segment's impairment is a sensory limitation (which could be either deafness or being hard of hearing). The sensory strength on which the marketer should focus is the visual, using vehicles such as print (newspaper or magazines), computer networks (video text commercials), or direct mail. There is a recognized need for duplication, for parallel methods that reflect the assumption that no one population with disabilities watches, reads, or listens in lockstep. This parallel media strategy runs at the same time but on different tracks. Pressing the analogy, the trains run on parallel tracks, picking up different passengers all along the way.

YOU CAN SAY THAT AGAIN

The issue of duplication in vehicles is an important matter to accept or reject before initiating disabilities communications strategy. The products or services best served by this approach are packaged goods (initial trial to reorder procedures) or recurring services (from banking or investment services to pest control to auto repair to book clubs) that are repurchased on a timely basis. During this cycle, the marketer has the opportunity to build a relationship, to demonstrate his or her company's understanding of the needs of these groups with disabilities.

Disabilities communications may not be appropriate for expensive, low-frequency purchases, such as homes or other highly discretionary, highly elastic products. Building long-term relationships is of little value to these marketers. Marketers of low-volume products try to achieve media efficiencies by tapping "qualified" leads. Disabilities communications strategy achieves its media effectiveness by expanding the reach of vehicles to produce a higher volume of frequently occurring purchases.

There are several vehicle significances to point out. First, the print medium can be examined for supporting communications with customers with visual impairments, short of blindness. Special actions can be taken with visual media such as direct mail—copy with enlarged type (say, body type in 14 to 24 points) might expand the size of the disability segment. For those who are blind, Braille announcements or audio cassettes might be an effective medium for customer communications. Using any specialized vehicles depends on the marketer's databases. Have a sufficient number of customers or prospects been assembled so that usage efficiencies can be relied upon?

Second, out-of-home media vehicles, such as outdoor, transit, or point of purchase advertising, have been excluded from the disabilities communications media "quiver" because of the inability to target them to physiographic groups. Disabilities communications brings the message to the market, rather than making the market come to the message. Certainly drivers or riders with disabilities come in contact with these out-of-home media, but the probability of segmentation is lost. Out-of-home media are generally used in a supporting role; however, in this disabilities-related strategy, marketing relationships are developed more quickly and directly utilizing primary media such as print or electronic channels. An analogy for primary versus support media has been discussed in terms of "concentric rings of influence" (Chapter 6); here the closer to the center of the target (those primary vehicles which establish direct communications with the prospects with disabilities), the more effective. Support media such as outdoor or transit advertising have diminished persuasive effects since support media are relegated to outlying circles with less frequent exposure.

REFERRALS PASS THE WORD

A third caveat addresses a nonadvertising aspect of disabilities communications. One of the best (if not the best and most powerful) persuasive sources, word-of-mouth referral, is a nonmedia vehicle. Yes, it can be carried over the news media which tend to classify it as nonpaid publicity exposure, but someone such as a public relations specialist or firm is compensated to generate the publicity.

But in addition to publicity, face-to-face exchanges give personal credibility to a product or service's value. This positive exposure is earned through performance, usually in rendering relief for or through stellar customer service to a client with a disability. An example is a feature story about a small pharmaceutical company that delivers prescriptions and files insurance reimbursements on behalf of their customers; the company merits a profile as a community leader. The local television station tapes an interview with the firm's president, and does a video tour of the facility. The reporter interviews several of the company's customers who confirm that the prescriptions service saves them time and money.

Publicity such as this builds reputations of truly exceptional companies. Reputations then spread to the circle of friends and relatives and beyond; the referral opportunities can be very influential through ensuing constructive and newsworthy publicity emanating from well-deserved public relations efforts. The marketer's endeavors can have a "halo" attached to all functions of the company or products or services; notwithstanding the bright light of admiration, the marketer's performance standards move higher and higher.

Publicity can be a most potent supporter, but it can be equally swift in exposing company or product shortcomings. The caution is that among the "controllable" channels by which to deliver messages, publicity stands apart because of its "uncontrollable" nature, often overpowering the players by the story content and relying on its own erratic timing, changeable interests, or unpredictable standards of accuracy. The risk of an unresponsive editor should be evaluated against the relationship the marketer might have with a news medium. The best of all possible worlds would result in positive, timely press coverage supplemented by well-placed paid media advertising. That's getting the word out.

ALLOW THE RECEIVER TO RESPOND

As disabilities communications reconstructs the capacities of the "outgoing" media disseminations, it also fosters a new appreciation for "incoming" feedback or response from the receiver, in this case, the customer or prospect with disabilities. Certain redundant media elements can be introduced to the communications process so as to facilitate the shopper with disabilities in receiving a marketer's message. Does this message decoding by the receiver end the communications process? No, the communications model presented so far is merely a monologue, a "one-way street" of the marketer telling the viewer, listener, or reader with disabilities about the product or service.

What disabilities communications establishes is a dialogue between the buyer and the marketer. A strategy of the media plan should be to cultivate those media that offer *interactivity* so that prospects and marketers can communicate directly to speed the purchase, satisfy the wants quicker, and reduce the interference between the buyer and seller.

If the goal is to advance interactivity of media channels, the marketer's highest aspiration for response capabilities is for an instantaneous reaction, to be able to call and ask questions by phone, to type an order by computer network, or to TDD a message as a complaint. One marketer's respect for this instantaneous reply is his company's policy of resolving customer dissatisfaction *while* the customer remains on the phone. Regardless of the employee's rank or department, if he or she settles the complaint within two hours, a $100 bonus is paid at the end of the month. If it's resolved in 24 hours, a $50 bonus is paid. This company deals with many subcontractors, so the more quickly problems are isolated, the less chance that "downstream" work is affected. This management clearly values timeliness and backs up its policies with rewards.

Levels of Response

But there are different levels of response methods and reaction times. Usually the telephone or TDD allows the quickest reply, instantly if an operator or voice response unit (VRU) forms the response system. The VRU is the series of recorded messages that a customer (or anyone for that matter) can call to learn of his or her checking account balance or to input the stockkeeping unit (SKU) code to make a purchase. VRUs can also record the caller's name if a voice capture is one of the modules or selection keys a user can push if the caller can or chooses to leave her or his name, address or phone number.

If timing is not critical to the purchase process, such as with monthly book club selections or magazine installments, the marketer could use the mail or other ground or air transportation services. But timing is very critical these days for time-sensitive sales promotions or dated advertising material or weekly newsletters. You have to decide how time affects your marketing process and act accordingly.

Many marketers are recognizing that making the ordering process easier goes beyond accepting major credit cards. It might mean keeping the order entry phones staffed until midnight Pacific standard time rather than shutting down the switchboard at 4:30 Eastern standard time. It might mean shortening 15-character account numbers that are easy to mistake and hard to transcribe. How does the marketer learn to make responding simpler?

Think back to the customers' preferences concerning communications vehicles; the marketer learned about the effort required by persons with disabilities by asking them, in formal and informal settings, with focus group research, in written surveys, and in personal interviews. The truth is not evasive. The fact remains that the capabilities of customers with disabilities are diverse; one size does not fit all.

Take this little test yourself. Get on the telephone, pose as a customer, and try opening an account. Ask to be shipped the initial order of your firm's goods. Keep in mind the physiographic conditions of mobility, hearing, sight, and speech impairments. (Few with speech impairments would even attempt the call.) How many times are you transferred from one department to another? How much listening, writing, or speaking is demanded? Would it be simpler to fax the account application? What is the tone of voice used by your operator? If you feign a hearing impairment, how patient is the operator with you?

There is a fine line between complaisant attitudes and responsible business policy; most marketers try to balance goodwill and profitability. Building your response mechanism must result in a system that customers with disabilities can test and use. Testing is important because the marketer can only assume the market will embrace the response vehicle. Changing consumer attitudes is difficult and costly; good ideas like videotext shopping services have foundered because

Figure 7.3–AT&T Demonstrates Silence for TDD Service

AT&T
"SILENCE" :30

(SILENCE THROUGHOUT) Open on an airplane taking off

(SILENCE THROUGHOUT) Cut to a small child covering her ears

(SILENCE THROUGHOUT) Cut to a woman walking through a crowded airport

(SILENCE THROUGHOUT) Cut to a cab driver who is yelling

(SILENCE THROUGHOUT) Cut to woman walking through a bustling airport

(SILENCE THROUGHOUT) Cut to a mother holding a crying child

(SILENCE THROUGHOUT) Cut to woman approaching AT&T Public Phone 2000

(SILENCE THROUGHOUT) She selects "Telecommunications Device for the Deaf" (TDD)

(SILENCE THROUGHOUT) and inserts her AT&T Calling Card

(SILENCE THROUGHOUT) Woman types the message: "Hi, I'm catching the earlier flight."

(SILENCE THROUGHOUT) A response comes onto the screen: "Wonderful. I'll be there. I've missed you."

(SILENCE THROUGHOUT) Cut to woman watching screen. She smiles.

(SILENCE THROUGHOUT) Cut to shot of AT&T cards

(SILENCE THROUGHOUT) Cut to arrivals curb at airport. Woman is waiting. She sees her husband through the crowd.

(SILENCE THROUGHOUT) She signs to him: "I love you." He mouths the words: "I love you too" and they embrace.

YOUNG & RUBICAM NEW YORK

The consequences of deafness is effectively portrayed in AT&T's television commercial, appropriately called "Silence" because it has no audio track. Using a "slice of life" execution, an actress goes about everyday activities in silence; the hearing person notices how odd traffic or airport scenes are without the accompanying noise. AT&T gains the attention of both consumer and business markets through its sensitivity to the communications needs of persons with hearing impairments.

(Used with permission of AT&T)

many shoppers didn't feel compelled to alter their shopping and pur-chase patterns.

Response Patterns

But response patterns of customers with disabilities are different. Casual shopping is less frequent and many times has to be planned weeks in advance to secure van, bus, or taxi transportation. Some health condi-tions allow virtually no mobility, so there are few if any opportunities to purchase in person, hence the necessity of easy-to-use, easy-to-order response methods. The more methods of direct response, the better the marketer will be able to facilitate the account holder with disabilities.

GIVE MEDIA A NEW TWIST

As media channels delve deeper into narrower segments, physiographic media mixes should be considered as alternatives to purchasing media via traditional methods, such as cost per thousand or cost per rating point comparisons. There are no rating figures to support disabilities communications' efficiency or inefficiency; likewise, there is no univer-sal agreement on cable television rating some 20 years after its introduc-tion as an advertising medium.

The challenge is to consider fresh, new ways to establish media cover-age, with intended duplication, to a hard to quantify yet newly emerg-ing economic population of diverse groups with disabilities. Solving a puzzle of this complexity requires creativity, perseverance, and sensitiv-ity.

CHAPTER EIGHT

APPLICATIONS OF DISABILITIES COMMUNICATIONS IN SALES PROMOTIONS

SUPPORTING THE TOOLS OF SALES PROMOTIONS

Part of the promotional mix available to the marketer is the variety of sales tools, such as special events, brochures, product catalogs, point of purchase displays, contests, and specialty advertising items, to name just a few. Marketing and advertising managers spend a great deal of time in the planning and implementation of imaginative promotional programs; many marketers devote significant attention to the smallest details of a multi-media promotion. Impressive promotional and merchandising tie-ins are evident in summer movie introductions of *Batman Returns* and *Dick Tracy*. High profile advertisers tie to the coattails of dazzling movie or TV stars, expecting that some stardust will rub off.

Less glamorous promotional programs are the more common rule among consumer products and services support. Attention to detail is still practiced so that positive impressions are chronicled by the media as well as recorded by prospective customers. An obvious error is quickly identified, polished out, and the promotion is placed back in the store window for all the world to see. But what happens to the less than obvious omission, the "collateral gap," where sales tools such as illegible or hard-to-handle brochures impact the prospect with a disability?

REHEARSAL BEFORE DISPERSAL

Marketers should be aware that persons with disabilities have different capabilities for gathering information on product or services purchases. One brochure—regardless of the graphic impact of the blind-embossed, double-varnished, gate-folding cover with die-cut rear pocket with loose but stepped insert sheets—does not serve all disabilities.

In the overall planning of effective marketing materials, a prospect with disabilities might wonder how much attention is given to communications tools that are circulated among his or her disabled peers. Problems with opening, handling, and reassembling loose pages are encountered by some with dexterity limitations; others with lower limb mobility conditions may not be able to circulate through the marketer's model home or a bookseller's tables and shelves or a trade show booth. While examples of missed opportunities in sales materials occur frequently, the way to avoid this insensitivity is to consider the consequences of the disabilities of persons you might be serving.

DESIGN FACTORS TO CONSIDER

Taking a lesson from the demographic profiles of desirable market segments, is there much uncertainty about whether consumers with disabilities can be found within the targets? No, it's quite likely that persons with mobility, hearing, sight, and speech impairments populate your user universe. Could any special touches assist the marketer's effort to improve the communications materials?

Recognizing the role of collateral materials such as brochures, maps, pamphlets, flyers, or point of purchase displays in marketing programs, is experienced based. Those support items created for one campaign might be inappropriate for another, and new disability-specific materials would need to be designed. Persons with fine motor impairments have limitations with mobility or manipulation, while visual impairments could limit the readability of the sales tool. The communications constant is persuasive content; this should not be forgotten. But rather than expecting the prospect to work to catch your attention, you should work to catch his or hers.

As you consider new sales aids, a review of the four major disability groups would be helpful. In general, hearing and speech impairments have little effect on the visual or information impacts of printed materials. Of course, if the audio medium were critical to the sales piece, such as with a music video or an audio cassette, a concerted action to provide a parallel medium to replace the audio portion must be explored. If no substitute medium can be found, the sales aid should be scrapped and supplanted with a new communications tool. It's better to err on the conservative side (to withhold distribution), than to distribute the piece liberally or with no sensitivity toward sensory discrimination.

You could start by categorizing the conditions of disabilities: mobility impairments, hearing impairments, sight impairments, and speech impairments. Each segment has different requisites, and anticipating and overriding "collateral gaps" takes a visionary mindset. Among persons with mobility impairments, plan to test the collateral for any awkwardness of use or any need for fine motor skills (like "rub-outs" on game cards or lottery tickets that require a strong finger grip to hold a coin or other abrasive item). This testing can be done informally by passing the piece among disabled relatives, friends, or co-workers for their comments, then incorporating these opinions, where possible, into the promotion.

Repeat the process for the other disabilities groups to see what accommodations, if any, should be considered. Sight impairments pose many obstacles in collateral materials; is there a method in which a prospect with a disability can access the product or service's promotional copy? Perhaps it can be accessed by telephone through an audiotext message or through readers on call?

The rehearsal could also audit the disabilities friendliness of various sales tools. How difficult are your sales brochures to handle? Can someone with one hand easily extract, open, and read one, then reassemble it? If not, why not?

In a mailing to members of various disabilities support groups, the publicity chair of an advocacy organization challenged a graphic designer to create an announcement that could be maneuvered with one hand. The designer took one large piece of paper and kept barrel-folding the panels over and over. The announcement unfolded five times, contained no loose inserts, and was a self-mailer with a postage indicia so no envelope was required. It remained closed by a gummed wafer that could be torn through with a fingertip. In addition, the large typeface (18-point) aided legibility. Thus a disabilities-friendly announcement design was beneficial to two large groups with disabilities, those with mobility and those with sight impairments.

If the promotion is one that cannot be accommodated to the physical skills of prospects with disabilities or if the accommodation totally changes the personality or intent of the game, should the promotion be discarded? Not in the least. Instead of watering down an exciting and imaginative sales promotion, merely give consideration to *additional* entry or participation methods that could be used by consumers with disabilities.

COKE AND THE OLYMPIC SPIRIT

Take a recent sales promotion in which Coca-Cola tied into the fascination Americans have with the Olympic Games. Inside cardboard 12-pack containers, Coke randomly inserted specially produced compact discs; the buyer might win a CD or cassette if he or she chose the right package. How would drinkers with disabilities be excluded from the contest? First, the person with mobility impairments might not be able to carry the 12-pack or might not have the strength to open the sealed cardboard box. For persons with sight impairments, there might be no way to identify the package ("Look for the specially marked carton") by touch; for those who are deaf, the premise of the promotion ("Enjoy specially produced Olympic music") might have little inducement.

But the marketer can anticipate accommodations for the groups that do wish to participate in the contest. If no purchase were necessary, those with mobility or sight impairments could telephone an 800 number to enter their names and addresses; a drawing would then select winners to be sent the CD prize. Or perhaps a registration process of mailing the name or logging onto a computer bulletin board would accommodate and duplicate the communications channels for users with disabilities.

FAST FOOD, SIGHT UNSEEN

Let's return to another example of disabilities-friendly sales aids currently in use at McDonald's. To facilitate customers who are blind, McDonald's has produced breakfast and dinner items on vinyl Braille menus, including drinks and dessert. For those patrons with speech or hearing loss, a quick scan of the "picture menu" allows the customer to point to the desired fare. This menu features full-color illustrations of each item; pointing to them is quick and easy.

KNOWING YOUR CUSTOMERS' NEEDS

Creativity can be defined as matching new combinations, taking a familiar situation and adding a new headline or vice versa. Experimenting with new sales promotions is no different; here the marketer attempts to differentiate her or his product or service by incorporating new twists to the elements of the marketing mix, either a unique approach to the tangible product or the intangible service, or to the promotional strategy or the price structure. Or as Jewel Food Stores, the Chicago-based grocer did in introducing a new distribution method of shopping by computer.

Called "Peapod," the new shopping system runs on specialized software and modem that allows shoppers to check prices and aisle locations, order, and have the goods delivered to their homes. A Peapod representative takes the order to a Jewel store and selects the merchandise. Both Jewel and Peapod are sensitive to cost; if the shopper is dissatisfied, the $49.95 software kit can be returned after a six-month trial for a full refund.

Another food merchandiser, Giant food stores in Washington, D.C., and the Baltimore area, expanded its order entry system for delicatessen goods by advertising a TDD number (341-HEAR) to accept orders Monday through Friday. The timing of this expanded advertising was excellent, running the week before Super Bowl Sunday.

Retailers can explore many more services that taken by themselves seem less than inventive. But if these merchandising accommodations are communicated to shoppers with disabilities, an instant appreciation is registered. As more marketers gain an empathy for the conditions of disabilities, many imaginative and assistive steps will be inaugurated. Let's review several suggestions for disabilities-friendly merchandising activities.

■ In retail or other service environments, consider creating a part-time staff position of "designated disabilities assistant" (DDA) who would be available on designated days (like Tuesday and Thursday afternoons) or at designated times daily; the DDA helps with shopping selection when requested.

Figure 8.1–Jewel Food Stores initiates home shopping service

Peapod makes grocery shopping as easy as...

1

You Order

You order your groceries from home or work using the Peapod software, a computer and a modem.

2

We Shop

Peapod receives your order and carefully shops for your groceries at Jewel.

3

We Deliver

Peapod delivers your groceries to your door... fast, fresh, and on time.

See how Peapod works for you ▣

Introduced in the Chicago area, a home delivery service promises convenience and full selection to Jewel grocery shoppers. Jewel Food Stores formed an alliance with Peapod to create a distinct advantage apart from competitors.

(Used with permission of Jewel Food Stores.)

- Equip the store with lap baskets for carrying selections to the checkout area.

- Hang a small lap desk or clipboard at checkout or pharmacy desks for use in signing orders, filling out forms, or other writing needs.

- For identification purposes, accept an alternative photo ID other than a driver's license, recognizing that many adults with disabilities do not drive automobiles. It will eliminate a potentially embarrassing explanation for both the purchaser and the clerk.

- Consider offering curbside delivery of telephone orders on Tuesday, Thursday, and Saturday afternoons or slower hours depending on store history.

TAKING CREDIT FOR INSTALLING A TDD

Many firms already have equipped their offices or stores with Telecommunications Devices for the Deaf in anticipation of the ADA enactment. TDD installation is a legal requirement for federal, state, and local government offices, but private and public companies view this telecommunications tool as a customer service enhancement. An array of businesses using TDDs include the following:

- Credit card service. Universal Card publishes its TDD number for account inquiries on the monthly statement.

- Hotel reservations. The Four Seasons Hotel in Toronto invites guests to make reservations via TDD.

- Investment information. Brokerage giant Merrill Lynch publishes a TDD number for account information in its monthly newsletter (see Figure 8.2); Van Kampen Merritt, a unit of Xerox Corporation, also offers financial services via TDD, as well as organizing a directory of TDD numbers.

- Airport telephones. Both AT&T and GTE feature TDD service in major airports around the nation.

- Account information for banking or mortgage services. Chase imprints its monthly statements with an announcement of TDD availability.

Not only did these responsible corporations launch TDD service to aid those customers with hearing impairments, they were also aggressive

Figure 8.2—Merrill Lynch responds to investors' needs

Accessibility . . .
Confidentiality . . .
Sensitivity . . .

MERRILL LYNCH DEAF/HARD-OF-HEARING INVESTOR SERVICES

The Merrill Lynch Deaf/Hard-of-Hearing Investor Services Information Card

Convenient, toll-free telephone numbers

1-800-765-4833 (TTY*): Referrals to TTY-equipped Financial Consultants; free financial brochures.

1-800-765-4464 (Voice amplifier for hard-of-hearing callers): Same as above

Financial Consultant _____

(TTY/v) _____

Merrill Lynch

(over)

Merrill Lynch

With 10,500 financial consultants nationwide, Merrill Lynch has been quick to recognize the opportunity presented by the ADA. In January, 1990, the financial services firm created the Deaf/Hard-of-Hearing Investor Services Program by providing direct communications accessibility for the hearing impaired community. This effort trained more than 75 financial consultants representing 40 states, equipping each with TDDs and speech amplifiers. Ninety percent of these financial consultants have some personal connection to the deaf/hard-of-hearing population; for example, some are deaf or hard-of-hearing themselves; some have deaf parents, children, friends, or relatives; some are former audiologists, pathologists, or teachers of the deaf.

(Used with permission of Merrill Lynch, Pierce, Fenner & Smith, Inc.)

enough to advertise or publicize the fact. One definition of public relations is "doing good and taking credit for it." All of these are stellar examples of credit where credit is due.

PRACTICAL ATTENTION TO COLLATERAL ITEMS

Here are a few proven tips for producing collateral materials to better match the needs of persons with disabilities; remember that making materials easier to handle or read is the most important consideration:

- If the brochure has multiple pages, think about stitching the text pages to the cover. This way the pieces won't fall out. Keep loose inserts to a minimum, for ease of handling.

- Be aware that some binding processes are preferable to others. Spiral binding, GBC binding, or three-hole punch tends to lie flat, making it easier to read by persons with upper body movement limitations; perfect binding tends to close back up. To keep it closed, a spot of Velcro does nicely.

- If you're using a series of loose inserts with no cover sleeve to hold them, use a mailing envelope (9" X 12") as an organizer.

- If an odd size (a size other than the standard 8 1/2" X 11" format) is desired, consider working in an oversized, rather than under-sized format. Undersized pieces, say the size of 5 1/4" floppy disk, are hard to handle. Insert sheets would have to be undersized, too, a design that is cute, but clumsy.

- Be sensitive to how easily reply cards or the detachable return portion of the statement fits the envelope. Too snug is much worse than too loose.

- For sight impairments, be alert to choosing easy-to-read typefaces, preferably a serif face, designed with a minimum body copy size of 14 points. Consider the amount of leading (the spacing between the lines); again more is better than less.

- Even if your collateral pieces are simple, be sensitive to legibility of printed documents; don't use a dot matrix (like the old nine-pin head) printer for reproducing spec sheets.

- Be sensitive to the colors of stock and ink so that visual contrast is crisp and legible.

■ If color selection is important in the purchase decision, how can an individual who is color-blind be assisted? Can descriptions, screens, or tints be used to differentiate the color choices?

■ To reduce glare, avoid gloss finishes of text stock; to eliminate glare, use a pass of varnish to produce a matte finish in the printing process.

■ Make sure perforations can be torn easily. Don't even bother with a printed dotted line and a scissors icon.

■ On registration cards, give the writer with disabilities a larger area to fill in, such as on a coupon or application. For audio responses, allow a longer time for spoken answers.

ONE PICTURE IS WORTH . . .

Photography adds realism to marketing materials regardless of the type of collateral aid. As real-life situations are portrayed in advertising copy, we are now seeing photography layouts that depict assumed users of products or services, including persons with disabilities. As we've noted in previous chapters, one in seven Americans has a functional limitation. It would seem only logical that in a group of 15 to 20 advertising models, most people would expect a wheelchair user or sight impaired person or two as part of the group.

Messages developed by Xerox, AT&T, and Budweiser have integrated people with disabilities into photo situations; the commercials were not patronizing nor saccharin-sweet but accurate portrayals of persons with disabilities participating in business conferences, making a telephone call from a busy airport, or exercising to build strength or fitness.

There has been a backlash from groups with disabilities toward firms using models or spokespeople who depicted disabled individuals but who in fact were not disabled themselves. Advertisers have been quick to apologize, noting their intent was to acknowledge the participation of persons with disabilities. In future commercials or training materials, advertisers have promised to employ both disabled and nondisabled models or spokespersons. Marketers should be able to anticipate their market's reaction, both potential kudos and criticism.

GIVE SALES DISPLAYS A WIDER BERTH

As more mobility impaired managers and convention-goers stretch their influence, trade booths and similar sales displays should be reassessed concerning the disabilities friendliness of the materials. In the graphics world many industrial designers are urged to place sale displays at "eye level," approximately 30 to 66 inches high. For the general population including persons with disabilities, this span of vision is appropriate, yet if the majority of show traffic is wheelchair users, maintaining the upper limit at 5 1/2 feet will cause neck strain if product discussions or demonstrations are at close proximity to higher graphics.

If the booth is not crowded and visuals can be easily seen, just have the demonstrators step away from the graphics to provide more comfortable viewing.

The biggest problem in trade show materials is not the height of the graphics, but the clutter of too many displays in too small a space. Again if your market is wheelchair users, room to enter, turn and exit a trade booth is needed. What's the turning radius for a wheelchair? According to guidelines from the *Federal Register*, a 5-by-5-foot area is the minimum turning space allowed. So in a 10-by-10-foot display area, not much room remains for video monitors, island displays, or slide projectors, much less tables and chairs.

Another improvement for serving those with mobility impairments is to lower the placement of literature racks or "take one" point of purchase stands. What is chest high to you probably isn't chest high to most purchasers in wheelchairs. Lowering the height or putting the brochure rack on a desk top might increase the ease by which a brochure can be accessed and read.

One last observation to access on trade show displays: The more sophistication added through computer-driven displays, the more frequently you will see a built-up booth floor; the raised floor accommodates cables and power cords to keep them safely out of sight. But the raised floor is a barrier to wheelchair users. A solution could be to add a ramp (but not to block the aisle) or wire overhead, dismissing the need for a raised floor, to simplify the display graphics by doing away with the computer booster.

A SURPRISE ENDING

Some years ago a home builder cosponsored a lavish special promotion with a local radio station in which, after a six-week entry period, a name would be selected randomly by the station's most popular disk jockey. The prize was a free $50,000 home, and during this month-and a-half period, the radio station's announcers built great excitement about the beautiful home and how lucky some winner would be on the day of the drawing. Media attention was piqued over the novelty of the contest and the generosity of the prize. At noon on the Saturday of the drawing, the news media, including newspaper, television, and the sponsoring radio's reporters were building audience interest. After much hoopla, the radio announcer reached into the fishbowl and selected a name. The winner was present; jumping up and down, he waved his hand to the officials. The television and radio reporters rushed to interview him. As he made his way to the podium, the reporters began to disperse, fading into the crowd.

The winner gave no interviews or acceptance comments; he was an individual both deaf and mute, unable to hear and speak. While the outcome was lucky for the winner, the sponsors lost some of the glitter, as they were unable to bask in the media spotlight. Who would have expected the special promotion to end on such a note? Perhaps this true story is just one more experience we can all learn from. Promotional programs do have ups and downs, and many uncontrollable factors, such as buyer response or media performance, are present. Rarely can the marketer anticipate all outcomes. If the marketer develops a sensitivity toward the abilities and limitations of the disabled target market, you can expect to reduce the number of promotional surprises.

APPLICATIONS OF DISABILITIES COMMUNICATIONS IN PUBLIC RELATIONS

THE POWER OF MEDIA RELATIONS

There is an opportunity to be pursued in adapting the public relations process to embrace disabilities communications: the communicator develops an adapted vision of what press offerings or public relations efforts can be targeted to narrower reader or viewer interests. The twist that disabilities communications adds is in *reorganizing* reader, listener, or viewer commonalities along the lines of physiographics; specifically the marketer should reconsider readership, listenership, or viewership interests by the four conditions groups, namely mobility, sight, hearing, or speech impairments.

151

The marketing premise underlying this public relations tactic should be familiar by now. The premises—that disabilities are diverse and that "traditional" publicity, the main weapon of public relations, has sufficient substance to consider testing disabilities communications—are a complement to media relations activities. This process could deny or confirm the presumption that "traditional" publicity excludes many Americans with disabilities possibly because of the channel interference among persons with disabilities.

WIDE TO NARROW APPEAL

Audiences for public relations programs can be as wide as national in scope, such as a presidential election, or can be as narrow as a neighborhood "crime watch" program. In the segmentation efforts discussed thus far, the marketer's task has been to penetrate to smaller user groups in a more direct fashion (with the assumption that flatter ordering and distribution systems would produce faster, more personalized response), which because of superior service, can result in long-term customer/provider bonds. How can we put the disabilities segmentation process to work as a portion of a larger-scope public relations effort?

HEALTH CONDITION AS THE SELECTOR

As economic uncertainties and fierce competition have complicated the health care industry, many medical providers are recognizing that effective marketing and community relations programs can attract new and diverse clients. Hospital management attitudes have changed too, resulting in services for both illness and wellness. The marketing challenge is to expand awareness among potential patients long before they actually need medical services. Innovative "maintenance" programs such as weight loss, smoking cessation, exercise, and women's health bring new faces to health care facilities, produce incremental revenues, and help, if only in a small way, to improve the general public's appreciation of an area's medical facility.

In a ranking of persuasion vehicles for health care organizations, marketing managers usually place public relations at the top. While ultimately uncontrollable, public relations is a "softer" messenger, viewed as more appropriate than advertising or sales promotions. Publicity is informative in nature and, while neutral in recommendation, a story or segment placed in the right vehicle can produce a tremendous response.

COMBINING SUBSTANCE AND CREDIBILITY

There is little doubt in most marketers' minds about the worth of positive, proactive efforts to shape a company's public image. A neutral third-party endorsement (understood frequently as a good publicity clip from a newspaper or magazine) can bring hordes of new prospects, subscribers, or investors to your doorstep. Let's define public relations as an ongoing process that attempts to shape the public image of an individual (such as an author or politician), an organization (such as a business like Coca-Cola or McDonald's, or a government entity like the U.S. Postal Service), or a cause (such as environmentalism or human rights). Editors and news directors, the press's "keepers of the gate," are attentive to story ideas that hold news value for their readers, listeners, and viewers. The job of these media experts is to report news or feature stories that their subscribers will value; they have no time for corporate self-aggrandizing. Nor do editors expect to be entertained by news releases or story outlines; all they want is the facts.

HOW NEWSWORTHY IS YOUR NEWS?

Many factors weigh in the planning of public relations programs, such as deciding if a story angle truly is newsworthy. Does it have news or feature story potential? If the story has news value, how important is timing? Is the story best developed as an exclusive (where the public relations specialist deals with only one vehicle) or as a customary news release, simultaneously sent to all vehicles? Is it of general interest, of interest to wider audiences, such as a daily newspaper or network television, or of value to special interest media, which deal more narrowly in audience breadth but with greater depth in writing?

Depending on the story angle, different press contacts and lists are used. Daily newspapers have become much more specific in story assignments. For example, the assignments editor of a daily newspaper may have a health care reporter, an insurance reporter, a real estate/development reporter, a marketing reporter, a banking reporter, and so forth. Don't mistake the pecking order of your press contacts: those who are reporters (who typically cover daily news events) versus those who are writers (who are considered of higher rank and who write feature stories and columns). Writers generally are allowed more time to research and develop articles; reporters usually have to react much more quickly, which could be critical in the placement strategy of your news release. As marketers or public relations resources becomes better acquainted with press contacts, they will be aware of editors' preferences.

Some editors will appreciate a written news release; others want only the briefest outline and a facts sheet so the reporter can flesh out the story in his or her own style. Yet others want only the tip and will pursue the story alone (which can be scary because you lose all "news control").

Also, different vehicles require different visuals, such as video footage for television, photography for newspaper or magazines, or recorded interviews for radio. And depending on unforeseen events, perhaps no visuals are needed; all the press might require is a telephone number or an address. Examples of general interest press vehicles are *USA Today* or "Good Morning America"; narrowly targeted media could include performance reviews (such as *Car and Driver*'s appeal to auto enthusiasts) or company performance (such as *Fortune* magazine's Service 500 rankings). Trade publications such as *Advertising Age* or *Progressive Grocer* also are narrowly focused on the information needs of their industry. Audience familiarity is vital to isolate the most appropriate story concepts that waste neither the editor's nor his or her readers' time.

The marketer or public relations director knows his or her customer profile and can match the profile with the specialty press requisites for consideration. Editors might take notice of special interest story ideas if the story concepts are targeted to the appropriate readership, are timely, and are accurately documented. None of this public relations primer suggests radical or "break-through" marketing strategy. Nor will there be any sensationalized or sympathetic releases; the objective is to move readers or viewers with disabilities into the mainstream of life, to blend in, not stand out.

COORDINATING THE ELEMENTS

Taking all of these factors into consideration, an enlightened regional medical center has produced a most gratifying example of the ability of public relations to serve its clients with disabilities. This medical center has organized its facilities into centers of excellence. The rehabilitation center is well known for its skills in resourceful physical, occupational, and recreational therapies. Of particular merit is the rehabilitation center's experience in treating head and spinal cord injuries. Its physiatrists, staff, and support services had already earned the health care industry's respect but public awareness, and more specifically benefits to the person with lower body dysfunction, needed a boost.

To test public relations' contribution to public awareness, the rehabilitation center's management chose to announce a new male fertility procedure called electroejaculation, or EEJ, in which a small amount of

Figure 9.1—Corporate sponsorships can breed success

Wheelchair racer Doug Kennedy admits that 1990 was a good year for winning. Rolling under the Red Lobster silks, Kennedy set the world of wheelchair racing on fire, as he produced world records in the five kilometer, the eight kilometer, the five mile, and was a national marathon champion. He was also a Gold medalist in the 1990 Goodwill Games. In the 1991 season, he medalled in 18 events, three producing world records. Abilities do command attention.

Kennedy began racing for Red Lobster following his victory in the Red Lobster 10K Classic in March 1990. His association with Red Lobster is part of a corporate program to recognize disabled communities all over the nation. This program included sponsorship of the summer and winter International Special Olympic Games as well as a hiring initiative that places developmentally disabled workers in most of the 528 Red Lobster restaurants in 45 states.

(Used with permission of Red Lobster, Inc.)

electrical current stimulates ejaculation. The ejaculate is then given to the partner through artificial insemination. Patients, because of spinal cord injury, do not feel any pain.

This procedure was selected for press exposure because of demographic trends and competitive forces. Because of modern medical technology, the lives of more and more accident victims are being saved, leaving them as persons with paraplegia or quadriplegia. Many are young persons who wish to rejoin the mainstream, and parenting is part of a rich and useful life. In addition to persons with spinal cord injuries, EEJ can be beneficial to males with testicular cancer or any type of nerve damage that might prohibit ejaculation.

The marketing director working closely with the administrators decided to publicly announce the procedure on two conditions:

1. That the fertility procedure was successful (The first two pregnancies were confirmed using EEJ, and one couple agreed to participate in the press conference.)

2. That the originator of the procedure would attend the announcement (The doctor was present at the press conference.)

A press conference was assembled, and local and regional press was generated through general interest media. In fact, the press activity was credited for attracting eight applicants to the program.

NARROWING THE SIGHTS

A second press activity was recommended, one that would target more specific prospect groups, rather than the general population. This publicity was directed to potential candidates for the procedure, males with head, spinal cord, or neurological impairments who were interested in parenting via artificial insemination.

A complementary press list developed; it was targeted to readers with mobility impairments involving limitations to the lower body, from injury, congenital, or health conditions, or because of nerve damage. The client might have received a disabling injury from an automobile or motorcycle accident, sports, or a work or diving accident; this male could have quadriplegia or paraplegia from neurological disorders.

The announcement of this procedure could be of great interest to certain groups with disabilities, yet we know how difficult (to impossible) it is to make direct contact with them because of confidentiality standards.

In some instances, there were no scheduled publications (with a regular monthly, bimonthly, or quarterly closing date); therefore, association newsletters or bulletin boards were selected for contact. Geography was expanded from county to state or national interests, based on the circulation area and editorial purposes of the publication. Depending on the marketer's area of influence, geographic distribution can be widened or reduced to fit.

Let's reconstruct the disabilities press list from our new strategy of physiographic segmentation, in this case mobility impairments with a focus on lower body dysfunction. As with many factors in implementing communications programs, the marketer in conjunction with the public relations staff will search and research the publications that target the appropriate physiographic group. This mobility impairment example of categories and publications for press contact (Checklist 9.1) was researched for the Tampa Bay area.

Checklist 9.1

National or Regional Associations

National Head Injury Foundation
        Southboro, MA
National Spinal Cord Injury Association
        Woburn, MA
National Multiple Sclerosis Society
        New York, NY
Muscular Dystrophy Association
        Tucson, AZ
Amyotrophic Lateral Sclerosis Association
        Woodland Hills, CA
Paralyzed Veterans of America
        Washington, DC
Advocacy Center for Persons with Disabilities
        Tallahassee, FL
Florida Medical Association
        Tampa Int'l Airport

Local Associations/Chapters

Self-Reliance Center for Independent Living
        Tampa, FL
Goodwill Industries—Suncoast Rehabilitation Center
        Tampa, FL

Spina Bifida Association of Tampa Bay, Inc.
        Tampa, FL
Amyotrophic Lateral Sclerosis Association of Tampa Bay
        Tampa, FL
March of Dimes Foundation
        Tampa, FL
Multiple Sclerosis Society, Florida Gulfcoast Chapter
        Tampa, FL
Paralyzed Veterans of America, Florida Gulfcoast Chapter
        Tampa, FL
United Cerebral Palsy Association of Tampa
        Tampa, FL

Publications/Newsletters

Outlook newsletter, Multiple Sclerosis Society, Florida Gulf Coast
Chapter
        Tampa, FL
MS Advocate
        New York, NY
Focus on You newsletter, Muscular Dystrophy Association
        St. Petersburg, FL
MDA News Magazine, Muscular Dystrophy Association
        Tucson, AZ
Paraplegia News
        Phoenix, AZ
Spinal Network
        Boulder, CO
Sports 'n Spokes
        Phoenix, AZ
LINK/Amyotrophic Lateral Sclerosis Association
        Woodland Hills, CA
LINKETTE/Amyotrophic Lateral Sclerosis Association, Tampa Bay
Chapter
        Tampa, FL
Eye on ALS newsletter, MDA/ALS Program
        New York, NY
Hospital News/Tampa Bay
        Tampa, FL
The Voice of Florida
        Margate, FL

Many newsletters welcome news materials of interest to their readers. Most health associations report that, as needs assessment surveys are conducted among their members or clients, the most frequently requested service is "information," about the health condition, services available, and how to make their lives more fulfilling. Frequently, newsletters are issued at two levels, from the national organization and from the local level or chapter. Some chapter newsletters may be simple in design, but are closely read for timely information, regardless of the sophistication of the graphics.

The larger magazines published by national associations are structured as most press vehicles are, with story materials submitted to the editor for consideration. The contact person at the national level can give you the names of local or regional associations and chapters; one phone call or letter usually generates three or four more press leads, most worthy of follow-up.

WHAT PRESS MATERIALS ARE NEEDED?

A conventional press kit used in general interest publicity efforts will do fine, with the "what, where, when" news release written to explain the new product or service's value to the publication's readers with disabilities. Likewise, background information such as company history or skills, details on clinical trials if appropriate, fact sheets or product photography with identifying captions are all helpful in rounding out the story.

In writing the news release, check the language for harsh or limiting terms. Offending phrases could be descriptions such as "an aid for the disabled," "perfect for the paraplegic confined to his wheelchair," "a victim of cancer," or "trying to lead a normal life." We've discussed the language and attitudes issues in Chapter 3. Persons with disabilities wish to eliminate labels, want to focus on the abilities, tend not to consider themselves victims or sufferers, and certainly don't like the idea of living an abnormal life. Consider the audience's self-concept and expectations.

Another caution: In communicating with a health or disability organization, you may well be writing to or conversing with an editor with a disability. Riding roughshod over language or etiquette, the marketer may make an indelible impression that can never be repaired, or at least not until a new editor replaces the offended incumbent. The point here is to use your head. If your target market is vision impaired, consider using only news releases printed in large type or submitted as audiocassettes. Or call the publication to ask which medium they prefer.

It would be foolish to correspond to deaf organizations without listing a working TDD telephone number. This is more than an issue of goodwill; it's a fundamental step toward dialogue. To converse, both parties must have "hearing" channels, and the TDD makes this exchange possible. Further, this tool shows that your company is sensitive to embracing organizations whose members are deaf or have severe hearing impairments.

A COVER LETTER GIVES A REASON WHY

Regardless if editors have a deluge or deficit of unsolicited press correspondence, sending a cover letter, personally addressed with the editor's correct name, is a courtesy that saves the editor and you time. It also ties the product or service to the mutual benefit of the heath organization's readership. One page in length is enough to summarize the high points. Then follow up with a phone call.

You should tailor your letter to the publication's interests. An example is a mobility product combining a nylon umbrella, PVC pipe, and large "balloon" tires; the manufacturer boasted it could be used in sand or snow, two surfaces that make the standard hard rubber tires of manual wheelchairs hard to maneuver. Potential purchasers would have different purposes for its use: a family beach resort could rent the "scooter" for conveying family members through the sand to the water's edge. The winter resort would see advantages in traversing snow conditions. A rehabilitation center might have uses involving swimming therapy for youngsters. Each of these press targets represent different industries, and each cover letter and news release should be drafted to speak to each trade's specific interests.

COMMANDING CONTROL AT PRESS CONFERENCES

It's the marketer's (or the public relations facilitator's) job to think of everything, impossible as it may seem. But let's think for a moment of how the face-to-face communications might be improved when meeting with the press. Obviously, most reporters will be nondisabled persons; however, if the product or service announcement is disabilities directed, you may well find a contingent of disabled reporters in the audience. What can be done to improve the communications and sensitivities atmosphere?

If the conference is in a large meeting room, pull the chairs away from the back tables so that wheelchair users don't have to scuff and scrape the chairs aside. If the auditorium has fixed seats, pull out the last row to provide a flat area for wheelchair users. Having to "park" in an inclined aisle is unsafe and a left-handed compliment to press people in wheelchairs.

Perhaps the reporter is hearing impaired. Consider holding the front row of chairs facing the speaker's table open (a tent card marked "reserved" is sufficient). Be sensitive to the lighting in the room; try to keep the speaker's face in full light, not shadows, so mouth and other facial expressions can be seen more easily. If the product is targeted to persons who are deaf, bringing a signing interpreter to sign the press conference would underscore your commitment to best serving the customer groups. Make available hard-copy transcripts of the meeting agenda and a full text of the speaker's comments as part of the press kit.

Try to stay away from rooms with stages, unless the stage is ramp accessible. If one of the speakers or panelists is in a wheelchair, the stage would prevent him or her from sitting with the panel. Also maintain a detachable podium, because the wheelchair speaker will be hidden behind the structure. A lavaliere microphone is suggested because some speakers with upper body impairments may not be able to manipulate a hand-held mike.

These communications enhancements will be noted and appreciated by both the press and the general public, particularly those with disabilities, and will make it easier for the press or investors or stockholders with disabilities to learn more about what your company does. Through thoughtful press relations, you're doing good and taking credit for it.

ADDING THE POWER OF IMPAIRMENTS TO CUSTOMER RELATIONS

A very delicate and important category of public relations is the practice of looking for ways to better serve the customer, from whose wells company revenues spring. Customer relations are those activities that improve customer-to-company or company-to-customer communications. Of course, these communications can produce great new product ideas, well-deserved compliments and complaints, and timely competitive intelligence. Can disabilities communications expand or enhance the dialogue in the current structure of your customer service program?

Let's start off by asking how often the company surveys current customers for their opinions, level of satisfaction, or unmet expectations. If the marketer can answer, "monthly," that's great. The more data points, the truer the fit to the line. (We are not going to discuss the "what" questions; this is a subject for an entire marketing research text.)

Figure 9.2—Taking advantage by phone

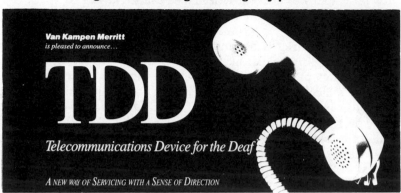

Fueled by personal experience and awareness of customer convenience, Van Kampen Merritt Companies' managers installed TDD service to assist client and broker communications. Rather than wait for the customer to "stumble" over the service, Van Kampen Merritt Companies advertised in the *National TDD Directory* and the Washington, D.C., telephone directory and created shareholder statement stuffers (like the one pictured here), prospectuses, and annual reports.

(Used with permission of Van Kampen Merritt, Inc.)

Assuming the marketer is proceeding with frequent customer contact, the question of disabilities exclusion should be reviewed. Suppose the customer communications program calls 250 randomly selected customer telephone numbers monthly. Could this procedure unknowingly eliminate a portion of the customer base? For many large national or regional retailers, the answer is yes; several groups with disabilities might remain outside of the telephone loop because of hearing or speech impairments. Or if written questionnaires were mailed to customers randomly, a customer with upper body mobility impairment might not be able to write responses to the questions. Nor will customers who are blind be able to read and react to written questionnaires. The potential number of customers with sensory impairments is great, estimated at 13 percent of the working-age population. Is there a way to better serve these markets?

To achieve the maximum survey coverage, plan to employ complementary communications channels of more than one response vehicle. Do the marketer's channels include a selection of verbal, written, videotext, TDD, or interactive TV response channels? Does the marketer's response system accept, if not all, at least two or three choices?

The issue is not a showcase of media with a high-tech veneer but rather an honest attempt to provide familiar vehicles that would support customer usage.

WILL CUSTOMERS USE CUSTOMER SERVICE CHANNELS?

The marketer is the best judge of customer interest in customer service. If telephone response is encouraged, does your company solicit customer contact by using toll-free phone numbers? What is the response to current programs; is the information gained helpful or disregarded? Does top management *read* the monthly summaries or just file them? If the latter action is taken, monies spent on customer service systems are wasted, no matter who the customer is, disabled or nondisabled.

But if management does pull together with marketing, to see that customer interests and input are heard, initiating any or all of these disabilities-friendly customer service channels such as toll-free phone numbers or personal computer networks, will build long-term relationships for the company.

REPAIR OR WARRANTY SERVICE COMMITMENTS

Customers who buy your products or services do so to solve their problems, not to have the new product create more. A great majority of manufacturers stand behind the quality of their product. "If there's anything wrong with it, wrap it up and send it back to us," is a well intentioned assurance, but for many buyers with disabilities, this offer is more easily said than done. Especially for persons with hand or arm mobility impairments or for those with sight impairments, reboxing, packing, wrapping, and delivering the defective CD player is a large problem.

What alternatives to packing and shipping could be substituted? Could repair by local retailers or alliances with existing warranty service vendors be explored? Are there any other ways to avoid the inconvenience of boxing and shipping? The customer-driven marketer will develop a warranty service process that delivers the promised satisfaction in purchasing the product and keeps the burden of repair on the manufacturer, not on the customer.

In seeking instructions for operating products or for troubleshooting advice, the customer with disabilities has little hesitation if the information channel available is one that he or she can use. In order to improve communications with disabled customers, consider adding a specialized disabilities-directed channel, such as a TDD phone and number, and place the number on the package, on company stationery, on monthly statements, in ads or news releases, in directory assistance; in short, make the phone number appear wherever possible. Then monitor the calls/transmissions from TDD users. Route them through one operator and keep track of the number of calls and the reason for the call (the subject, department, or inventory questions, for example). Test this disability service for at least 12 months, to allow dissemination of the TDD number, before deciding if it produces any incremental revenue or if it helps to identify problems that users who are deaf encounter. User trial takes time; don't pull the test plug too soon.

Perhaps the written medium is easier for your customers to use. Keep in mind the advice on envelope size, strength necessary to open, strength required to tear the perforation, ease of handling (as in one-handed opening), sufficient space to fill in the blanks, paid postage permits, and other response accommodations.

The marketer must recognize that certain response vehicles function better than others, depending on the disability. The issue of customer service is to solve problems and keep a pulse of the marketplace. Without parallel communication channels, the customer service representative could be listening only for the front door, while many other friends stand unnoticed at the back, side, and patio doors.

Disabilities communications will work well when marketers make time to manage relationships with the organization's audiences. The publics of public relations can be information disseminators, such as the news media; information seekers, such as prospects or customers with disabilities; or investors or regulators with disabilities. Sensitivity to public scrutiny requires a marketer to be anticipatory. The better you plan for pubic exposure, the more friends you're going to make.

CHAPTER TEN

APPLICATIONS OF DISABILITIES COMMUNICATIONS IN PERSONAL SELLING

GETTING UP CLOSE AND PERSONAL

Market segments. Product adaption. Media mixes. Parallel channels. All these strategies sound good in theory but aren't worth a plug nickel if your staff's personal selling techniques are left to chance. Good marketers know that nothing can be assumed and that all programs gravitate to chaos if left alone. Rather than relinquish control, what's to bring us back to communicating in the most effective manner: both the marketer and prospect speaking, face-to-face?

This dialogue between a marketer and a purchaser with a disability doesn't have to be a casual, one-time encounter, but can instead become

165

the basis of a long-term relationship. And when the marketer finds a successful marketing mix that puts him or her at the prospect's front door or on the prospect's monitor, the marketer had better be ready with some persuasive reason for calling the meeting.

WHEN SENSITIVITY REALLY COUNTS

A *Wall Street Journal* article recently chronicled the attempts of catalog merchants who were targeting "consumers' special physical needs." Several retailers were lamenting the uncertainty of the fashion business.

"As the fashion business becomes more specialized, retailers are increasingly capitalizing on what they call 'consumer conditions.' Cheery conditions, such as pregnancy, are simple enough to exploit. But sensitive ones—such as arthritis, paraplegia, and obesity—are a different story. Consumers with such conditions are hard to identify. Unless every aspect of the retailer's approach is examined for sensitivity, consumers may wind up feeling more wounded than wooed."[1]

The fashion business is not the only industry affected; any organization that spends great amounts of time on personal selling or providing personal service to disabled customers should look for methods that improve selling satisfaction. Put your current sales policies aside for the moment to look from the viewpoint of the customer with disabilities. What are their expectations? Does your sales team spend enough time learning about disabled customers' needs? Do they recognize that all disabilities are not the same? Does their sales plan overlook any significant prospect group with disabilities? How comfortable are they in dealing with buyers with disabilities? How comfortable are persons with disabilities in dealing with your organization?

Thought should be given to these simple questions and more because modifications to sales programs may be needed. Many retail businesses are reviewing customer expectations and the resulting adjustments required of their company's communications programs. Dealing in appearance-enhancing products, such as fashions, can be highly sensitive and subjective, and it makes good sense for a marketer to be cautious by planning the most effective and honest ways to improve personal communications with purchasers with disabilities.

---

1 Helliker, Kevin, "Fashion Catalogs Focus on Consumers' Special Needs," *Wall Street Journal* (New York, NY: Dow Jones, April 16, 1992), B-1.

READJUSTING SALES ATTITUDES

Many sales tactics and reactions are intuitive. They are probably the result of years of experience, sharpened by agile sparring with heavy-handed purchasing managers or tight-fisted retail buyers. This combative landscape has great potential for disaster if the marketer takes this "one size fits all" approach into personal selling situations. As purchasing agents or buyers with disabilities earn positions as department managers, the selling process, commonly called the sales call, should be reconsidered. Besides possibly needing disabilities-friendly sales collateral of larger type specs sheets or inventory lists formatted to a 5 1/4" floppy disk (discussed in Chapter 8), nonverbal attitudes and sales techniques may need adjustment when selling to disabled buyers.

What shouldn't be done is to instinctively read, then process body language of businesspeople with disabilities. For many marketing or sales managers, body language such as assertive gestures or posture telegraph nonverbal cues concerning a sales prospect's self-confidence or decision-making capabilities. This is particularly true in the initial sales meeting, with the customer or client with disabilities encountering a new sales representative from your firm. It's easy to pass judgment by reading between the lines of those signs not spoken, to form an indelible first impression. But using only those criteria that are physically visible may rob the sales representative of the chance of forming a long-term relationship with a disabled owner's company.

SENSITIVITY TRAINING TO OPEN THEIR EYES

Encourage your sales team to be open-minded and aggressive toward serving the needs of customers with disabilities. But arm them with knowledge first.

Consider sensitivity training that simulates the disabled buyer/seller situation; this training is an excellent way to build awareness and dispel doubt about disabilities among the salespeople in the field. A lesson salespeople could learn from, for example, is that verbal messages should be evaluated on information, not style. Why? Glibness may not be an accurate measure of the performance of the purchasing agent with disabilities. Someone with cerebral palsy might be slower in responding to questions or explaining what the inventory needs are. As we've discussed, different people have different strengths and weaknesses, disabled or not. Help the sales staff adapt personal expectations accordingly.

Figure 10.1—Customer newsletters are vital links for announcing new services.

Support for the Hearing Impaired

Merrill Lynch maintains a special toll-free TDD* number for CBA clients. For up-to-date information, hearing impaired clients can call Client Services at 1-800-262-3340. There is also a TDD number especially for questions about our products and services, 1-800-765-4TDD (1-800-765-4833).

Currently, Merrill Lynch has 70 Financial Consultants representing 33 states, each equipped with a TDD and a telephone speech amplifier.

* A "TDD" is a Telecommunication Device for the Deaf which allows one party to type out messages to another party using similar equipment. ■

Even before Merrill Lynch had completed its Deaf/Hard-of-Hearing program, TDD services were made available via the Capital Builder Account (CBA) newsletter.

(Used with permission of Merrill Lynch, Pierce, Fenner & Smith Inc.

Here's another "field-leveling" idea: change the "selling setting" to a venue or channel that is more disabilities friendly. Perhaps verbal communication is vexing; it might be easier for the customer to communicate or order by fax or videotext if an interactive menu is available. The concept of dual media channels surfaces again, but this time as a personal selling tool. Employing a nonpersonal response channel in place of the face-to-face sales process is somewhat paradoxical to the marketing manager, but not to the client.

Besides customer convenience, there are other reasons to adapt your expectations of verbal communications skills; understand that certain persons with disabilities need more time to process information in response to your questions. The correct answer will be returned; it might not be as prompt or as crisp as you would expect from others. But remember that intelligence is not the issue but rather the customer's use of a "slower communications transmitter."

Another accommodation could be to take your goods or services, particularly those that can be demonstrated, to the market rather than forcing the markets with disabilities to come to you. Examples are numerous, such as bringing out computer units with several types of keyboard adaptions, or "roadside" repairs of damaged equipment, or personal phone calls to check satisfaction with the performance of the vendor and his or her products. Taking the extra step sets the seller apart from the competition.

Accommodations can facilitate "custom routing" of product or service access. But before we focus on product or service delivery, how can salespeople get to know the prospect better?

SUBSTITUTING THE POWER HANDSHAKE

As you greet a disabled customer for the first time, recognize that a strong handshake, steady eye contact or attentive posture may be physically unattainable for your new acquaintance. Neuromuscular involvement may restrict upper body control, for example, but in no way restricts the experience or knowledge of your client with a disability.

Personality traits such as reluctance to participate in receptions or dinner parties may also be mistaken as "antisocial" behavior. This really is an indication of the comfort level an individual has in socializing with friends or among strangers; imagine the potential for social discomfort. For those with upper limb limitations, bringing a cup to the mouth or relying on an aide for feeding may be embarrassing in formal business receptions. Or the amplified din of cocktail chatter might prove to be an annoying atmosphere for the client with a hearing impairment. Repeating missed questions is troublesome for both the impaired listener and the questioner.

Viewpoint 10.1—Reasons why disabled people's mobility or social activities are limited

Based on a Harris survey of persons who say their disability limits their mobility or activities:

Reason	Total Disab pers 559	Slightly to Moderately 165	Somewhat to Severely 378
	%	%	%
Because of fear that your disability or health problem might cause you to get hurt, sick, or victimized by crime	59	58	59
Because you need someone to go with you or help you, but don't always have someone available	56	48	59
Because you are not able to use public transportation or because you can't get special transportation or someone to give you a ride when you need one	49	44	51
Because you are self-conscious about your disability	40	40	40
Because you come across many public buildings and places that you can't get into or that have bathrooms you can't use	40	38	40
Because you have difficulty in seeing, talking or hearing	37	32	39

Source: Louis Harris and Associates, 1986

So anticipating the atmosphere in which selling relationships are built or destroyed is a beneficial training exercise for field sales representatives. The client's hesitancy to join in social settings is not job related and should have no bearing on how well-qualified the person with disabilities is to perform his or her job. Social stigmas can exist on both sides of the fence, for the marketer and the client alike. Recognizing the difference between "public" work behavior and "private" social behavior gives the marketing manager the proper frame of reference in attempting to fraternize with clients or customers with disabilities. If the comfort level is there, great. If not, don't take the turndown personally.

CONSIDER OTHER SALES ACCOMMODATIONS

One thing that impresses a prospect with disabilities is when the vendor takes the initiative to offer more help or guidance than was expected in past purchases; here's an example. In buying a wheelchair, a hospital bed or other durable (and likely expensive) goods, most insurance companies or health agencies such as the Muscular Dystrophy Association require price quotes and equipment specifications from three sources.

To assist the process, the disabled individual begins to contact vendors to learn more about the product and its functions, and product information, brochures and spec sheets grow and grow into a perplexing array of choices. Knowing little about power-drive wheelchairs, the person checks with his or her friends who already have the product; the amount of advice also expands quickly. Setting aside confusion, the buyer with a disability presses on and makes the three phone calls to three referred health care retailers.

The first telephone call produces a seemingly knowledgeable sales representative who wants to know which chair is preferred. The caller states that he has no idea what chair he wants, much less which is best. The salesperson assures the purchaser with a disability that she has worked with MDA before and knows from the phone call which power chair is best. The phone interview ends with a promise to submit a bid and a promise to send a brochure on the equipment specified.

The second telephone call results in an appointment to measure the prospective buyer since different chairs have different seat and frame widths as well as wheel sizes, pneumatic versus solid rubber tires, spokes versus sport wheels, controller types, battery types, articulating versus fixed footrests, options, colors, the list goes on. During an in-home visit, the second sales representative takes a measurement, leaves colorful brochures depicting active use, and promises a written quotation. While photos of the power chair are informative, a test drive could answer all of the prospect's questions.

The third telephone call produces a second house call. Again, measurements and brochures are exchanged, but this time the sales representative reads a hint of frustration and uncertainty. In an effort to match the wheelchair user with the proper power chair, the sales representative offers to contact the manufacturer to assemble a replica of the power chair the representative thinks will best fit the user's needs. From this Wednesday appointment, a Saturday date is set to check the fit of the chair and to test the controller. On Saturday, the power chair is ready (it's not the right color, has different wheels, and no swing-away controller arm, but that's no problem; these cosmetic selections don't affect the performance in the mind of the prospect) and charged to go. This demonstration is attributable to the sensitive sales representative working in tandem with a proactive distributor who both went out of their way to simplify and reassure the purchaser with disabilities that he is making the prudent decision. Nor did they have any assurance that they would win the order. But this take-charge effort does win referral response from the buyer, family, and friends, and has priceless value in building long-term reputations and relationships.

WHAT TO DO IF THE MARKET HAS TO COME TO YOU

Many products and services can't be duplicated and delivered for trial. No one expects an appliance or automotive shop to bring its selection of refrigerators or hydraulic grease racks to a client's driveway. Equipment may be too expensive, too delicate, or too bulky to be portable. Likewise, the cost of a skilled technician, such as a dental appliance maker or a machinist might be prohibitive for making house calls.

So what can a marketing or sales manager do to make store or office visits easier? In Chapter 3, "Assessing Your Organization," access issues were discussed via a checklist of physical accommodations in a financial institution. Rather than starting in the parking lot, the marketer should begin at the home of the account holder with disabilities, to understand how much of a journey it is to visit your store or office.

Getting to the Store

■ Check with the advertising department to make certain that store addresses, hours of operation, phone numbers, and directional copy are correct and included in all ads.

■ Be sure the person at the reception desk is familiar with any public transportation systems that run past the store. Be familiar with the routes, stops, and schedules. Take a test ride on the bus, train, or metro line that serves your office or store; this is a good way to empathize with your disabled customers.

■ Offer to reimburse your customers who ride public transit for the trip on which they purchase your company's good or services. This gesture is predicated on the retailer maintaining sufficient margins to absorb the 50 cents to three dollar fee.

■ Inform the staff where the nearest disabled parking spaces or passenger loading zones are located.

   • Is this loading area protected overhead from rain or snow?

   • The entry door should be accessible with one-handed strength; can the door pressure be adjusted or can a touch-plate automatic opener be installed?

■ Be sensitive to the aisle width, even for one-day "sidewalk" sales. Keep a safe clearance sufficiently wide to accommodate wheelchairs at 36 inches. Make sure that temporary displays are sturdy and secure.

■ Instruct the sales staff to be familiar with the location of handicapped facilities, bathrooms, fountains, elevators, public phones; if you're in a mall, prepare a handout map of facilities, and access and emergency evacuation routes.

Creating a Better Selling Atmosphere

■ Consider training your staff in personal communications skills for dealing with the four physiographic groups; assist the sales staff in understanding the differences in the disabilities and in recognizing nonverbal signals (such as posture or eye contact) to improve face-to-face encounters with customers with disabilities.

■ Consider training in sales communications, such as instructing employees to make mental adjustments to allow extra time to service disabled persons' needs. For example, a person with arthritic hands or joints takes longer to undress and dress. An empathetic salesperson attitude will strongly support any advertising or publicity claims of disabilities-friendly retailing services.

■ Use an alternative document as proof of identity rather than automatically demanding a driver's license; many persons with disabilities do not drive. Perhaps an employee or student ID might suffice.

■ Are oversized bags or tote bags available in all departments to make handling and carrying purchases easier and more manageable?

■ Consider purchasing and learning to use a TDD for better serving customers who are deaf. These devices cost about $150 and open a whole new channel of sales communications. Use the TDD number in store ads for newspapers and the Yellow Pages. Make sure everyone knows how to use the machine to save the store from the embarrassing situation of advertising a TDD number but employing no one who can operate it.

■ At the next special event, perhaps a fashion show or an author's autograph party, hire a signing interpreter and advertise the signing service to the deaf community. This could attract a whole new segment expecting ongoing service to customers who are deaf.

These suggestions are by no means exhaustive; they merely scratch the surface of selling mindsets and programs that can improve face-to-face selling dialogue. With proper commitment by the marketing and sales managers, perhaps in the not-too-distant future some of these ideas will have become standard operating procedure for all retail and service providers.

CHAPTER ELEVEN

TEN TIPS TO IMPROVE COMMUNICATIONS WITH CONSUMERS WITH DISABILITIES

TURNING THE LEARNING CURVE INTO A SMILE

After all the arguments are made and positions defended or revised, it soon becomes time to implement the disabilities communications strategy. Product-development goals have been established between top management and the marketing director; the goals are clearly understood, compatible with company strengths, and realistic in scope and time expectations. A test-product or service has been adapted according to the preferences of users with disabilities, and the test-market area has likewise been designated. Geography has been defined to produce a manageable area of control so that concerns of over- or under-commu-

175

nicating are minimized. Distribution, sales, and service resources are in place, and now the potential prospect needs to be defined.

LET'S GET PHYSICAL

The marketer has quantified the targeted disabilities markets, and sufficient numbers of users or prospects appear to populate "common interest" segments. Commonalities are then grouped according to the physiographic profile that invisibly binds someone with debilitating arthritis to the upper body impairments of an individual with paralysis to the finger-numbing exacerbations of multiple sclerosis to the one-handedness of someone who lost an arm to cancer and amputation. These four circumstances may seem independent as health conditions, but all result in limitations to full hand or arm movement. Organizing by physiographic factors produces an in-depth understanding of strengths and weaknesses of most elements of the marketing process, from product or service design to convenience in ordering to accessible packaging to ease of delivery to simplified operating instructions to convenience in after-sale customer communications. All these facilitating efforts benefit customers with disabilities as well as nondisabled customers who value convenience, too.

LEFT-BRAIN CREATIVITY

We are moving closer to that looming abyss into which the marketer shouts, not knowing for sure if anyone is listening, and awaits an echo of response. Every marketer hopes for an avalanche rather than a trickle of buyer interest; no promises can be made here about "guaranteed" level of sales. Too many factors impact the marketing terrain over which the communications strategy has no control—poorly conceived or adapted products, lack of sales representation or no distribution support, ill-prepared or trained customer service people. With proper planning, though, a disabilities communications strategy can become the relationship-building bridge spanning from corporate objectives on one side to satisfied customers on the other.

Knowing that there is no replacement for the proper product sporting a fair price, with convenience-oriented distribution and an interested buyer segment, are there any tips or admonitions to make the last "P," promotion in general, more effective to those managers who are contemplating a test of the strategy? Yes. Here is a list of the ten most important determinants in establishing, molding, and equalizing attitudes that will help to mainstream marketing efforts to persons with disabilities. Some of these thoughts deal with facts, others with attitudes, some with communications techniques; all address the issue of getting to know the individual with disabilities better and honestly embracing him or her as an economically-attractive market segment.

TEN TIPS FOR IMPROVING COMMUNICATIONS

1. **Recognize that the needs and motivations of persons with disabilities are diverse; disabled people are not all alike**. Good communicators make an extra effort to learn more about sensitivity; different people want different things. Markets with disabilities contain diverse groups, yet the segments can be organized according to physiographic characteristics of mobility, hearing, sight, and speech impairments. Learn how each health condition limits marketing communications performance. This entails more work, yes, but also more reward.

2. **Don't single out the disabled person in headlines or copy**. Talk directly to the person, not to the disability. Focus on skills and achievement, not on limitations or sympathy. The best headline to get the attention of a mobility impaired executive or a hearing impaired business owner probably is, "Hey, here's the benefit." The reader with a disability will then decide whether to investigate the product further.

3. **Show persons with disabilities as part of the whole in stills or video**. The issue is mainstreaming, showing persons with disabilities participating thoroughly in daily life. Show disabled individuals or couples reacting naturally in social settings like family gatherings, business meetings, in teaching or other professional roles, leading civic events, competing as athletes, or as cheering spectators. Picture them with kids, with older and younger people, with pets . . . in situations just like anyone else.

4. **Offer advice or solutions that will better their lives; don't dwell on problems or negative consequences**. Persons with disabilities are aware of their limitations; many have lived with their disability all their lives. You don't have to remind them. How can your product or service make their lives better? What's the benefit, in time or money or effort? Tell them quickly because their time is as valuable (maybe more so) as others'.

5. **Offer persons with disabilities choices**. In the past, many disabled customers' choices in products, styles, colors, models, and price could be counted on one thumb. Send the product design team into the field to meet with rehabilitation engineers or physical therapists. Call competitors for their product catalogs and read them cover to cover. Talk to your potential customers via focus groups and listen closely. Challenge your thinking to provide variety in product development; don't be afraid to err on the side of too much choice rather than too little.

6. **Take your message to the market; don't expect the disabled market to come to you**. How do your disabled customers learn of your business, products, or services? Do you presently have any customers with disabilities? Don't take for granted that account holders with disabilities wait by their doorsteps for news about your merchandise. For disabled customers to know of special promotions or programs, be aware that more than in-store point of purchase merchandising is needed. Because many of them don't get "in-store" casually, they must be given a reason to stop by. Remember that advertising is a one-way street; it produces no dialogue. So in your advertising, don't be cute; what might be funny to a brash young copywriter might be glaringly offensive to a somber politician with a disability. Leave humor to the personal selling task, where the sender can watch the receiver's reactions and adjust accordingly if the pun falls flat on its face.

7. **Mix your message with the mainstream; recognize that various groups of disabilities use media differently**. Sight, hearing, speech, or mobility impairments reduce each medium's effectiveness in market coverage. Depending on which physiographic groups are being targeted, the marketer may need a mix of media to cover an annual sale adequately, meaning some print, some electronic, and some direct mail to reach various groups of customers with disabilities. Some duplicate coverage by vehicles may result because of differences in abilities to see, hear, or handle each medium.

8. **Make it easy to order**. Remember that different disabilities have different capabilities when it comes to ordering and purchasing your goods. This point is twofold. Consider facilitating the initial order (and offering an incentive for reordering). For example, the prescription refill, telephone reorder is standard. But what about the speech or hearing impaired customer? Substitute

a TDD in some stores or a postage-paid reorder card as a package stuffer in all checkouts.

9. **Make it easy to open, and easy to read**, including the direct mail envelope and the product packaging. Test the strengths of glues, friction, papers, staples, and other materials that could make package opening difficult. Keep body type size at a minimum of 12 points for legibility. Separate the body copy lines with extra leading for an open look. These suggestions should benefit older customers as well.

10. **As you construct communications for consumption by Americans with disabilities, show them contributing and building, with desirable and expanding skills**. Persons with disabilities want to work, earn money, enjoy life's pleasures, and achieve recognition resulting from their abilities, not to be known for their disabilities. This competency may be showcased by skills in craftsmanship or art; or by earning advanced degrees that contribute knowledge to science or technology that improve life for everyone; or through hard-won experience devoted to social consciousness or other worthy endeavors. Persons with disabilities populate all societies and cultures. They like what you like. Make it a point to bring them into the "consumer communications loop."

INTO THE ECONOMIC MAINSTREAM

Reasons abound why embracing consumers with disabilities in communications and commercial endeavors is socially responsible and makes for building long-term relationships. Persons with disabilities form the segmentation targets, while relatives, friends and other caregivers can also participate in generating goodwill and sales patronage to those manufacturers or services providers who dispense satisfaction. The disabilities markets exist, will continue to grow, and are looking for benefits only a visionary marketer can identify. With this mindset toward consumer satisfaction, reorganize your product or service into the situation analysis and strategy process of disabilities marketing. If this marketing logic appears to fit, the likely result will be a win-win relationship for market and marketer alike.

MYTHS WILL DISAPPEAR

As marketers put their heads together to face the future, it is apparent that the broad markets of the old days will be long gone, replaced by "splinter" segments composed of special interests, each citing special needs. Marketers can only drive so far downward before the economies of mass marketing are lost. At this point, marketers should have the option to "reconstitute" splinter segments, rebundled by new physiographic organization. This strategy assumes that consumer goods and services marketers harbor an honest interest in learning more about how disabilities affect their customers' lives and how brand loyalty can be enhanced by auditing and applying disabilities marketing techniques.

Interest in disabilities issues has been heightened with the passage of the Americans with Disabilities Act; the influence of the law can impact attitudes as well as opportunities in a positive fashion. Regardless of national or regional marketing responsibilities, the marketer can demonstrate efficiency, as in the ability to control costs based on scale. Effectiveness should be measured, too, in recombining splinter groups with commonalities in ability or disability. This observation applies not only to disabled populations but also to general markets who wish to upgrade their shopping access by time (when I want it) and convenience (to my door). In addressing time, companies are mostly at the starting gate, with a few prescient national marketers off and running. These firms, for example, DuPont, Merrill Lynch, Van Kampen Merritt, or AT&T, had already recognized the value of serving people with disabilities before the ADA mandate was passed.

Embracing the law can bring opportunity to the marketer in building long-term customer relations. The marketing mix of advertising, sales promotion, public relations, and personal selling can be bolstered when targeting consumers with disabilities; disabilities communications techniques smooth media and response interference. Given the influence of the Americans with Disabilities Act, shouldn't these efforts be readily identified as tools for contact and dialogue with disabled consumers?

Often, it is only the restrictive attitudes of others that prevent persons with disabilities from achieving their goals of independence, participation, and self-esteem. Attitudes toward disabilities are frequently negative because the public doesn't understand them. Nondisabled persons may feel uncomfortable in unfamiliar situations serving someone with a disability; we all try to ignore or forget those experiences that result in fear or uncertainty. Fear can be reduced by education, and rather than engaging in a cover-up, we encourage questions and information that makes disabilities more comprehensible. As improved accessibility and accommodations integrate greater numbers of people with disabilities into society's mainstream, many myths and misconceptions will continue to disappear.

Marketers who initiate disabilities marketing efforts will be further up the learning curve. These savvy marketers will already be at the "transaction" level of commerce, while the ADA-ignorant manager may be long lost, still weighing the "action" need for marketing intervention.

Where do you want your company to be? Ahead of or behind the learning curve?

APPENDIX A

POPULATION STATISTICS*

PREVALENCE OF CHRONIC CONDITIONS

Table 1 presents estimates of the number of selected chronic conditions and rate per 1,000 persons in the total population, by four age groups (under 45 years, 45–69 years, 70–84 years, and 85 years and over) and by gender. Age groupings vary among tables (such as 18 years and under or 18–45 years), so care must be taken to match equal segments (as in "apples to apples" comparisons.) Information on chronic health conditions are grouped into six categories: skin conditions, musculoskeletal conditions, impairments, digestive conditions, circulatory conditions, and miscellaneous conditions. Impairments are divided further to mainly functional or structural musculoskeletal and neuromuscular im-

---

*   The Tables listed in this Appendix are from the National Institute on Disability and Rehabilitation Research, *Data on Disability from the National Health Interview Survey 1983–1985.* Washington, D.C.: U.S. Department of Education, 1988, pp. 62–88.

pairments and other impairments of visual and auditory senses and intelligence.

The conditions listed on Table 1 are only those that can be meaningfully estimated from the checklists. Table 1, therefore, presents data on selected chronic conditions only. Within each of the six condition categories presented in Table 1, for example, is a residual group of conditions. They do not represent all other conditions, only those "select" ones asked on the survey checklist that are not enumerated separately in the table. Some minor conditions that do appear on the checklists, acne for example, are not presented in Table 1 because they rarely cause a disability.

The five most prevalent conditions based on rates per 1,000 persons are sinusitis, arthritis, hypertension, deafness and other hearing impairments, and heart disease. Per 1,000 persons in the total population, about 134.6 report sinusitis as a chronic condition; 130.0 report rheumatoid arthritis or osteoarthritis and other arthropathies; 123.5 report hypertension; 90.8 report deafness and other hearing impairments, and 89.7 report some form of heart disease. The relative ranking of conditions depends on how the conditions are grouped. For example, if all deformities and orthopedic impairments are combined, they would rank fourth, at 121 cases per 1,000 persons.

Ranking based on rates presented in Table 1 show some differences between men and women. Per 1,000 men, sinusitis (116.8), hypertension (108.7), deafness and other hearing impairments (105.9), arthritis (95.3), and heart disease (84.5) are reported most often. Per 1,000 women, arthritis (164.3), sinusitis (151.2), hypertension (137.3), heart disease (94.4), and hay fever (90.4) rank as the top five conditions.

Table 1A–Prevalence of activity limitation due to chronic conditions, by main cause of limitation, age, and gender: United States civilian noninstitutionalized population, 1983–1985 (three-year average)

Males

Main Cause of Limitation	All Ages		Under 18		18-44		45-69		70-84		85+	
	Number of conditions in thousands and percent distribution											
All conditions	15,178	100.0	1,900	100.0	4,236	100.0	6,469	100.0	2,235	100.0	340	100.0
Skin and musculoskeletal												
Rheumatoid arthritis	137	0.9	*3	*0.2	*8	*0.2	82	1.3	22	1.0	.	.
Osteoarthritis/other arthropathies	1,024	6.7	*5	*0.3	150	3.5	595	9.2	233	10.4	40	11.9
Intervertebral disk disorders	741	4.9	*2	*0.1	354	8.4	354	5.5	31	1.4	*1	*0.3
Osteomyelitis/bone disorders	109	0.7	*16	*0.8	31	0.7	49	0.8	*12	*0.5	.	.
Bursitis	54	0.4	*1	*0.0	21	0.5	24	0.4	*7	*0.3	.	.
Psoriasis and dermatitis	38	0.2	*6	*0.3	*15	*0.3	17	0.3	*1	*0.0	.	.
Skin cancer	*15	*0.1			*5	*0.1	*6	*0.1	*4	*0.2	.	.
Bone cancer	17	0.1					*9	*0.1	*8	*0.4	*1	*0.3
Other skin and musculoskeletal	118	0.8	*2	*0.1	27	0.6	61	0.9	24	1.1	*4	*1.2
Impairments												
Absence of arm(s)/hand(s)	24	0.2	*3	*0.2	*8	*0.2	*9	0.1	*4	*0.2	*4	*1.2
Absence of leg(s)	103	0.7	*1	*0.1	26	0.6	48	0.7	24	1.1	*1	*0.3
Absence of fingers, toes, feet	48	0.3	0	0.0	23	0.5	22	0.3	*2	*0.1		
Other absence, NEC	58	0.4	*5	*0.2	23	0.5	22	0.3	*8	*0.3	*1	*0.4
Complete paralysis of extremities	146	1.0	*3	*0.2	56	1.3	70	1.1	17	0.8	*1	*0.4
Cerebral palsy	78	0.5	41	2.1	29	0.7	*8	*0.1				
Partial paralysis of extremities	82	0.5	*6	*0.3	26	0.6	36	0.6	*12	*0.6	*2	*0.7
Paralysis of other sites	33	0.2	*7	*0.4	*13	*0.3	*10	*0.2	*2	*0.1	*1	*0.4
Curvature of back or spine	144	1.0	*10	*0.5	99	2.3	30	0.5	*4	*0.2	*1	*0.2
Other impairment of back	1,020	6.7	*11	*0.6	506	11.9	450	7.0	49	2.2	*6	*1.7
Spina bifida	17	0.1	*7	*0.4	*8	*0.2	*2	*0.0				
Impairment of upper extremities	332	2.2	19	1.0	193	4.6	110	1.7	*11	*.5	17	5.0
Impairment of lower extremities	1,028	6.8	74	3.9	524	12.4	322	5.0	91	4.1	*1	*0.2
Other orthopedic impairment	66	0.4	*2	0.1	32	0.7	26	0.4	*5	*0.2	*1	*0.4
Speech impairment	155	1.0	136	7.2	*15	*0.4	*3	*0.0	*1	*0.0		
Blind in both eyes	106	0.7	*7	*0.4	23	0.6	37	0.6	27	1.2	*11	*3.4
Cataracts	81	0.5	*2	*0.1	*9	*0.2	29	0.5	33	1.5	*7	*2.1
Glaucoma	56	0.4			*6	*0.1	23	0.4	18	0.8	*9	*2.5
Other visual impairment/eye disorders	461	3.0	49	2.6	175	4.1	137	2.1	76	3.4	24	6.9
Deaf in both ears	76	0.5	*14	*0.7	28	0.7	19	0.3	*11	*0.5	*5	*1.4
Other hearing impairment/ear disorders	367	2.4	115	6.1	101	2.4	88	1.4	50	2.2	*13	*3.9

* Figure has low statistical reliability or precision (relative standard error exceeds 30 percent)

SOURCE: National Health Interview Surveys, 1983-1985: original tabulations from public use tapes

Table 1A—(Continued)

Males

Main Cause of Limitation	All Ages		Under 18		18-44		45-69		70-84		85+	
		Number of conditions in thousands and percent distribution										
Digestive												
Ulcers	72	0.5	*2	*0.1	24	0.6	38	0.6	*8	*0.4		
Abdominal hernia	145	1.0	*3	*0.2	45	1.1	70	1.1	23	1.0	*3	*0.9
Enteritis and colitis	27	0.2	*1	*0.0	*13	*0.3	*13	*0.2	1	0.1		
Cancer of digestive sites	67	0.4			*7	*0.2	44	0.7	*11	*0.5	*5	*1.3
Other digestive disorders	107	0.7	*10	*0.5	24	0.6	55	0.8	17	0.7	*1	*0.2
Circulatory												
Rheumatic fever	34	0.2	*2	*0.1	*10	*0.2	20	0.3	*1	*0.1		
Ischemic heart disease	1,090	7.2	*1	*0.0	62	1.5	788	12.2	227	10.2	*12	*3.6
Heart rhythm disorders	138	0.9	17	0.9	*15	*0.3	73	1.1	32	1.4	*1	*0.4
Other heart disease	709	4.7	30	1.6	52	1.2	419	6.5	179	8.0	29	8.5
Hypertension	406	2.7	*5	*0.3	52	1.2	270	4.2	76	3.4	*2	*0.6
Cerebrovascular disease	340	2.2	*2	*0.1	*10	*0.2	163	2.5	145	6.5	19	5.5
Arteriosclerosis	91	0.6			*3	*0.1	53	0.8	27	1.2	*9	*2.5
Phlebitis, varicose veins	68	0.4			*15	*0.4	41	0.6	*11	*0.5	*1	*0.2
Other circulatory	164	1.1	*1	*0.1	*14	*0.3	93	1.4	48	2.1	*7	*2.2
Respiratory												
Chronic bronchitis	59	0.4	*16	*0.8	*10	*0.2	23	0.4	*11	*0.5		
Asthma	657	4.3	343	18.1	183	4.3	104	1.6	26	1.2		
Hay fever	92	0.6	38	2.0	47	1.1	*8	*0.1				
Sinusitis	27	0.2	*5	*0.3	*5	*0.1	*11	*0.2	*5	*0.2	*1	*0.2
Emphysema	466	3.1			*10	*0.2	299	4.6	153	6.9	*3	*1.0
Lung or bronchial cancer	62	0.4			*2	*0.1	38	0.6	19	0.9	*2	*0.6
Other respiratory disease	209	1.4	19	1.0	26	0.6	108	1.7	54	2.4	*3	*0.8

* Figure has low statistical reliability or precision (relative standard error exceeds 30 percent)

SOURCE: National Health Interview Surveys, 1983-1985: original tabulations from public use tapes

Table 1A—(Continued)

Males

Number of conditions in thousands and percent distribution

Miscellaneous

Main Cause of Limitation	All Ages		Under 18		18-44		45-69		70-84		85+	
Diabetes	346	2.3	*9	*0.5	82	1.9	202	3.1	48	2.1	*5	*1.6
Anemias	25	0.2	*10	*0.5	*7	*0.2	*2	*0.0	*3	*0.1	*2	*0.6
Kidney disorders	51	0.3	*5	*0.3	*14	*0.3	23	0.4	*7	*0.3	*1	*0.4
Female genital disorders	na	na	na	na	na	na	na	na	na	na	na	na
Schizophrenia/other psychoses	130	0.9	*15	*0.8	75	1.8	35	0.5	*4	*0.2	*1	*0.2
Neuroses/personality disorders	147	1.0	31	1.6	61	1.4	48	0.7	*7	*0.3		
Other mental illness	274	1.8	180	9.5	41	1.0	46	0.7	*6	*0.3		
Alchohol or drug dependency	56	0.4	*5	*0.3	32	0.7	18	0.3	*1	*0.0		
Mental retardation	583	3.8	368	19.4	176	4.2	36	0.6	*2	*0.1	*1	*0.2
Epilepsy	186	1.2	33	1.7	110	2.6	37	0.6	*6	*0.3		
Multiple sclerosis	40	0.3			*16	*0.4	22	0.3	*2	*0.1		
Senility	141	0.9					*20	*0.3	70	3.1	51	15.1
Parkinson's disease	53	0.3			*2	*0.0	21	0.3	27	1.2	*3	*0.8
Other nervous disorders	250	1.6	34	1.8	84	2.0	87	1.3	38	1.7	*5	*1.5
Tuberculosis (all sites)	21	0.1			*7	*0.2	*11	*0.2	*3	*0.2		
Other infectious/parasitic diseases	49	0.3	*6	*0.3	28	0.7	*12	*0.2	*3	*0.1	*1	*0.2
Leukemia	23	0.2	*7	*0.4	*2	*0.0	*10	*0.2	*5	*0.2		
Cancer of genitourinary sites	49	0.3	*1	*0.0	*2	*0.1	25	0.4	19	0.9	*2	*0.5
Cancer of all other sites, NEC	75	0.5	*5	*0.3	*13	*0.3	44	0.7	*12	*0.5	*1	*0.2
Surgical/medical complications	76	0.5	*5	*0.3	22	0.5	37	0.6	*13	*0.6	*1	*0.2
Other injuries	103	0.7	*13	*0.7	47	1.1	30	0.5	*11	*0.5	*3	*0.9
Other ill-defined conditions	314	2.1	36	1.9	100	2.4	137	2.1	37	1.7	*5	*1.5
All other chronic conditions	423	2.8	96	5.1	132	3.1	135	2.1	48	2.1	*12	*3.4

* Figure has low statistical reliability or precision (relative standard error exceeds 30 percent)

SOURCE: National Health Interview Surveys, 1983-1985: original tabulations from public use tapes

Table 1A—(Continued)

Main Cause of Limitation	All Ages		Under 18		18-44		45-69		70-84		85+	
					Number of conditions in thousands and percent distribution							
All conditions	17,362	100.0	1,293	100.0	4,144	100.0	7,675	100.0	3,461	100.0	789	100.0
Skin and musculoskeletal												
Rheumatoid arthritis	389	2.2	*7	*0.6	78	1.9	228	3.0	68	2.0	*7	*0.8
Osteoarthritis/other arthropathies	2,450	14.1	*6	*0.5	198	4.8	1,310	17.1	774	22.3	162	20.6
Intervertebral disk disorders	683	3.9			274	6.6	358	4.7	46	1.3	5	0.6
Osteomyelitis/bone disorders	251	1.4	*12	*0.9	35	0.9	124	1.6	67	1.9	*12	*1.5
Bursitis	85	0.5	*1	*0.0	30	0.7	43	0.6	*11	*0.3	*1	*0.1
Psoriasis and dermatitis	69	0.4	*10	*0.8	34	0.8	21	0.3	*3	*0.1		
Skin cancer	*12	*0.1			*2	*0.1	*7	*0.1	*1	*0.0	*1	*0.1
Bone cancer	26	0.1	*1	*0.0	*2	*0.1	*12	*0.2	*10	*0.3	*1	*0.1
Other skin and musculoskeletal	159	0.9	*4	*0.3	36	0.9	81	1.1	31	0.9	*7	*0.9
Impairments												
Absence of arm(s)/hand(s)	*4	*0.0	*1	*0.1	*2	*0.0	*1	*0.0				
Absence of leg(s)	43	0.2	*1	*0.0	*4	*0.1	19	0.2	17	0.5	*2	*0.3
Absence of fingers, toes, feet	*15	*0.1	*3	*0.2	*3	*0.1	*4	*0.1	*5	*0.2		
Other absence, NEC	52	0.3	*3	*0.2	*10	*0.2	28	0.4	*10	*0.3		
Complete paralysis of extremities	69	0.4	*6	*0.5	17	0.4	31	0.4	*13	*0.4	*3	*0.4
Cerebral palsy	73	0.4	34	2.6	31	0.7	*7	*0.1	*1	*0.0		
Partial paralysis of extremities	50	0.3			*5	*0.1	28	0.4	*16	*0.5	*1	*0.1
Paralysis of other sites	24	0.1	*2	*0.2	*6	*0.2	*10	*0.1	*4	*0.1	*1	*0.2
Curvature of back or spine	280	1.6	32	2.5	153	3.7	74	1.0	20	0.6	*1	*0.1
Other impairment of back	1,102	6.3	*13	*1.0	512	12.3	476	6.2	89	2.6	*13	*1.6
Spina bifida	*15	*0.1	*7	*0.5	*7	*0.2	*1	*0.0	*1	*0.0		
Impairment of upper extremities	200	1.2	*9	*0.7	88	2.1	77	1.0	20	0.6	*6	*0.7
Impairment of lower extremities	945	5.4	81	6.3	308	7.4	301	3.9	193	5.6	61	7.8
Other orthopedic impairment	70	0.4	*4	*0.3	22	0.5	31	0.4	*11	*0.3	*2	*0.3
Speech impairment	83	0.5	67	5.2	*7	*0.2	*8	*0.1	*2	*0.0	*1	*0.1
Blind in both eyes	98	0.6	*2	*0.2	*14	*0.3	22	0.3	40	1.2	18	2.3
Cataracts	145	0.8	*3	*0.2	*5	*0.1	44	0.6	66	1.9	27	3.4
Glaucoma	79	0.5			*3	*0.1	29	0.4	41	1.2	*5	*0.7
Other visual impairment/eye disorders	414	2.4	32	2.5	81	2.0	128	1.7	115	3.3	57	7.2
Deaf in both ears	72	0.4	*14	*1.1	23	0.6	18	0.2	*13	*0.4	*3	*0.4
Other hearing impairment/ear disorders	298	1.7	85	6.6	66	1.6	82	1.1	49	1.4	*16	*2.0

* Figure has low statistical reliability or precision (relative standard error exceeds 30 percent)

SOURCE: National Health Interview Surveys, 1983-1985: original tabulations from public use tapes

Table 1A–(Continued)

Main Cause of Limitation	All Ages		Under 18		18-44		45-69		70-84		85+	
					Females							
					Number of conditions in thousands and percent distribution							
Digestive												
Ulcers	54	0.3	*2	*0.2	*14	*0.3	27	0.4	*10	*0.3	*1	*0.1
Abdominal hernia	125	0.7	*3	*0.3	36	0.9	70	0.9	*14	*0.4	*2	*0.3
Enteritis and colitis	50	0.3	*2	*0.2	17	0.4	26	0.3	*3	*0.1	*1	*0.1
Cancer of digestive sites	60	0.3	*1	*0.1	*5	*0.1	35	0.5	17	0.5	*1	*0.2
Other digestive disorders	171	1.0	*12	*0.9	45	1.1	73	0.9	34	1.0	*7	*0.8
Circulatory												
Rheumatic fever	114	0.7	*4	*0.3	30	0.7	62	0.8	17	0.5	*1	*0.2
Ischemic heart disease	702	4.0			20	0.5	410	5.3	242	7.0	30	3.8
Heart rhythm disorders	186	1.1	*10	*0.8	38	0.9	78	1.0	52	1.5	*7	*0.9
Other heart disease	763	4.4	20	1.5	83	2.0	362	4.7	238	6.9	60	7.6
Hypertension	834	4.8	*2	*0.1	114	2.8	567	7.4	135	3.9	17	2.1
Cerebrovascular disease	270	1.6	*3	*0.2	*14	*0.3	97	1.3	125	3.6	31	4.0
Arteriosclerosis	76	0.4			*2	*0.0	24	0.3	33	1.0	*16	*2.1
Phlebitis, varicose veins	203	1.2	*2	*0.2	51	1.2	125	1.6	23	0.7	*3	*0.3
Other circulatory	144	0.8	*2	*0.2	26	0.6	70	0.9	40	1.1	*6	*0.8
Respiratory												
Chronic bronchitis	78	0.4	17	1.3	*13	*0.3	33	0.4	*14	*0.4	*2	*0.2
Asthma	754	4.3	225	17.4	284	6.8	198	2.6	43	1.3	*4	*0.4
Hay fever	91	0.5	23	1.8	48	1.2	18	0.2	*2	*0.1		
Sinusitis	31	0.2	*4	*0.3	*7	*0.2	18	0.2	*2	*0.0		
Emphysema	183	1.1	*1	*0.1	*6	*0.2	128	1.7	47	1.3	*2	*0.2
Lung or bronchial cancer	30	0.2			*1	*0.0	22	0.3	*7	*0.2		
Other respiratory disease	112	0.6	*14	*1.1	19	0.5	62	0.8	17	0.5		

* Figure has low statistical reliability or precision (relative standard error exceeds 30 percent)

SOURCE: National Health Interview Surveys, 1983-1985: original tabulations from public-use tapes

Table 1A–(Continued)

Females

Number of conditions in thousands and percent distribution

Main Cause of Limitation	All Ages		Under 18		18-44		45-69		70-84		85+	
Miscellaneous												
Diabetes	539	3.1	*10	*0.8	79	1.9	304	4.0	134	3.9	*12	*1.5
Anemias	75	0.4	*16	*1.2	25	0.6	25	0.3	*6	*0.2	*4	*0.4
Kidney disorders	95	0.5	*8	*0.6	32	0.8	44	0.6	*10	*0.3	*1	*0.1
Female genital disorders	141	0.8	*11	*0.8	68	1.6	55	0.7	*7	*0.2		
Schizophrenia/other psychoses	74	0.4	*3	*0.2	34	0.8	32	0.4	*4	*0.1	*2	*0.2
Neuroses/personality disorders	156	0.9	*13	*1.0	65	1.6	64	0.8	*11	*0.3	*3	*0.3
Other mental illness	164	0.9	58	4.5	41	1.0	48	0.6	*15	*0.4	*1	*0.1
Alchohol or drug dependency	20	0.1	*3	*0.3	*13	*0.3	*3	*0.0				
Mental retardation	364	2.1	205	15.9	123	3.0	31	0.4	*3	*0.1	*1	*0.1
Epilepsy	139	0.8	27	2.1	84	2.0	23	0.3	*5	*0.1	*1	*0.1
Multiple sclerosis	78	0.4			31	0.8	41	0.5	*5	*0.1		
Senility	266	1.5					45	0.6	102	2.9	119	15.1
Parkinson's disease	46	0.3			*1	*0.0	17	0.2	22	0.6	*6	*0.8
Other nervous disorders	359	2.1	21	1.6	122	2.9	155	2.0	56	1.6	*5	*0.6
Tuberculosis (all sites)	59	0.3	*3	*0.2	18	0.4	29	0.4	*9	*0.3		
Other infectious/parasitic diseases	48	0.3	*4	*0.3	19	0.4	*13	*0.2	*12	*0.3	*1	*0.1
Leukemia	17	0.1	*2	*0.1	*4	*0.1	*7	*0.1	*4	*0.1		
Cancer of female breast	93	0.5			*15	*0.4	60	0.8	17	0.5	*2	*0.3
Cancer of genitourinary sites	56	0.3	*1	*0.0	*14	*0.3	35	0.5	*6	*0.2	*1	*0.1
Cancer of all other sites, NEC	69	0.4	*4	*0.3	17	0.4	34	0.4	*11	*0.3	*2	*0.3
Surgical/medical complications	135	0.8			32	0.8	74	1.0	24	0.7	*5	*0.6
Other injuries	103	0.6	*5	*0.4	35	0.8	43	0.6	*14	*0.4	*6	*0.7
Other ill-defined conditions	393	2.3	24	1.9	118	2.8	177	2.3	62	1.8	*11	*1.4
All other chronic conditions	593	3.4	86	6.6	222	5.4	207	2.7	70	2.0	*7	*0.9

* Figure has low statistical reliability or precision (relative standard error exceeds 30 percent)

SOURCE: National Health Interview Surveys, 1983-1985: original tabulations from public use tapes

Table 1B—Prevalence of activity limitation due to chronic conditions, by all causes of limitation, age, and gender: United States civilian noninstitutionalized population, 1983–1985 (three-year average)

Number of conditions in thousands and percent distribution

All Causes of Limitation	All Ages		Under 18		18-44		45-69		70-84		85+	
All conditions	52,718	100.0	3,817	100.0	10,895	100.0	25,027	100.0	10,884	100.0	2,097	100.0
Skin and musculoskeletal												
Rheumatoid arthritis	646	1.2	*11	*0.3	121	1.1	388	1.5	118	1.1	*8	*0.4
Osteoarthritis/other arthropathies	5,484	10.4	*14	*0.4	469	4.3	3,099	12.4	1,594	14.6	308	14.7
Intervertebral disk disorders	1,699	3.2	*2	*0.0	668	6.1	904	3.6	117	1.1	*8	*0.4
Osteomyelitis/bone disorders	552	1.0	33	0.9	91	0.8	280	1.1	128	1.2	21	1.0
Bursitis	253	0.5	*1	*0.0	76	0.7	140	0.6	35	0.3	*1	*0.0
Psoriasis and dermatitis	189	0.4	31	0.8	75	0.7	69	0.3	*11	*0.1	*2	*0.1
Skin cancer	44	0.1			*8	*0.1	20	0.1	*13	*0.1	*3	*0.1
Bone cancer	52	0.1	*1	*0.0	*5	*0.0	24	0.1	20	0.2	*2	*0.1
Other skin and musculoskeletal	573	1.1	*13	*0.3	94	0.9	315	1.3	128	1.2	23	1.1
Impairments												
Absence of arm(s)/hand(s)	35	0.1	*5	*0.1	*10	*0.1	*13	*0.1	*7	*0.1	*8	*0.4
Absence of leg(s)	191	0.4	*2	*0.0	33	0.3	93	0.4	55	0.5	*2	*0.1
Absence of fingers, toes, feet	109	0.2	*6	*0.1	39	0.4	49	0.2	*13	*0.1	*1	*0.0
Other absence, NEC	186	0.4	*11	*0.3	47	0.4	88	0.4	39	0.4	*16	*0.8
Complete paralysis of extremities	373	0.7	*10	*0.3	93	0.9	172	0.7	82	0.8		
Cerebral palsy	177	0.3	86	2.2	72	0.7	18	0.1	*1	*0.0		
Partial paralysis of extremities	380	0.7	*9	*0.2	*48	0.4	164	0.7	137	1.3	22	1.1
Paralysis of other sites	122	0.2	*13	0.4	25	0.2	53	0.2	25	0.2	*6	*0.3
Curvature of back or spine	534	1.0	56	1.5	287	2.6	155	0.6	33	0.3	*3	*0.1
Other impairment of back	2,593	4.9	25	0.7	1,154	10.6	1,186	4.7	200	1.8	27	1.3
Spina bifida	36	0.1	*14	*0.4	17	0.2	*5	*0.0	*1	*0.0		
Impairment of upper extremities	822	1.6	35	0.9	361	3.3	341	1.4	73	0.7	*12	*0.6
Impairment of lower extremities	2,791	5.3	183	4.8	1,047	9.6	1,014	4.0	433	4.0	115	5.5
Other orthopedic impairment	211	0.4	*11	*0.3	75	0.7	84	0.3	32	0.3	*8	*0.4
Speech impairment	421	0.8	234	6.1	53	0.5	83	0.3	44	0.4	*7	*0.3
Blind in both eyes	301	0.6	*15	*0.4	53	0.5	88	0.4	100	0.9	46	2.2
Cataracts	572	1.1	*9	*0.2	25	0.2	189	0.8	256	2.3	93	4.4
Glaucoma	312	0.6	*1	*0.0	19	0.2	122	0.5	131	1.2	38	1.8
Other visual impairment/eye disorders	1,715	3.3	141	3.7	404	3.7	575	2.3	438	4.0	158	7.5
Deaf in both ears	221	0.4	31	0.8	56	0.5	62	0.2	50	0.5	10	1.0
Other hearing impairment/ear disorders	1,184	2.2	249	6.5	227	2.1	371	1.5	249	2.3	89	4.2

* Figure has low statistical reliability or precision (relative standard error exceeds 30 percent)

SOURCE: National Health Interview Surveys, 1983-1985; original tabulations from public use tapes

Table 1B–(Continued)

All Causes of Limitation	All Ages		Under 18		18-44		45-69		70-84		85+	
	Number of conditions in thousands and percent distribution											
Digestive												
Ulcers	429	0.8	*6	*0.1	81	0.7	257	1.0	78	0.7	*8	*0.4
Abdominal hernia	595	1.1	*9	*0.1	105	1.0	336	1.3	128	1.2	17	0.8
Enteritis and colitis	138	0.3	*8	*0.2	43	0.4	75	0.3	*10	*0.1	*2	*0.1
Cancer of digestive sites	185	0.4	*1	*0.0	*14	*0.1	114	0.5	48	0.4	*9	*0.4
Other digestive disorders	775	1.5	36	0.9	142	1.3	387	1.5	176	1.6	34	1.6
Circulatory												
Rheumatic fever	204	0.4	*7	*0.2	52	0.5	114	0.5	27	0.3	*3	*0.1
Ischemic heart disease	2,423	4.6	*1	*0.0	97	0.9	1,581	6.3	683	6.3	61	2.9
Heart rhythm disorders	598	1.1	39	1.0	79	0.7	288	1.1	170	1.6	23	1.1
Other heart disease	2,350	4.5	67	1.8	187	1.7	1,230	4.9	714	6.6	151	7.2
Hypertension	3,506	6.6	*10	*0.3	311	2.9	2,313	9.2	780	7.2	92	4.4
Cerebrovascular disease	939	1.8	*6	*0.1	34	0.3	430	1.7	396	3.6	74	3.5
Arteriosclerosis	363	0.7			*6	*0.1	153	0.6	151	1.4	52	2.5
Phlebitis, varicose veins	470	0.9	*3	*0.1	84	0.8	307	1.2	70	0.6	*7	*0.3
Other circulatory	612	1.2	*4	*0.1	60	0.6	329	1.3	182	1.7	37	1.8
Respiratory												
Chronic bronchitis	301	0.6	40	1.0	41	0.4	151	0.6	62	0.6	*6	*0.3
Asthma	1,783	3.4	608	15.9	547	5.0	493	2.0	127	1.2	*8	*0.4
Hay fever	253	0.5	76	2.0	112	1.0	56	0.2	*9	*0.1		
Sinusitis	135	0.3	*11	*0.3	23	0.2	69	0.3	28	0.3	*4	*0.2
Emphysema	994	1.9	*2	*0.0	29	0.3	650	2.6	297	2.7	*16	*0.8
Lung or bronchial cancer	125	0.2			*4	*0.0	81	0.3	39	0.4	*2	*0.1
Other respiratory disease	564	1.1	41	1.1	65	0.6	330	1.3	119	1.1	*8	*0.4

* Figure has low statistical reliability or precision (relative standard error exceeds 30 percent)

SOURCE: National Health Interview Surveys, 1983-1985: original tabulations from public use tapes

Table 1B—(Continued)

All Causes of Limitation	All Ages		Under 18		18-44		45-69		70-84		85+	
	Number of conditions in thousands and percent distribution											
Miscellaneous												
Diabetes	2,111	4.0	23	0.6	222	2.0	1,284	5.1	535	4.9	47	2.2
Anemias	168	0.3	29	0.8	46	0.4	57	0.2	23	0.2	*13	*0.6
Kidney disorders	344	0.7	20	0.5	75	0.7	174	0.7	61	0.6	*14	*0.7
Female genital disorders	271	0.5	*12	*0.3	111	1.0	118	0.5	28	0.3	*1	*0.1
Schizophrenia/other psychoses	253	0.5	21	0.5	127	1.2	88	0.4	*13	*0.1	*4	*0.2
Neuroses/personality disorders	410	0.8	54	1.4	158	1.4	168	0.7	26	0.2	*3	*0.2
Other mental illness	601	1.1	269	7.1	124	1.1	162	0.6	44	0.4	*2	*0.1
Alchohol or drug dependency	104	0.2	*10	*0.3	56	0.5	36	0.1	*2	*0.0		
Mental retardation	1,047	2.0	629	16.5	334	3.1	75	0.3	*7	*0.1	*2	*0.1
Epilepsy	444	0.8	78	2.0	244	2.2	105	0.4	*16	*0.1	*1	*0.1
Multiple sclerosis	127	0.2			53	0.5	66	0.3	*9	*0.1		
Senility	469	0.9					81	0.3	201	1.8	187	8.9
Parkinson's disease	146	0.3			*4	*0.0	53	0.2	74	0.7	*15	*0.7
Other nervous disorders	884	1.7	70	1.8	279	2.6	388	1.6	133	1.2	*14	*0.7
Tuberculosis (all sites)	114	0.2	*3	*0.1	29	0.3	66	0.3	*15	*0.1	*1	*0.0
Other infectious/parasitic diseases	137	0.3	*11	*0.3	55	0.5	45	0.2	22	0.2	*3	*0.2
Leukemia	58	0.1	*9	*0.2	*7	*0.1	29	0.1	*13	*0.1	*1	*0.0
Cancer of female breast	159	0.3			19	0.2	101	0.4	34	0.3	*5	*0.2
Cancer of genitourinary sites	173	0.3	*2	*0.1	20	0.2	96	0.4	48	0.4	*8	*0.4
Cancer of all other sites, NEC	190	0.4	*10	*0.3	36	0.3	100	0.4	39	0.4	*5	*0.2
Surgical/medical complications	454	0.9	*10	*0.3	96	0.9	240	1.0	96	0.9	*13	*0.6
Other injuries	359	0.7	23	0.6	114	1.0	152	0.6	58	0.5	*12	*0.6
Other ill-defined conditions	1,361	2.6	78	2.0	334	3.1	681	2.7	228	2.1	40	1.9
All other chronic conditions	1,814	3.4	233	6.1	484	4.4	752	3.0	300	2.8	45	2.2

* Figure has low statistical reliability or precision (relative standard error exceeds 30 percent)

SOURCE: National Health Interview Surveys, 1983-1985: original tabulations from public use tapes

Table 1B—(Continued)

	Males											
	All Ages		Under 18		18-44		45-69		70-84		85+	
All Causes of Limitation	Number of conditions in thousands and percent distribution											
All conditions	23,581	100.0	2,279	100.0	5,380	100.0	11,113	100.0	4,195	100.0	613	100.0
Skin and musculoskeletal												
Rheumatoid arthritis	172	0.7	*4	*0.2	33	0.6	104	0.9	31	0.7		
Osteoarthritis/other arthropathies	1,686	7.1	*6	*0.3	190	3.5	1,016	9.1	412	9.8	62	10.1
Intervertebral disk disorders	887	3.8	*2	*0.1	379	7.0	453	4.1	52	1.2	*2	*0.3
Osteomyelitis/bone disorders	161	0.7	20	0.9	43	0.8	77	0.7	20	0.5	*1	*0.2
Bursitis	98	0.4	*1	*0.0	30	0.6	52	0.5	*15	0.4		
Psoriasis and dermatitis	73	0.3	18	0.8	21	0.4	29	0.3	*3	*0.1	*1	*0.1
Skin cancer	25	0.1			*6	*0.1	*11	*0.1	*6	*0.1	*2	*0.3
Bone cancer	21	0.1			*1	*0.0	*10	*0.1	*9	*0.2	*1	*0.2
Other skin and musculoskeletal	265	1.1	*5	*0.2	44	0.8	148	1.3	60	1.4	*8	*1.4
Impairments												
Absence of arm(s)/hand(s)	30	0.1	*3	*0.1	*8	*0.2	*13	*0.1	*6	*0.1		
Absence of leg(s)	136	0.6	*1	*0.1	29	0.5	67	0.6	34	0.8	*5	*0.8
Absence of fingers, toes, feet	86	0.4	*2	*0.1	36	0.7	38	0.3	*7	*0.2	*2	*0.4
Other absence, NEC	93	0.4	*7	*0.3	28	0.5	43	0.4	*15	*0.4		
Complete paralysis of extremities	232	1.0	*4	*0.2	67	1.2	108	1.0	45	1.1	*8	*1.3
Cerebral palsy	94	0.4	48	2.1	36	0.7	*10	*0.1				
Partial paralysis of extremities	207	0.9	*7	*0.3	34	0.6	94	0.8	63	1.5	*9	1.4
Paralysis of other sites	71	0.3	*9	*0.4	*16	*0.3	32	0.3	*10	*0.2	*3	*0.5
Curvature of back or spine	182	0.8	*15	0.6	115	2.1	45	0.4	*6	*0.1	*1	*0.1
Other impairment of back	1,241	5.3	*12	0.5	569	10.6	575	5.2	76	1.8	*9	*1.4
Spina bifida	19	0.1	*7	*0.3	*9	*0.2	*3	*0.0				
Impairment of upper extremities	472	2.0	22	1.0	238	4.4	188	1.7	24	0.6		
Impairment of lower extremities	1,437	6.1	90	3.9	646	12.0	529	4.8	146	3.5	26	4.3
Other orthopedic impairment	99	0.4	*4	*0.2	45	0.8	36	0.3	*10	*0.2	*4	*0.6
Speech impairment	273	1.2	157	6.9	35	0.7	51	0.5	27	0.6	*2	*0.3
Blind in both eyes	152	0.6	*11	0.5	30	0.6	50	0.5	44	1.1	17	2.8
Cataracts	209	0.9	*5	*0.2	*13	*0.2	76	0.7	89	2.1	25	4.1
Glaucoma	122	0.5	*1	*0.1	*12	*0.2	49	0.4	44	1.1	*14	*2.3
Other visual impairment/eye disorders	842	3.6	90	3.9	267	5.0	274	2.5	167	4.0	46	7.4
Deaf in both ears	111	0.5	*15	0.7	31	0.6	32	0.3	22	0.5	*10	*1.6
Other hearing impairment/ear disorders	641	2.7	141	6.2	141	2.6	197	1.8	128	3.1	33	5.4

* Figure has low statistical reliability or precision (relative standard error exceeds 30 percent)

SOURCE: National Health Interview Surveys, 1983-1985: original tabulations from public use tapes

Table 1B—(Continued)

Males

All Causes of Limitation	All Ages		Under 18		18-44		45-69		70-84		85+	
	Number of conditions in thousands and percent distribution											
Digestive												
Ulcers	209	0.9	*3	*0.1	45	0.8	125	1.1	33	0.8	*2	*0.3
Abdominal hernia	272	1.2	*4	*0.2	55	1.0	153	1.4	51	1.2	*8	*1.3
Enteritis and colitis	42	0.2	*3	*0.1	*15	*0.3	20	0.2	*4	*0.1		
Cancer of digestive sites	98	0.4			*8	*0.1	64	0.6	20	0.5	*5	*0.9
Other digestive disorders	267	1.1	*15	*0.7	50	0.9	141	1.3	54	1.3	*7	*1.1
Circulatory												
Rheumatic fever	48	0.2	*3	*0.1	*12	*0.2	28	0.3	*4	*0.1		
Ischemic heart disease	1,395	5.9	*1	*0.0	72	1.3	998	9.0	311	7.4	*14	*2.3
Heart rhythm disorders	252	1.1	25	1.1	25	0.5	129	1.2	68	1.6	*5	*0.8
Other heart disease	1,073	4.5	42	1.8	71	1.3	627	5.6	286	6.8	47	7.6
Hypertension	1,172	5.0	*7	*0.3	105	2.0	807	7.3	236	5.6	*16	*2.6
Cerebrovascular disease	507	2.1	*2	*0.1	*14	*0.3	255	2.3	209	5.0	26	4.2
Arteriosclerosis	188	0.8			*4	*0.1	106	1.0	64	1.5	*14	*2.3
Phlebitis, varicose veins	124	0.5	*1	*0.0	20	0.4	77	0.7	26	0.6	*1	*0.1
Other circulatory	313	1.3	*1	*0.1	22	0.4	182	1.6	93	2.2	*15	*2.4
Respiratory												
Chronic bronchitis	122	0.5	19	0.8	*15	*0.3	64	0.6	23	0.6		
Asthma	785	3.3	363	15.9	205	3.8	169	1.5	46	1.1	*2	*0.4
Hay fever	116	0.5	47	2.0	54	1.0	13	0.1	*3	0.1		
Sinusitis	58	0.2	*6	*0.3	*9	*0.2	26	0.2	*15	*0.4	*2	*0.3
Emphysema	683	2.9	*1	*0.0	17	0.3	445	4.0	207	4.9	*13	*2.2
Lung or bronchial cancer	87	0.4			*3	*0.1	53	0.5	29	0.7	*2	*0.3
Other respiratory disease	360	1.5	23	1.0	37	0.7	208	1.9	85	2.0	6	0.9

* Figure has low statistical reliability or precision (relative standard error exceeds 30 percent)

SOURCE: National Health Interview Surveys, 1983-1985: original tabulations from public-use tapes

Table 1B–(Continued)

	Males											
	Number of conditions in thousands and percent distribution											
All Causes of Limitation	All Ages		Under 18		18-44		45-69		70-84		85+	

Miscellaneous

All Causes of Limitation	All Ages		Under 18		18-44		45-69		70-84		85+	
Diabetes	830	3.5	*10	*0.4	107	2.0	528	4.7	170	4.1	*15	*2.4
Anemias	42	0.2	*11	*0.5	*10	*0.2	*11	*0.1	*6	*0.1	*3	*0.6
Kidney disorders	123	0.5	*9	*0.4	24	0.4	63	0.6	24	0.6	*4	*0.6
Female genital disorders	na	na	na	na	na	na	na	na	na	na	na	na
Schizophrenia/other psychoses	158	0.7	*16	*0.7	88	1.6	44	0.4	*7	*0.2	*2	*0.3
Neuroses/personality disorders	193	0.8	37	1.6	77	1.4	68	0.6	*10	*0.3	na	na
Other mental illness	355	1.5	207	9.1	59	1.1	73	0.7	*15	*0.4	na	na
Alcohol or drug dependency	77	0.3	*6	*0.3	39	0.7	30	0.3	*2	*0.0	·	·
Mental retardation	646	2.7	407	17.9	195	3.6	39	0.3	*3	*0.1	*1	*0.2
Epilepsy	257	1.1	41	1.8	136	2.5	68	0.6	*10	*0.2	*1	*0.1
Multiple sclerosis	47	0.2	·	·	20	0.4	23	0.2	*3	*0.1	·	·
Senility	162	0.7	·	·	·	·	24	0.2	80	1.9	58	9.4
Parkinson's disease	80	0.3	·	·	*2	*0.0	30	0.3	44	1.0	*4	*0.6
Other nervous disorders	344	1.5	44	1.9	107	2.0	135	1.2	52	1.2	6	0.9
Tuberculosis (all sites)	34	0.1	·	·	*8	*0.2	21	0.2	*4	*0.1	*1	*0.1
Other infectious/parasitic diseases	69	0.3	*6	*0.3	33	0.6	23	0.2	*6	*0.1	*1	*0.1
Leukemia	31	0.1	*7	*0.3	*2	*0.0	*15	*0.1	*7	*0.2	*1	*0.1
Cancer of genitourinary sites	91	0.4	*1	*0.0	*2	*0.0	46	0.4	37	0.9	*5	*0.8
Cancer of all other sites, NEC	99	0.4	*6	*0.3	*16	*0.3	56	0.5	20	0.5	*1	*0.1
Surgical/medical complications	167	0.7	*6	*0.3	38	0.7	80	0.7	39	0.9	*4	*0.6
Other injuries	178	0.8	*15	*0.6	68	1.3	69	0.6	22	0.5	*4	*0.6
Other ill-defined conditions	551	2.3	43	1.9	150	2.8	273	2.5	75	1.8	*12	*1.9
All other chronic conditions	741	3.1	132	5.8	185	3.4	288	2.6	118	2.8	18	3.0

* Figure has low statistical reliability or precision (relative standard error exceeds 30 percent)

SOURCE: National Health Interview Surveys, 1983-1985: original tabulations from public use tapes

Table 1B—(Continued)

	Females											
	Number of conditions in thousands and percent distribution											
All Causes of Limitation	All Ages		Under 18		18-44		45-69		70-84		85+	
All conditions	29,136	100.0	1,537	100.0	5,514	100.0	13,913	100.0	6,689	100.0	1,482	100.0
Skin and musculoskeletal												
Rheumatoid arthritis	474	1.6	*7	*0.5	88	1.6	284	2.0	87	1.3	*8	*0.5
Osteoarthritis/other arthropathies	3,797	13.0	*8	*0.5	279	5.1	2,083	15.0	1,181	17.7	245	16.6
Intervertebral disk disorders	812	2.8			289	5.2	451	3.2	65	1.0	*6	*0.4
Osteomyelitis/bone disorders	391	1.3	*13	*0.8	49	0.9	203	1.5	108	1.6	19	1.3
Bursitis	155	0.5	*1	*0.0	46	0.8	87	0.6	20	0.3	*1	*0.0
Psoriasis and dermatitis	116	0.4	*13	*0.8	54	1.0	40	0.3	*8	*0.1	*1	*0.1
Skin cancer	18	0.1			*2	*0.0	*8	*0.1	*7	*0.1	*1	*0.0
Bone cancer	31	0.1	*1	*0.0	*4	*0.1	*14	*0.1	*11	*0.2	*1	*0.1
Other skin and musculoskeletal	308	1.1	*8	*0.5	50	0.9	168	1.2	68	1.0	*14	*1.0
Impairments												
Absence of arm(s)/hand(s)	*5	*0.0	*1	*0.1	*2	*0.0	*1	*0.0	*1	*0.0		
Absence of leg(s)	55	0.2	*1	*0.0	*5	*0.1	26	0.2	21	0.3	*2	*0.2
Absence of fingers, toes, feet	24	0.1	*4	*0.2	*3	*0.1	*11	*0.1	*6	*0.1		
Other absence, NEC	92	0.3	*7	*0.2	19	0.3	45	0.3	24	0.4		*0.0
Complete paralysis of extremities	141	0.5	*7	*0.5	26	0.5	64	0.5	38	0.6	*9	*0.6
Cerebral palsy	83	0.3	37	2.4	36	0.7	*8	*0.1	*1	*0.0		
Partial paralysis of extremities	172	0.6	*7	*0.1	*14	*0.2	70	0.5	74	1.1	*14	*0.9
Paralysis of other sites	51	0.2	*4	*0.3	*9	*0.2	20	0.1	*15	*0.2	*3	*0.2
Curvature of back or spine	352	1.2	42	2.7	172	3.1	109	0.8	27	0.4	*2	*0.1
Other impairment of back	1,352	4.6	*14	*09	585	10.6	611	4.4	123	1.8	18	1.2
Spina bifida	18	0.1	*7	*0.5	*8	*0.1	*2	*0.0	*1	*0.0		
Impairment of upper extremities	350	1.2	*13	*0.9	122	2.2	153	1.1	49	0.7	*12	*0.8
Impairment of lower extremities	1,354	4.6	94	6.1	401	7.3	484	3.5	287	4.3	88	5.9
Other orthopedic impairment	111	0.4	*7	*0.5	30	0.5	48	0.3	22	0.3	*4	*0.3
Speech impairment	148	0.5	77	5.0	18	0.3	31	0.2	17	0.3	*5	*0.3
Blind in both eyes	149	0.5	*4	*0.3	23	0.4	38	0.3	55	0.8	29	1.9
Cataracts	363	1.2	*3	*0.2	*12	*0.2	113	0.8	166	2.5	67	4.5
Glaucoma	190	0.7			*7	*0.1	72	0.5	87	1.3	24	1.6
Other visual impairment/eye disorders	872	3.0	51	3.3	137	2.5	300	2.2	271	4.1	112	7.6
Deaf in both ears	110	0.4	*15	*1.0	25	0.5	30	0.2	28	0.4	*11	*0.8
Other hearing impairment/ear disorders	543	1.9	108	7.0	86	1.6	174	1.3	121	1.8	55	3.7

* Figure has low statistical reliability or precision (relative standard error exceeds 30 percent)

SOURCE: National Health Interview Surveys, 1983-1985: original tabulations from public use tapes

Table 1B–(Continued)

	Females											
All Causes of Limitation	**All Ages**		**Under 18**		**18-44**		**45-69**		**70-84**		**85+**	

Number of conditions in thousands and percent distribution

All Causes of Limitation	All Ages		Under 18		18-44		45-69		70-84		85+	
Digestive												
Ulcers	221	0.8	*3	*0.2	36	0.6	132	0.9	45	0.7	*6	*0.4
Abdominal hernia	323	1.1	*4	*0.3	50	0.9	183	1.3	76	1.1	*9	*0.6
Enteritis and colitis	96	0.3	*4	*0.3	29	0.5	55	0.4	*6	*0.1	*2	*0.1
Cancer of digestive sites	88	0.3	*1	*0.1	*6	*0.1	50	0.4	27	0.4	*4	*0.2
Other digestive disorders	508	1.7	21	1.3	92	1.7	246	1.8	122	1.8	27	1.8
Circulatory												
Rheumatic fever	156	0.5	*4	*0.3	40	0.7	86	0.6	24	0.4	*3	*0.2
Ischemic heart disease	1,028	3.5			25	0.5	583	4.2	372	5.6	47	3.2
Heart rhythm disorders	346	1.2	*14	*0.9	53	1.0	159	1.1	101	1.5	18	1.2
Other heart disease	1,277	4.4	25	1.6	117	2.1	603	4.3	428	6.4	104	7.0
Hypertension	2,334	8.0	*2	*0.2	206	3.7	1,506	10.8	544	8.1	76	5.1
Cerebrovascular disease	432	1.5	*3	*0.2	19	0.4	175	1.3	186	2.8	48	3.2
Arteriosclerosis	174	0.6			*2	*0.0	47	0.3	87	1.3	38	2.5
Phlebitis, varicose veins	347	1.2	*2	*0.1	64	1.2	230	1.6	44	0.7	*6	*0.4
Other circulatory	299	1.0	*3	*0.2	38	0.7	147	1.1	89	1.3	22	1.5
Respiratory												
Chronic bronchitis	179	0.6	21	1.4	27	0.5	87	0.6	39	0.6	*6	*0.4
Asthma	998	3.4	245	15.9	342	6.2	325	2.3	81	1.2	*6	*0.4
Hay fever	137	0.5	30	1.9	58	1.1	43	0.3	6	0.1		
Sinusitis	77	0.3	*4	*0.3	*14	*0.3	42	0.3	*13	*0.2	*2	*0.1
Emphysema	311	1.1	*1	*0.0	*12	*0.2	205	1.5	91	1.4	*3	*0.2
Lung or bronchial cancer	38	0.1			*1	*0.0	28	0.2	*10	*0.1		
Other respiratory disease	204	0.7	17	1.1	28	0.5	123	0.9	34	0.5	*3	*0.2

* Figure has low statistical reliability or precision (relative standard error exceeds 30 percent)

SOURCE: National Health Interview Surveys, 1983-1985: original tabulations from public use tapes

Table 1B—(Continued)

Number of conditions in thousands and percent distribution

All Causes of Limitation	Females											
	All Ages		Under 18		18-44		45-69		70-84		85+	
Miscellaneous												
Diabetes	1,281	4.4	*12	*0.8	115	2.1	756	5.4	365	5.5	32	2.2
Anemias	126	0.4	18	1.2	36	0.7	46	0.3	17	0.3	*9	*0.6
Kidney disorders	221	0.8	*11	*0.7	51	0.9	111	0.8	38	0.6	*11	*0.7
Female genital disorders	270	0.9	*12	*0.8	111	2.0	118	0.8	28	0.4	*1	*0.1
Schizophrenia/other psychoses	95	0.3	*4	*0.3	39	0.7	44	0.3	*6	*0.1	*2	*0.2
Neuroses/personality disorders	216	0.7	17	1.1	80	1.5	100	0.7	*16	*0.2	*3	*0.2
Other mental illness	246	0.8	62	4.0	65	1.2	89	0.6	29	0.4	*2	*0.1
Alcohol or drug dependency	27	0.1	*3	*0.2	17	0.3	*7	*0.0				
Mental retardation	401	1.4	222	14.4	139	2.5	36	0.3	*4	*0.1	*1	*0.1
Epilepsy	187	0.6	37	2.4	107	1.9	37	0.3	*6	*0.1	*1	*0.0
Multiple sclerosis	81	0.3			33	0.6	43	0.3	*5	*0.1		
Senility	306	1.1					57	0.4	120	1.8	129	8.7
Parkinson's disease	66	0.2			*1	*0.0	23	0.2	30	0.5	*12	*0.8
Other nervous disorders	540	1.9	24	1.6	172	3.1	255	1.8	81	1.2	*7	*0.5
Tuberculosis (all sites)	80	0.3	*3	*0.2	20	0.4	44	0.3	*12	*0.2	*1	*0.1
Other infectious/parasitic diseases	68	0.2	*5	*0.3	22	0.4	22	0.2	17	0.2	*3	*0.2
Leukemia	27	0.1	*2	*0.1	*5	*0.1	*14	*0.1	*7	*0.1		
Cancer of female breast	159	0.5			19	0.3	101	0.7	34	0.5	*5	*0.3
Cancer of genitourinary sites	82	0.3	*1	*0.1	18	0.3	50	0.4	*11	*0.2	*3	*0.2
Cancer of all other sites, NEC	91	0.3	*4	*0.3	20	0.4	45	0.3	18	0.3	*4	*0.3
Surgical/medical complications	287	1.0	*4	*0.2	57	1.0	159	1.1	57	0.9	*9	*0.6
Other injuries	182	0.6	*9	*0.6	46	0.8	82	0.6	36	0.5	*9	*0.6
Other ill-defined conditions	810	2.8	35	2.3	184	3.3	409	2.9	153	2.3	28	1.9
All other chronic conditions	1,074	3.7	101	6.6	299	5.4	465	3.3	182	2.7	27	1.8

* Figure has low statistical reliability or precision (relative standard error exceeds 30 percent)

SOURCE: National Health Interview Surveys, 1983-1985: original tabulations from public use tapes

Table 1C—Prevalence of work limitation due to chronic conditions, by main cause of limitation, age, and gender: United States civilian noninstitutionalized population, ages 18–69, 1983–1985 (three-year average)

Main Cause of Limitation	All Ages		18-44		45-69		Males All Ages		Males 18-44		Males 45-69	
					Number of conditions in thousands and percent distribution							
All conditions	17,395	100.0	5,983	100.0	11,412	100.0	8,461	100.0	3,059	100.0	5,402	100.0
Skin and musculoskeletal												
Rheumatoid arthritis	324	1.9	77	1.3	247	2.2	94	1.1	25	0.8	69	1.3
Osteoarthritis/other arthropathies	1,692	9.7	225	3.8	1,468	12.9	576	6.8	94	3.1	482	8.9
Intervertebral disk disorders	1,068	6.1	504	8.4	563	4.9	584	6.9	296	9.7	288	5.3
Osteomyelitis/bone disorders	176	1.0	46	0.8	130	1.1	59	0.7	20	0.7	39	0.7
Bursitis	72	0.4	30	0.5	42	0.4	26	0.3	*13	*0.4	*13	*0.2
Psoriasis and dermatitis	58	0.3	26	0.4	32	0.3	21	0.3	*7	*0.2	*14	*0.3
Skin cancer	*13	*0.1	*2	*0.0	*11	*0.1	*5	*0.1	*1	*0.0	*5	*0.1
Bone cancer	22	0.1	*2	*0.0	20	0.2	*8	*0.1			*8	*0.1
Other skin and musculoskeletal	148	0.8	38	0.6	110	1.0	58	0.7	*16	*0.5	42	0.8
Impairments												
Absence of arm(s)/hand(s)	*14	*0.1	*9	*0.1	*6	*0.0	*12	*0.1	*7	*0.2	*6	*0.1
Absence of leg(s)	85	0.5	25	0.4	61	0.5	64	0.8	22	0.7	43	0.8
Absence of fingers, toes, feet	39	0.2	19	0.3	19	0.2	33	0.4	17	0.6	*16	*0.3
Other absence, NEC	60	0.3	24	0.4	35	0.3	33	0.4	17	0.5	*16	*0.3
Complete paralysis of extremities	159	0.9	68	1.1	91	0.8	116	1.4	52	1.7	64	1.2
Cerebral palsy	69	0.4	55	0.9	*14	*0.1	36	0.4	28	0.9	*8	*0.1
Partial paralysis of extremities	83	0.5	29	0.5	54	0.5	55	0.7	25	0.8	30	0.6
Paralysis of other sites	35	0.2	18	0.3	17	0.2	22	0.3	*13	*0.4	*10	*0.2
Curvature of back or spine	271	1.6	183	3.1	88	0.8	100	1.2	77	2.5	23	0.4
Other impairment of back	1,424	8.2	727	12.1	697	6.1	716	8.5	362	11.8	354	6.6
Spina bifida	*14	*0.1	*12	*0.2	*3	*0.0	*7	*0.1	*5	*0.2	*2	*0.0
Impairment of upper extremities	330	1.9	192	3.2	138	1.2	210	2.5	126	4.1	85	1.6
Impairment of lower extremities	883	5.1	440	7.3	443	3.9	501	5.9	269	8.8	232	4.3
Other orthopedic impairment	87	0.5	39	0.6	49	0.4	48	0.6	24	0.8	23	0.4
Speech impairment	31	0.2	19	0.3	*12	*0.1	17	0.2	*14	*0.5	*4	*0.1
Blind in both eyes	91	0.5	35	0.6	56	0.5	56	0.7	21	0.7	35	0.6
Cataracts	67	0.4	*12	*0.2	54	0.5	29	0.3	*8	*0.2	22	0.4
Glaucoma	52	0.3	*7	*0.1	45	0.4	26	0.3	*4	*0.1	22	0.4
Other visual impairment/eye disorders	385	2.2	168	2.8	217	1.9	219	2.6	114	3.7	105	1.9
Deaf in both ears	76	0.4	47	0.8	29	0.3	40	0.5	25	0.8	*15	*0.3
Other hearing impairment/ear disorders	210	1.2	89	1.5	120	1.1	107	1.3	45	1.5	62	1.1

* Figure has low statistical reliability or precision (relative standard error exceeds 30 percent)

SOURCE: National Health Interview Surveys, 1983-1985; original tabulations from public use tapes

Table 1C—(Continued)

Number of conditions in thousands and percent distribution

Main Cause of Limitation	All Ages		18-44		45-69		Males All Ages		Males 18-44		Males 45-69	
Digestive												
Ulcers	82	0.5	26	0.4	56	0.5	49	0.6	*15	*0.5	34	0.6
Hernia	167	1.0	61	1.0	106	0.9	86	1.0	33	1.1	53	1.0
Enteritis and colitis	56	0.3	23	0.4	33	0.3	20	0.2	*11	*0.3	*9	*0.2
Cancer of digestive sites	82	0.5	*12	*0.2	70	0.6	46	0.5	*6	*0.2	39	0.7
Other digestive disorders	152	0.9	48	0.8	104	0.9	67	0.8	18	0.6	50	0.9
Circulatory												
Rheumatic fever	96	0.5	32	0.5	64	0.6	26	0.3	*9	*0.3	18	0.3
Ischemic heart disease	1,109	6.4	70	1.2	1,039	9.1	746	8.8	53	1.7	693	12.8
Heart rhythm disorders	148	0.8	30	0.5	117	1.0	69	0.8	*9	*0.3	60	1.1
Other heart disease	780	4.5	98	1.6	682	6.0	414	4.9	39	1.3	375	6.9
Hypertension	757	4.3	115	1.9	642	5.6	254	3.0	36	1.2	218	4.0
Cerebrovascular disease	263	1.5	20	0.3	243	2.1	166	2.0	*9	*0.3	157	2.9
Arteriosclerosis	67	0.4	*5	*0.1	62	0.5	49	0.6	*3	*0.1	46	0.8
Phlebitis, varicose veins	183	1.1	47	0.8	136	1.2	42	0.5	*10	*0.3	33	0.6
Other circulatory	167	1.0	30	0.5	138	1.2	88	1.0	*11	*0.4	77	1.4
Respiratory												
Chronic bronchitis	55	0.3	*14	*0.2	41	0.4	28	0.3	*6	*0.2	22	0.4
Asthma	491	2.8	270	4.5	221	1.9	185	2.2	109	3.6	76	1.4
Hay fever	65	0.4	51	0.9	*14	*0.1	29	0.3	28	0.9	*1	*0.0
Sinusitis	30	0.2	*7	*0.1	23	0.2	*11	*0.1	*3	*0.1	*9	*0.2
Emphysema	379	2.2	*13	*0.2	366	3.2	271	3.2	*8	*0.3	264	4.9
Lung or bronchial cancer	57	0.3	*2	*0.0	55	0.5	37	0.4	*2	*0.0	36	0.7
Other respiratory disease	175	1.0	31	0.5	145	1.3	110	1.3	18	0.6	93	1.7

* Figure has low statistical reliability or precision (relative standard error exceeds 30 percent)

SOURCE: National Health Interview Surveys, 1983-1985: original tabulations from public use tapes

Table 1C—(Continued)

Number of conditions in thousands and percent distribution

Main Cause of Limitation	All Ages		18-44		45-69		Males All Ages		Males 18-44		Males 45-69	
Miscellaneous												
Diabetes	516	3.0	119	2.0	396	3.5	228	2.7	62	2.0	165	3.1
Anemias	44	0.3	20	0.3	23	0.2	*6	*0.1	*4	*0.1	*2	*0.0
Kidney disorders	90	0.5	34	0.6	57	0.5	32	0.4	*12	*0.4	19	0.4
Female genital disorders	84	0.5	48	0.8	36	0.3						
Schizophrenia/other psychoses	174	1.0	106	1.8	68	0.6	108	1.3	73	2.4	35	0.7
Neuroses/personality disorders	229	1.3	123	2.1	106	0.9	107	1.3	60	2.0	46	0.9
Other mental illness	156	0.9	71	1.2	85	0.7	77	0.9	35	1.1	42	0.8
Alchohol or drug dependency	60	0.3	39	0.7	21	0.2	46	0.5	27	0.9	18	0.3
Mental retardation	350	2.0	283	4.7	68	0.6	201	2.4	164	5.4	36	0.7
Epilepsy	212	1.2	159	2.7	53	0.5	126	1.5	92	3.0	34	0.6
Multiple sclerosis	92	0.5	39	0.7	53	0.5	35	0.4	*15	*0.5	20	0.4
Senility	53	0.3	.	.	53	0.5	17	0.2			17	0.3
Parkinson's disease	37	0.2	*2	*0.0	36	0.3	22	0.3	*2	*0.0	21	0.4
Other nervous disorders	359	2.1	156	2.6	202	1.8	141	1.7	67	2.2	74	1.4
Tuberculosis (all sites)	55	0.3	22	0.4	34	0.3	*14	*0.2	*7	*0.2	*8	*0.1
Other infectious/parasitic diseases	49	0.3	31	0.5	18	0.2	26	0.3	17	0.6	*9	*0.2
Leukemia	22	0.1	*4	*0.1	17	0.1	*11	*0.1	*2	*0.0	*10	*0.2
Cancer of female breast	61	0.4	13	0.2	49	0.4	na	na	na	na	na	na
Cancer of genitourinary sites	66	0.4	*9	*0.2	57	0.5	25	0.3	*1	*0.0	24	0.4
Cancer of all other sites, NEC	90	0.5	20	0.3	70	0.6	48	0.6	*9	*0.3	39	0.7
Surgical/medical complications	129	0.7	40	0.7	89	0.8	51	0.6	19	0.6	32	0.6
Other injuries	115	0.7	60	1.0	55	0.5	56	0.7	32	1.0	24	0.4
Other ill-defined conditions	448	2.6	171	2.9	277	2.4	205	2.4	83	2.7	121	2.2
All other chronic conditions	509	2.9	245	4.1	264	2.3	206	2.4	97	3.2	109	2.0

* Figure has low statistical reliability or precision (relative standard error exceeds 30 percent)

SOURCE: National Health Interview Surveys, 1983-1985: original tabulations from public use tapes

Table 1C—(Continued)

Main Cause of Limitation	Females					
	All Ages		18-44		45-69	
	Number of conditions in thousands and percent distribution					
All conditions	8,934	100.0	2,924	100.0	6,010	100.0
Skin and musculoskeletal						
Rheumatoid arthritis	230	2.6	52	1.8	178	3.0
Osteoarthritis/other arthropathies	1,116	12.5	130	4.5	986	16.4
Intervertebral disk disorders	484	5.4	208	7.1	275	4.6
Osteomyelitis/bone disorders	117	1.3	26	0.9	91	1.5
Bursitis	46	0.5	17	0.6	29	0.5
Psoriasis and dermatitis	37	0.4	19	0.7	18	0.3
Skin cancer	*8	*0.1	*1	*0.0	*6	*0.1
Bone cancer	*14	*0.2	*2	*0.1	*12	*0.2
Other skin and musculoskeletal	89	1.0	21	0.7	68	1.1
Impairments						
Absence of arm(s)/hand(s)	*2	*0.0	*2	*0.1		
Absence of leg(s)	21	0.2	*3	*0.1	18	0.3
Absence of fingers, toes, feet	*6	*0.1	*2	*0.1	*4	*0.1
Other absence, NEC	27	0.3	*8	*0.3	19	0.3
Complete paralysis of extremities	44	0.5	16	0.5	27	0.4
Cerebral palsy	33	0.4	27	0.9	*6	*0.1
Partial paralysis of extremities	28	0.3	*4	*0.1	23	0.4
Paralysis of other sites	*13	*0.1	*6	*0.2	*7	*0.1
Curvature of back or spine	171	1.9	106	3.6	65	1.1
Other impairment of back	708	7.9	365	12.5	343	5.7
Spina bifida	*7	*0.1	*6	*0.2	*1	*0.0
Impairment of upper extremities	120	1.3	67	2.3	53	0.9
Impairment of lower extremities	381	4.3	170	5.8	211	3.5
Other orthopedic impairment	40	0.4	*15	*0.5	25	0.4
Speech impairment	*15	*0.2	*6	*0.2	*9	*0.1
Blind in both eyes	36	0.4	*14	*0.5	21	0.4
Cataracts	37	0.4	*5	*0.2	32	0.5
Glaucoma	26	0.3	*3	*0.1	23	0.4
Other visual impairment/eye disorders	166	1.9	54	1.8	113	1.9
Deaf in both ears	36	0.4	21	0.7	*15	*0.2
Other hearing impairment/ear disorders	103	1.2	45	1.5	59	1.0

* Figure has low statistical reliability or precision (relative standard error exceeds 30 percent)

SOURCE: National Health Interview Surveys, 1983-1985, original tabulations from public use tapes

Table 1C—(Continued)

Main Cause of Limitation	Females					
	All Ages		18-44		45-69	
	Number of conditions in thousands and percent distribution					

Main Cause of Limitation	All Ages		18-44		45-69	
Digestive						
Ulcers	32	0.4	*11	*0.4	22	0.4
Hernia	81	0.9	28	1.0	53	0.9
Enteritis and colitis	36	0.4	*12	*0.4	24	0.4
Cancer of digestive sites	36	0.4	*5	*0.2	30	0.5
Other digestive disorders	84	0.9	30	1.0	54	0.9
Circulatory						
Rheumatic fever	69	0.8	23	0.8	46	0.8
Ischemic heart disease	363	4.1	17	0.6	346	5.8
Heart rhythm disorders	79	0.9	21	0.7	58	1.0
Other heart disease	366	4.1	59	2.0	306	5.1
Hypertension	502	5.6	78	2.7	424	7.1
Cerebrovascular disease	97	1.1	*10	*0.4	86	1.4
Arteriosclerosis	19	0.2	*2	*0.1	17	0.3
Phlebitis, varicose veins	141	1.6	37	1.3	104	1.7
Other circulatory	79	0.9	18	0.6	61	1.0
Respiratory						
Chronic bronchitis	27	0.3	*8	*0.3	19	0.3
Asthma	306	3.4	161	5.5	146	2.4
Hay fever	36	0.4	23	0.8	13	0.2
Sinusitis	18	0.2	*4	*0.1	*14	*0.2
Emphysema	108	1.2	*5	*0.2	102	1.7
Lung or bronchial cancer	20	0.2	*1	*0.0	19	0.3
Other respiratory disease	65	0.7	*13	*0.4	52	0.9

* Figure has low statistical reliability or precision (relative standard error exceeds 30 percent)

SOURCE: National Health Interview Surveys, 1983-1985: original tabulations from public use tapes

Table 1C—(Continued)

Main Cause of Limitation	Females			
	All Ages	18-44	45-69	
	Number of conditions in thousands and percent distribution			
Miscellaneous				
Diabetes	288	3.2	57	1.9	231	3.8
Anemias	37	0.4	*16	*0.5	21	0.4
Kidney disorders	58	0.7	21	0.7	37	0.6
Female genital disorders	83	0.9	48	1.6	36	0.6
Schizophrenia/other psychoses	66	0.7	33	1.1	33	0.6
Neuroses/personality disorders	122	1.4	63	2.1	59	1.0
Other mental illness	78	0.9	35	1.2	43	0.7
Alchohol or drug dependency	*14	*0.2	*12	*0.4	*2	*0.0
Mental retardation	150	1.7	118	4.0	31	0.5
Epilepsy	86	1.0	67	2.3	19	0.3
Multiple sclerosis	57	0.6	24	0.8	32	0.5
Senility	36	0.4	.	.	36	0.6
Parkinson's disease	*15	*0.2	.	.	*15	*0.2
Other nervous disorders	216	2.4	89	3.0	128	2.1
Tuberculosis (all sites)	41	0.5	*15	*0.5	26	0.4
Other infectious/parasitic diseases	23	0.3	*14	*0.5	*9	*0.1
Leukemia	*10	*0.1	*3	*0.1	*7	*0.1
Cancer of female breast	61	0.7	*13	*0.4	49	0.8
Cancer of genitourinary sites	41	0.5	*9	*0.3	33	0.5
Cancer of all other sites, NEC	43	0.5	*12	*0.4	31	0.5
Surgical/medical complications	78	0.9	21	0.7	57	0.9
Other injuries	59	0.7	28	1.0	31	0.5
Other ill-defined conditions	243	2.7	88	3.0	155	2.6
All other chronic conditions	303	3.4	149	5.1	155	2.6

* Figure has low statistical reliability or precision (relative standard error exceeds 30 percent)

SOURCE: National Health Interview Surveys, 1983-1985: original tabulations from public use tapes

Table 1D–Prevalence of work limitation due to chronic conditions, by all causes of limitation, age, and gender: United States civilian noninstitutionalized population, ages 18–69, 1983–1985 (three-year average)

							Males					
All Causes of Limitation	All Ages		18-44		45-69		All Ages		18-44		45-69	
				Number of conditions in thousands and percent distribution								
All conditions	28,316	100.0	7,962	100.0	20,354	100.0	13,623	100.0	4,018	100.0	9,606	100.0
Skin and musculoskeletal												
Rheumatoid arthritis	401	1.4	88	1.1	312	1.5	117	0.9	28	0.7	89	0.9
Osteoarthritis/other arthropathies	2,738	9.7	326	4.1	2,412	11.8	986	7.2	131	3.3	855	8.9
Intervertebral disk disorders	1,261	4.5	540	6.8	721	3.5	691	5.1	320	8.0	371	3.9
Osteomyelitis/bone disorders	279	1.0	63	0.8	216	1.1	92	0.7	30	0.7	63	0.7
Bursitis	150	0.5	49	0.6	100	0.5	58	0.4	20	0.5	38	0.4
Psoriasis and dermatitis	101	0.4	43	0.5	58	0.3	36	0.3	*10	*0.2	26	0.3
Skin cancer	19	0.1	*3	*0.0	*16	*0.1	*11	*0.1	*2	*0.0	*9	*0.1
Bone cancer	27	0.1	*4	*0.1	23	0.1	*10	*0.1	*1	*0.0	*9	*0.1
Other skin and musculoskeletal	318	1.1	58	0.7	259	1.3	153	1.1	28	0.7	125	1.3
Impairments												
Absence of arm(s)/hand(s)	18	0.1	*9	*0.1	*10	*0.0	*16	*0.1	*7	*0.2	*10	*0.1
Absence of leg(s)	111	0.4	28	0.3	84	0.4	83	0.6	24	0.6	59	0.6
Absence of fingers, toes, feet	72	0.3	32	0.4	40	0.2	61	0.4	30	0.7	32	0.3
Other absence, NEC	106	0.4	35	0.4	71	0.4	59	0.4	22	0.5	38	0.4
Complete paralysis of extremities	241	0.9	87	1.1	155	0.8	163	1.2	64	1.6	100	1.0
Cerebral palsy	82	0.3	67	0.8	*15	*0.1	44	0.3	35	0.9	*9	*0.1
Partial paralysis of extremities	187	0.7	45	0.6	142	0.7	118	0.9	33	0.8	84	0.9
Paralysis of other sites	72	0.3	22	0.3	49	0.3	46	0.3	*14	*0.4	31	0.3
Curvature of back or spine	345	1.2	212	2.7	132	0.6	126	0.9	89	2.2	37	0.4
Other impairment of back	1,734	6.1	835	10.5	899	4.4	876	6.4	415	10.3	461	4.8
Spina bifida	18	0.1	*13	*0.2	*5	*0.0	*9	*0.1	*6	*0.2	*3	*0.0
Impairment of upper extremities	521	1.8	258	3.2	263	1.3	319	2.3	167	4.2	152	1.6
Impairment of lower extremities	1,356	4.8	592	7.4	764	3.8	767	5.6	356	8.9	411	4.3
Other orthopedic impairment	124	0.4	58	0.7	66	0.3	69	0.5	36	0.9	32	0.3
Speech impairment	123	0.4	49	0.6	74	0.4	80	0.6	33	0.8	48	0.5
Blind in both eyes	134	0.5	49	0.6	85	0.4	76	0.6	27	0.7	48	0.5
Cataracts	170	0.6	21	0.3	148	0.7	74	0.5	*11	*0.3	62	0.6
Glaucoma	113	0.4	*13	*0.2	100	0.5	53	0.4	*8	*0.2	45	0.5
Other visual impairment/eye disorders	735	2.6	277	3.5	458	2.3	403	3.0	186	4.6	217	2.3
Deaf in both ears	104	0.4	50	0.6	54	0.3	54	0.4	28	0.7	26	0.3
Other hearing impairment/ear disorders	414	1.5	132	1.7	282	1.4	226	1.7	73	1.8	154	1.6

* Figure has low statistical reliability or precision (relative standard error exceeds 30 percent)

SOURCE: National Health Interview Surveys, 1983-1985; original tabulations from public use tapes

Table 1D—(Continued)

Number of conditions in thousands and percent distribution

All Causes of Limitation	All Ages		18-44		45-69		Males All Ages		Males 18-44		Males 45-69	
Digestive												
Ulcers	283	1.0	63	0.8	220	1.1	152	1.1	36	0.9	117	1.2
Hernia	346	1.2	79	1.0	266	1.3	170	1.2	40	1.0	130	1.4
Enteritis and colitis	91	0.3	31	0.4	59	0.3	27	0.2	*11	*0.3	*15	*0.2
Cancer of digestive sites	115	0.4	*13	*0.2	102	0.5	67	0.5	*7	*0.2	60	0.6
Other digestive disorders	428	1.5	111	1.4	318	1.6	172	1.3	41	1.0	131	1.4
Circulatory												
Rheumatic fever	128	0.5	41	0.5	86	0.4	36	0.3	*11	*0.3	26	0.3
Ischemic heart disease	1,460	5.2	80	1.0	1,379	6.8	952	7.0	60	1.5	892	9.3
Heart rhythm disorders	279	1.0	49	0.6	230	1.1	128	0.9	18	0.4	111	1.2
Other heart disease	1,225	4.3	143	1.8	1,082	5.3	628	4.6	57	1.4	572	5.9
Hypertension	2,057	7.3	231	2.9	1,826	9.0	787	5.8	80	2.0	707	7.4
Cerebrovascular disease	413	1.5	29	0.4	385	1.9	254	1.9	13	0.3	241	2.5
Arteriosclerosis	134	0.5	*6	*0.1	129	0.6	96	0.7	*4	*0.1	92	1.0
Phlebitis, varicose veins	310	1.1	60	0.8	249	1.2	80	0.6	*13	*0.3	67	0.7
Other circulatory	317	1.1	43	0.5	274	1.3	172	1.3	17	0.4	155	1.6
Respiratory												
Chronic bronchitis	149	0.5	28	0.4	121	0.6	68	0.5	*10	*0.3	57	0.6
Asthma	705	2.5	326	4.1	379	1.9	260	1.9	125	3.1	136	1.4
Hay fever	96	0.3	60	0.8	36	0.2	39	0.3	33	0.8	*6	*0.1
Sinusitis	70	0.2	*15	*0.2	55	0.3	29	0.2	*7	*0.2	22	0.2
Emphysema	592	2.1	25	0.3	566	2.8	414	3.0	*15	*0.4	399	4.2
Lung or bronchial cancer	78	0.3	*3	*0.0	75	0.4	53	0.4	*2	*0.1	50	0.5
Other respiratory disease	333	1.2	50	0.6	284	1.4	215	1.6	28	0.7	187	1.9

* Figure has low statistical reliability or precision (relative standard error exceeds 30 percent)

SOURCE: National Health Interview Surveys, 1983-1985; original tabulations from public use tapes

Table 1D–(Continued)

	All Causes of Limitation						Males					
	All Ages		18-44		45-69		All Ages		18-44		45-69	

Number of conditions in thousands and percent distribution

Miscellaneous

	All Ages		18-44		45-69		All Ages		18-44		45-69	
Diabetes	1,217	4.3	168	2.1	1,049	5.2	556	4.1	84	2.1	471	4.9
Anemias	75	0.3	29	0.4	46	0.2	17	0.1	*6	*0.1	*11	*0.1
Kidney disorders	207	0.7	58	0.7	149	0.7	79	0.6	21	0.5	57	0.6
Female genital disorders	156	0.6	76	0.9	81	0.4						
Schizophrenia/other psychoses	204	0.7	120	1.5	85	0.4	127	0.9	84	2.1	44	0.5
Neuroses/personality disorders	300	1.1	147	1.9	152	0.7	139	1.0	75	1.9	64	0.7
Other mental illness	244	0.9	105	1.3	139	0.7	120	0.9	53	1.3	67	0.7
Alchohol or drug dependency	80	0.3	48	0.6	32	0.2	61	0.4	34	0.8	27	0.3
Mental retardation	388	1.4	314	3.9	74	0.4	222	1.6	184	4.6	39	0.4
Epilepsy	299	1.1	204	2.6	95	0.5	178	1.3	115	2.9	63	0.7
Multiple sclerosis	100	0.4	45	0.6	55	0.3	40	0.3	19	0.5	22	0.2
Senility	58	0.2			58	0.3	20	0.1	na		20	0.2
Parkinson's disease	51	0.2	*3	*0.0	48	0.2	30	0.2	*2	*0.1	28	0.3
Other nervous disorders	526	1.9	213	2.7	313	1.5	200	1.5	86	2.1	114	1.2
Tuberculosis (all sites)	82	0.3	26	0.3	56	0.3	26	0.2	*8	*0.2	18	0.2
Other infectious/parasitic diseases	73	0.3	38	0.5	35	0.2	41	0.3	22	0.5	19	0.2
Leukemia	31	0.1	*4	*0.1	26	0.1	17	0.1	*2	*0.0	*15	*0.2
Cancer of female breast	94	0.3	*14	*0.2	80	0.4	na		na		na	
Cancer of genitourinary sites	97	0.3	*11	*0.1	86	0.4	43	0.3	*1	*0.0	43	0.4
Cancer of all other sites, NEC	111	0.4	25	0.3	86	0.4	60	0.4	*11	*0.3	49	0.5
Surgical/medical complications	274	1.0	74	0.9	200	1.0	106	0.8	34	0.8	72	0.7
Other injuries	204	0.7	85	1.1	119	0.6	113	0.8	51	1.3	62	0.6
Other ill-defined conditions	819	2.9	258	3.2	561	2.8	358	2.6	126	3.1	231	2.4
All other chronic conditions	945	3.3	351	4.4	595	2.9	393	2.9	143	3.6	250	2.6

* Figure has low statistical reliability or precision (relative standard error exceeds 30 percent)

SOURCE: National Health Interview Surveys, 1983-1985: original tabulations from public use tapes

Table 1D—(Continued)

All Causes of Limitation	Females					
	All Ages		18-44		45-69	
	Number of conditions in thousands and percent distribution					
All conditions	14,693	100.0	3,944	100.0	10,749	100.0
Skin and musculoskeletal						
Rheumatoid arthritis	284	1.9	60	1.5	224	2.1
Osteoarthritis/other arthropathies	1,752	11.9	195	4.9	1,557	14.5
Intervertebral disk disorders	570	3.9	220	5.6	351	3.3
Osteomyelitis/bone disorders	187	1.3	33	0.8	154	1.4
Bursitis	91	0.6	29	0.7	63	0.6
Psoriasis and dermatitis	65	0.4	33	0.8	32	0.3
Skin cancer	*8	*0.1	*1	*0.0	*7	*0.1
Bone cancer	17	0.1	*3	*0.1	*14	*0.1
Other skin and musculoskeletal	164	1.1	30	0.8	134	1.2
Impairments						
Absence of arm(s)/hand(s)	*2	*0.0	*2	*0.1		
Absence of leg(s)	28	0.2	*4	*0.1	24	0.2
Absence of fingers, toes, feet	*11	*0.1	*2	*0.1	*9	*0.1
Other absence, NEC	47	0.3	*13	*0.3	34	0.3
Complete paralysis of extremities	78	0.5	23	0.6	55	0.5
Cerebral palsy	37	0.3	32	0.8	*6	*0.1
Partial paralysis of extremities	69	0.5	*11	*0.3	58	0.5
Paralysis of other sites	26	0.2	*8	*0.2	18	0.2
Curvature of back or spine	219	1.5	123	3.1	95	0.9
Other impairment of back	858	5.8	420	10.6	438	4.1
Spina bifida	*9	*0.1	*7	*0.2	*2	*0.0
Impairment of upper extremities	202	1.4	91	2.3	111	1.0
Impairment of lower extremities	590	4.0	236	6.0	354	3.3
Other orthopedic impairment	55	0.4	22	0.6	33	0.3
Speech impairments	42	0.3	*16	*0.4	27	0.3
Blind in both eyes	58	0.4	21	0.5	37	0.3
Cataracts	96	0.7	*10	*0.3	86	0.8
Glaucoma	60	0.4	*5	*0.1	55	0.5
Other visual impairment/eye disorders	332	2.3	91	2.3	241	2.2
Deaf in both ears	49	0.3	22	0.6	27	0.3
Other hearing impairment/ear disorders	188	1.3	60	1.5	128	1.2

* Figure has low statistical reliability or precision (relative standard error exceeds 30 percent)

SOURCE: National Health Interview Surveys, 1983-1985; original tabulations from public use tapes

Table 1D—(Continued)

All Causes of Limitation	Females					
	All Ages		18-44		45-69	
	Number of conditions in thousands and percent distribution					

Digestive

Ulcers	130	0.9	27	0.7	103	1.0
Hernia	176	1.2	39	1.0	136	1.3
Enteritis and colitis	64	0.4	20	0.5	44	0.4
Cancer of digestive sites	48	0.3	*5	*0.1	42	0.4
Other digestive disorders	257	1.7	70	1.8	187	1.7

Circulatory

Rheumatic fever	91	0.6	31	0.8	61	0.6
Ischemic heart disease	508	3.5	20	0.5	487	4.5
Heart rhythm disorders	150	1.0	32	0.8	119	1.1
Other heart disease	597	4.1	86	2.2	510	4.7
Hypertension	1,270	8.6	151	3.8	1119	10.4
Cerebrovascular disease	159	1.1	*15	*0.4	143	1.3
Arteriosclerosis	39	0.3	*2	*0.1	37	0.3
Phlebitis, varicose veins	230	1.6	48	1.2	182	1.7
Other circulatory	145	1.0	27	0.7	118	1.1

Respiratory

Chronic bronchitis	81	0.6	18	0.5	63	0.6
Asthma	444	3.0	201	5.1	243	2.3
Hay fever	58	0.4	28	0.7	30	0.3
Sinusitis	41	0.3	*8	*0.2	33	0.3
Emphysema	178	1.2	*11	*0.3	167	1.6
Lung or bronchial cancer	25	0.2	*1	*0.0	24	0.2
Other respiratory disease	117	0.8	21	0.5	96	0.9

* Figure has low statistical reliability or precision (relative standard error exceeds 30 percent)

SOURCE: National Health Interview Surveys, 1983-1985: original tabulations from public use tapes

Table 1D—(Continued)

	Females					
	All Ages		18-44		45-69	
All Causes of Limitation	Number of conditions in thousands and percent distribution					
Miscellaneous						
Diabetes	662	4.5	84	2.1	578	5.4
Anemias	58	0.4	24	0.6	34	0.3
Kidney disorders	128	0.9	36	0.9	91	0.9
Female genital disorders	156	1.1	76	1.9	80	0.7
Schizophrenia/other psychoses	77	0.5	36	0.9	41	0.4
Neuroses/personality disorders	161	1.1	72	1.8	88	0.8
Other mental illness	125	0.9	52	1.3	72	0.7
Alchohol or drug dependency	19	0.1	*14	*0.4	*5	*0.0
Mental retardation	165	1.1	131	3.3	35	0.3
Epilepsy	121	0.8	89	2.3	32	0.3
Multiple sclerosis	59	0.4	26	0.7	33	0.3
Senility	38	0.3			38	0.4
Parkinson's disease	20	0.1	*1	*0.0	20	0.2
Other nervous disorders	326	2.2	127	3.2	199	1.9
Tuberculosis (all sites)	55	0.4	17	0.4	38	0.4
Other infectious/parasitic diseases	32	0.2	*16	*0.4	*16	*0.1
Leukemia	*14	*0.1	*3	*0.1	*11	*0.1
Cancer of female breast	94	0.6	*14	*0.4	80	0.7
Cancer of genitourinary sites	54	0.4	*10	*0.3	43	0.4
Cancer of all other sites, NEC	51	0.3	*14	*0.4	37	0.3
Surgical/medical complications	169	1.1	41	1.0	128	1.2
Other injuries	91	0.6	34	0.9	57	0.5
Other ill-defined conditions	462	3.1	133	3.4	329	3.1
All other chronic conditions	552	3.8	208	5.3	344	3.2

* Figure has low statistical reliability or precision (relative standard error exceeds 30 percent)

SOURCE: National Health Interview Surveys, 1983-1985: original tabulations from public use tapes

GOVERNMENT AGENCIES AND OTHER RESOURCES

The following is a listing of agencies and resources available to assist you in understanding and complying with the ADA.

AMERICANS WITH DISABILITIES ACT HANDBOOK

Prepared by the U.S. Equal Employment Opportunity Commission, and the U.S. Department of Justice. For sale by the U.S. Government Printing Office. To order a resource directory, call:

SUPERINTENDENT OF DOCUMENTS
Washington, DC 20402-9328
(202) 783-3238

CIVIL RIGHTS DIVISION
Office on the Americans with Disabilities Act
U.S. Department of Justice
P.O. Box 66118
Washington, DC 20035-6118
(202) 514-0301 (Voice and TDD)

Source for regulations, technical assistance, and enforcement for Title II
(public services) and Title III (public accommodations)

EQUAL EMPLOYMENT OPPORTUNITY COMMISSION
1801 L Street NW
Washington, DC 20507
(202) 669-EEOC (Voice); (800) 800-3302 (TDD)

Source for regulations, technical assistance, and enforcement for Title I
(employment)

DEPARTMENT OF TRANSPORTATION
400 Seventh Street SW
Room 10424
Washington, DC
(202) 366-9305; (202) 755-7687 (TDD)

Source for regulations, technical assistance, and enforcement for Title II
and Title III (transportation) provisions

ARCHITECTURAL AND TRANSPORTATION BARRIERS COMPLIANCE BOARD
1111 18th Street NW
 Suite 501
Washington, DC 20036
(800) USA-ABLE (Voice and TDD)

For information concerning the minimum ADA accessibility guidelines
(called Americans with Disabilities Act Accessibilities Guide, or ADAAG)
required under Title III and for technical assistance on architectural,
transportation, and communications accessibility issues.

FEDERAL COMMUNICATIONS COMMISSION
1919 M Street NW
Washington, DC 20554
(202) 632-7260 (Voice); (202) 632-6999 (TDD)

For regulations, technical assistance, and enforcement for Title IV (telecommunications).

U.S. DEPT. OF THE TREASURY-INTERNAL REVENUE SERVICE
Office of Chief Counsel
P.O. Box 7604
Ben Franklin Station
Washington, DC 20224
(202) 566-3292 (Voice only)

The Internal Revenue Service provides technical assistance on various tax code provisions designated to encourage businesses to hire people with disabilities.

NATIONAL COUNCIL ON DISABILITY
800 Independence Avenue SW
Suite 814
Washington, DC 20591
(202) 267-3846 (Voice); (202) 267-3232 (TDD)

This agency is charged by statute with responsibility for developing recommendations for federal disability policy and overseeing the research priorities for the National Institute on Disability and Rehabilitation Research.

SMALL BUSINESS ADMINISTRATION
Office of Advocacy/Office of Economic Research
409 Third Street SW, Fifth Floor
Washington, DC 20416
(202) 205-6530 (Voice only)

PRESIDENT'S COMMITTEE ON EMPLOYMENT OF PEOPLE WITH DISABILITIES
1331 F Street NW, Third Floor
Washington, DC 20004-1107
(202) 376-6200 (Voice); (202) 376-6205 (TDD)

Provides information, referral, and technical assistance to employers as well as employees with disabilities and others interested in employment of individuals with disabilities, specifically on employment provisions of ADA directly or through its Governors' Committees on Employment of People with Disabilities.

REHABILITATION SERVICES ADMINISTRATION
U.S. Department of Education
400 Maryland Avenue SW
Washington, DC 20202-2572
(202) 708-5366 (Voice and TDD)

The administrative office for educational rehabilitation services for students.

NATIONAL INSTITUTE ON DISABILITY AND REHABILITATION RESEARCH
U.S. Department of Education
400 Maryland Avenue SW
Washington, DC 20202-2572
(202) 708-5366 (Voice and TDD)

Administers the principal federal disability research programs, the Technology Related Assistance for Individuals with Disabilities Act, and ADA technical assistance centers.

PUBLIC HEALTH SERVICE
U.S. Department of Health and Human Services
Centers for Disease Control
Mail Stop C09
1600 Clifton Road NE
Atlanta, GA 30333
(404) 639-2237 (Voice only)

The ADA in certain circumstances permits the reassignment of individuals with certain contagious diseases specified by the Public Health Service from food-handling jobs to other jobs if the risk posed by the individual can not be eliminated by a reasonable accommodation.

SOCIAL SECURITY ADMINISTRATION
Office of Disability
Room 545, Altimeyer Building
6401 Security Boulevard,
Baltimore, MD 21235
(301) 965-3424 (Voice only)

SSA administers programs that provide incentives for individuals receiving Social Security Disability Insurance or Supplemental Security Income to obtain gainful employment.

Access Board
(800) 872-2253 (Voice/TDD); (202) 653-7848 (Voice/TDD)

Disability Rights Education and Defense Fund
(800) 466-4232 (Voice/TDD); (510) 644-2555 (Voice);
(510) 644-2629 (TDD)

Equal Employment Opportunity Fund
(800) 669-3362 (Voice); (800) 800-3302 (TDD)

Federal Communications Commission
(202) 632-7260 (Voice); (202) 632-6999 (TDD)

Job Accommodations Network
(800) ADA-WORK; (800) 526-7234 (Voice/TDD);
(800) 526-4698 (Voice/TDD for West Virginia only)

National Association for Protection and Advocacy Systems
(202) 408-9514 (Voice); (202) 408-9521 (TDD)

National Association of the Deaf
(301) 587-1788 (Voice); (301) 587-1789 (TDD)

National Association for Law and the Deaf
(202) 651-5373 (Voice/TDD)

National Institute on Disability and Rehabilitation Research
(202) 732-1139 (Voice); (202) 732-5316 (TDD)

President's Committee on Employment of People with Disabilities
(202) 376-6200 (Voice); (202) 376-6205 (TDD)

Project Action
(202) 347-3066 (Voice); (202) 347-7385 (TDD)

Rehabilitation Services Administration
(202) 732-1331 (Voice); (202) 732-4538 (TDD)

U.S. Department of Justice
(202) 514-0301 (Voice); (202) 514-0381 or 0383

U.S. Department of Transportation
(202) 366-9306 or 4011 (Voice); (202) 755-7687 or 366-2979 (TDD)

ORGANIZATIONS AND RESOURCES

NATIONAL ORGANIZATIONS FOR DISABILITIES INTERESTS
These organizations represent special interests of health, government, or business members throughout the nation.

American Occupational Therapy Association
P.O. Box 1725
1383 Piccard Drive
Rockville, MD 20850
(301) 948-9626

American Physical Therapy Association
1111 North Fairfax Street
Alexandria, VA 22314
(703) 684-2782

Apple Office of Special Education Programs/Apple Computer
20825 Marina Avenue
MS23D
Cupertino, CA 95104
(407) 973-6484

Provides information on computer hardware and software to assist a disabled person's use of the computer.

Association for Severely Handicapped Individuals
7010 Roosevelt Way, NE
Seattle, WA 98115
(206) 523-8446 (Voice); (206) 524-6198 (TDD)

Association of Persons in Supported Employment
5001 W. Broad Street, Suite 34
Richmond, VA 23230
(800) 282-3655 (Voice only)

Building Owners and Managers Association International
1201 New York Avenue NW, Suite 300
Washington, DC 20005
(202) 408-2662
Building accessibility issues.

IBM National Support Center for Persons with Disabilities
P.O. Box 2150
Atlanta, Georgia 30055
(800) IBM-2133 (Voice/TDD)

Responds to requests for technical assistance and information on computers as a resource for people with disabilities.

Industry-Labor Council
National Center for Disabilities Studies
201 I.U. Willets Road
Albertson, New York 11507
(516) 747-6323 (Voice); (516) 747-5355 (TDD)

A nonprofit membership organization serving 152 mostly Fortune 500 corporations and labor unions committed to integrating persons with disabilities into the work force. Assists in planning and implementing affirmative action plans and provides architectural accessibility surveys.

Institute for Rehabilitation and Disability Management (IRDM)
Washington Business Group on Health
229 1/2 Pennsylvania Avenue, S.E.
Washington, DC 20003
(202) 547-6644 (Voice/TDD)

Works with corporations on hiring and retention of disabled employees.

Inter-National Association of Business, Industry and Rehabilitation
P.O. Box 15242
Washington, DC 20003
(202) 543-6353 (Voice only)

Represents businesses, labor unions, and job placement service organizations sponsoring federally funded Projects With Industry (PWI) programs. These organizations are public-private partnerships that competitively employ people with disabilities.

Job Accommodation Network (JAN)
West Virginia University
809 Allen Hall, P.O. Box 468
Morgantown, West Virginia 26506
(800) 526-7234; (304) 293-7186

Free consulting resource able to assist with questions concerning practical solutions to accommodate functional limitations of employees and applicants with disabilities.

Mainstream, Inc.
1200 15th Street, NW
Washington, DC 20005
(202) 833-1136 (Voice/TDD)

Customized training, mostly for businesses, associations, and service providers on the aspects of employing persons with disabilities. Produces ADA-related materials; placement projects in Dallas and Washington, DC.

National Alliance for the Mentally Ill
2101 Wilson Blvd., Suite 302
Arlington, VA 22201
(703) 524-7600 (Voice only)

National Association for the Physically Handicapped
4230 Emerick Street
Saginaw, MI 48602
(517) 799-3060 (Voice only)

National Council on Independent Living
Troy Atrium, Fourth and Broadway
Troy, NY 12180
(518) 274-1979 (Voice); (518) 274-0701 (TDD)

Represents community-based independent living centers. Will provide referral information on services offered by centers, and will locate the center closest to the inquirer.

National Easter Seals Society
1350 New York Avenue
Washington, DC 20005
(202) 347-3066 (Voice); (202) 347-7385 (TDD)

National Organization on Disability (NOD)
910 16th Street NW, Suite 600
Washington, DC 20006
(202) 293-5960 (Voice); (202) 293-5968 (TDD)

Operates an information clearing house, directing inquirers to a variety of resources.

National Rehabilitation Association
633 South Washington Street
Alexandria, VA 22314
(703) 836-0850

ORGANIZATIONS FOR PERSONS WHO ARE BLIND

American Council of the Blind
1115 15th Street NW, Suite 720
Washington, DC 20005
(202) 467-5081 (Voice only); (800) 424-8666 (Mon-Fri 3 to 5:30 EST only)

American Foundation for the Blind
15 West 16th Street
New York, NY 10011
(212) 620-2000 (Voice); (212) 620-2158 (TDD)

American Printing House for the Blind
1839 Frankfort Avenue, Louisville, KY 40206-0085
(502) 895-2405 (Voice only)

Institute for the Visually Impaired
1200 W. Godfrey Avenue
Philadelphia, PA 19141
(215) 276-6295

Job Opportunities for the Blind: National Federation of the Blind
1800 Johnson Street
Baltimore, Maryland 21230
(301) 659-9314, (800) 638-7518

A free nationwide job listing and job referral system.

National Association for the Visually Handicapped
22 West 21st Street
New York, NY 10010
(212) 889-3141

National Federation of the Blind
1800 Johnson Street
Baltimore, MD 21230
(301) 659-9314

National Library Services for the Blind and Physically Handicapped
1291 Taylor Street NW
Washington, DC 20542
(202) 707-5100 (Voice); (202) 707-0744 (TDD)

DEAFNESS ORGANIZATIONS

Alexander Graham Bell Association for the Deaf
3417 Volta Place NW
Washington, DC 20007
(202) 337-5220 (Voice and TDD)

National Center on Employment of the Deaf (NCED)
National Institute for the Deaf, Rochester Institute of Technology
Lyndon Baines Johnson Building
Rochester, NY 14623-0887
(716) 475-6219 (Voice); (716) 475-6205 (TDD)

Offers a range of services designed to assist in the employment of people
who are deaf.

National Information Center on Deafness
Gallaudet University
800 Florida Avenue N.E.
Washington, DC
(202) 651-5052 (Voice); (202) 651-5976 (TDD)

Self-Help for Hard of Hearing People
7800 Wisconsin Avenue NW
Bethesda, MD, 20814
(301) 657-2248 (Voice); (301) 657-2249 (TDD)

Serves consumers and professionals; also provides technical assistance to
hospitals on meeting the needs of individuals with hearing impairments.

Telecommunications for the Deaf
8719 Colesville Road, Suite 300
Silver Spring, MD
(301) 589-3786 (Voice); (301) 589-3006 (TDD)

Publishes and sells a nationwide Telecommunications Device for the
Deaf (TDD) directory; information on visually-based accommodations
for deaf and hearing impaired people, such as alarms, decoders, and
TDDs. Sells decoders and a videotape on how to use a TDD.

SPEECH-RELATED ORGANIZATIONS

American Speech-Language-Hearing Association
10801 Rockville Pike
Rockville, MD 20852
(301) 897-5700 (Voice and TDD); (800) 638-8255 (Voice and TDD)

National Stuttering Project
1269 7th Avenue
San Francisco, CA 94122

National Council on Stuttering
P.O. Box 8171
Grand Rapids, MI 49508

Speak Easy International
233 Concord Drive
Paramus, NJ 07652

DISABILITIES ORGANIZATIONS

International Center for the Disabled
340 East 24th Street
New York, NY 20010
(212) 679-0100

National Rehabilitation Information Center (NARIC)
8455 Colesville Road, Suite 935
Silver Spring, MD 20910-3319
(800) 346-2742

Louis Harris & Associates
630 Fifth Avenue, 11th Floor
New York, NY 10111
(212) 698-9600

World Institute on Disability
510 16th Street, Suite 100
Oakland, CA 94612
(415) 763-4100 (Voice and TDD)

American Amputee Foundation
Little Rock, AR
(501) 666-2523 (Voice only)

American Cancer Society
Atlanta, GA
(404) 320-3333

American Heart Association
Dallas, TX
(214) 373-6300

Arthritis Foundation
Atlanta, GA
(404) 872-7100; (800) 283-7800

Eastern Paralyzed Veterans Association
Jackson Heights
New York, NY
(800) 444-0120

Epilepsy Foundation of America
Landover, MD
(301) 459-3700

Goodwill Industries of America
Landover, MD
(301) 530-6500

Learning Disabilities Association
Pittsburgh, PA
(412) 341-1515

Learning Disabilities Network
Hingham, MA
(617) 740-2327

Mended Hearts
Dallas, TX
(214) 706-1442

Muscular Dystrophy Association
New York, NY
(212) 586-0808

National AIDS Network
Washington, DC
(202) 293-2437

National Amputee Foundation
Whitestone, NY
(718) 767-8400

National Association for Retarded Citizens
Washington, DC
(202) 785-3388 (Voice); (202) 785-3411 (TDD)

National Center for Learning Disabilities
New York, NY
 (212) 687-7211

National Cerebral Palsy Associations
Washington, DC
(202) 842-1266 (Voice only)

National Diabetes Information Clearinghouse
Rockville, MD
(301) 468-2162

National Easter Seal Society
Chicago, IL
(312) 726-6200, (312) 726-4258 (TDD), (800) 221-6827

National Head Injury Foundation
Southboro, MA
(508) 485-9950

National Industries for the Severely Handicapped
Vienna, VA
(703) 560-6800

National Information System/Developmental Disabilities
Columbia, SC
(803) 777-4435

National Mental Health Association
1021 Prince Street
Alexandria, VA 22314-2971
(703) 684-7722

National Multiple Sclerosis Society
New York, NY
(212) 986-3240; (800) 624-8236

National Organization for Rare Disorders
New Fairfield, CT
(800) 999-6673 (Voice only); (203) 746-6518 (Voice only)

National Spinal Cord Injury Association
Woburn, MA
(617) 935-2722 (Voice only)

National Stroke Information Service Referral Clearing House
Washington, DC
(202) 429-9091; (800) 336-4797

Paralyzed Veterans of America
Washington, DC
(202) 872-1300 (Voice only)

Spina Bifida Association
Rockville, MD
(301) 770-7222; (800) 621-3141

United Cerebral Palsy Association
New York, NY
(212) 268-6655; (800) 872-1827

U.S. Chamber of Commerce/Labor and Human Resources Department
1615 H Street NW
Washington, DC 20062
(202) 463-5502 (Voice only)

National Association of Wholesale Distributors
1725 K Street NW, Suite 700
Washington, DC 20006
(202) 872-0885 (Voice only)

National Restaurant Association
1200 17th Street NW
Washington, DC 20036
(202) 331-5988 (Voice only)

National Retail Federation
701 Pennsylvania Avenue, Suite 710
Washington, DC 20004
(202) 783-7971 (Voice only)

Society for Human Resources Management
606 North Washington Street
Alexandria, VA 22314
(703) 548-3440 (Voice only)

STATE ORGANIZATIONS
Each state has many resources to support disabilities services; you might consult the telephone directory of the state capital for disabilities listings. Here is a listing of the State of Florida's services, as an example.

Florida Governor's Alliance for the Employment of Disabled Citizens
345 South Magnolia Drive, Suite A-17
Tallahassee, FL 32301-2947
(904)487-2222 (Voice), (904) 487-0925 (TDD)

A public/private advocacy group that monitors disabilities issues such as employment opportunities, legislation, and awareness of the rights of persons with disabilities.

Division of Vocational Rehabilitation
Department of Labor and Employment Security
1709-A Mahan Drive
Tallahassee, FL 32399
(904) 488-6210

Can offer employers assistance with information on supported employment, rehabilitation and assistive technology, and on employment of people with disabilities. Information can be sought from local district Vocational Rehabilitation offices.

Division of Blind Services
State organization that oversees services rendered to persons who are blind.
Department of Education
2540 Executive Center Circle West
Tallahassee, FL 32301 (904) 488-1330

Advocacy Center for Persons with Disabilities, Inc.
2671 Executive Center West, Suite 100
Tallahassee, FL 32301-5024
(800) 342-0823 (Voice), (800) 346-4127 (TDD)

The Corporate Initiative (TCI)
1-800-741-4180

A network of large and small businesses committed to supported employment and employment of persons with disabilities. Available to share information and training concepts.

Florida Council for Community Mental Health
111 Gadsden Street
Tallahassee, FL 32301
(904) 224-6048

Florida Council for the Hearing Impaired
The Florida Education Center
Suite 622-C
Tallahassee, FL 32399-0401

Local District Offices of Vocational Rehabilitation
Division of Vocational Rehabilitation
4437 Park Blvd.
Pinellas Park, FL 34665
(813) 893-2261

Division of Blind Services
3637 4th Street, Suite 310
St. Petersburg, FL 33704
(813) 893-2341

Pinellas Deaf Services Center
7190 76th Street No.
Pinellas Park, FL 34665-3739
(813) 541-4488

J. Clifford MacDonald Center
4304 Boy Scout Blvd.
Tampa, FL 33607
(813) 871-1300

Center for Independent Living, District VI
Self-Reliance, Inc.
12310 N. Nebraska Avenue
Tampa, FL 33612
(813) 977-6338

Abilities of Florida
2735 Whitney Road
Clearwater, FL 34618
(813) 530-0617

Goodwill Industries—Suncoast, Inc.
P.O. Box 14456
St. Petersburg, FL 33733-4456
(813) 576-3819

Paralyzed Veterans Chapters
Florida Gulf Coast Chapter/Paralyzed Veterans of America
121 W. 122nd Avenue
Tampa FL 33612
(813) 935-6540

LOCAL REHABILITATION CENTERS
(Check Yellow Pages under listings, "Associations" or "Social Services")

INDEX

About the Publisher

PROBUS PUBLISHING COMPANY

Probus Publishing Company fills the informational needs of today's business professional by publishing authoritative, quality books on timely and relevant topics, including:

- Investing
- Futures/Options Trading
- Banking
- Finance
- Marketing and Sales
- Manufacturing and Project Management
- Personal Finance, Real Estate, Insurance and Estate Planning
- Entrepreneurship
- Management

Probus books are available at quantity discounts when purchased for business, educational or sales promotional use. For more information, please call the Director, Corporate/Institutional Sales at 1-800-998-4644, or write:

Director, Corporate/Institutional Sales
Probus Publishing Company
1925 N. Clybourn Avenue
Chicago, Illinois 60614
FAX (312) 868-6250